Contents

It so happens that for the first six months of 1941, the author and I served together as Midshipmen in HMS Valiant, in the Mediterranean Fleet. The whole naval war in the eastern Mediterranean never lacked for incident, but those early months in 1941 were a veritable baptism of fire for us inexperienced Midshipmen. The author has vividly captured the essential features of the 'learning-curve' which we attempted to climb.

No written account can ever match the real thing, but, in my view, the author has produced as true a picture of the life of very junior officers during those dramatic events as is reasonably possible. This may be a 'worms eye view' of great events, but it is from these lucid first-hand accounts that good history is ultimately written.

Philip

Acknowledgements

My grateful thanks are due to the following, without whose help and encouragement my task as author would have been infinitely more difficult. I would add that the names are not listed chronologically, nor reflect the degree of assistance given.

Mr Philip Knightley, author and biographer of Kim Philby, who introduced me to the world of publishing and gave me valuable advice on how to construct my book.

Mrs Christina Petyan, whose knowledge of the Italian language was invaluable in translating the records of the frogmen's attack and in telephone conversations with the late Admiral Luigi de la Penne.

The late Admiral Luigi de la Penne, whose courage was only matched by his willingness to assist me with his recollections of the frogmen's attack.

The late Commander Antonio Marceglia, who described to my wife and myself in vivid detail how he carried out his attack on HMS *Queen Elizabeth*.

Mrs Daphne Bruton and Mrs Pamela Griffin of AD Secretarial Services of Nailsworth, Gloucestershire, for typing the remainder of my manuscript.

Mr Leo Cooper, military publisher, for help and advice.

Doctor Christopher Dowling of the Imperial War Museum, together with his colleagues Mr Roderick Suddaby, Keeper of Documents, and Mr Paul Kemp of the Photographic Department.

The staff of the Public Record Office, Kew.

Captain J.H. Gault, Royal Australian Navy, of the Australian High Commission, London.

The Naval Historical Officer, Department of Defence (Navy), Canberra.

Mr J.C. Woods, of the Naval Historical Branch, Great Scotland Yard.

The Construction Department, Ministry of Defence, Bath.

Amrniraglio di Divisione (R) Carlo Gottardi, of the Conservatore Museo Storico, Venice.

Amrniraglio di Squadra Enzo Consolo.

Professor Francesco Berlingieri.

Mr Tony Sheldon for introducing me to his publisher daughter, Miss Caroline Sheldon.

Mr Paul Sampson, of Messrs. Osbome Clarke, Solicitors, of Bristol, for legal advice.

Mr Brian Power, himself a published author, for introducing me to my original publisher, Mr John Thorpe, whose courtesy and help I have greatly valued.

Mr John Hamilton, whose magnificent painting of the Battle of Matapan is reproduced on the cover, photographed by Martin Stone. Also to Vice Admiral Sir Roderick Macdonald, who was there at the time, for his painting of the Stuka attack, 10 January, 1941.

To Mr Evert Abendanon and Mr Peter Lapping for correcting my Afrikaans spelling. Commander John McGregor for detailed information on the enemy minefields off Tripoli.

My wife for assistance in proof reading.

Mrs Gillian Grim, who assisted greatly with the bulk of the proof reading and whose objective views on the text were of great help.

Last but not least, Mr Stan Clark of Minchinhampton, Gloucestershire, who also served in the Royal Navy, and to whom I am indebted for a constant supply of naval journals.

The author and publishers would like to thank the following for the use of copyright material: p. 13 Royal Naval College, Dartmouth; pp. 2, 13, 42, 44, 47, 52, 53, 77, 137, 166 and 204 author's collection; pp. 127, 135, 141, 143, 175, 177 and 212 Imperial War Museum; p. 82 from the painting by Vice-Admiral Sir Roderick Macdonald; pp. 99 and 101 from *The Battle of Matapan* by S.W.C. Pack, published by Batsford; p. 147 Blandford Press; pp. 179 and 181 from *Battleship Barham* by Geoffrey Jones, published by William Kimber, an imprint of Harper Collins Publishers Ltd; p. 204 Museo Storico Navale, Venezia.

Introduction

It was with great trepidation and misgiving that I decided to add to the thousands of books which have been written about the Second World War.

The keeping of diaries by anyone in the armed forces of the Crown was strictly forbidden during wartime. I suppose therefore that is why so many senior officers kept copious records of their often top secret decisions and doings which later formed the basis for their remunerative memoirs after the cessation of hostilities. But midshipmen, Royal Navy, were in a very different category as regards being latter-day Pepys. We were not only allowed to keep a day-to-day record of our duties and the movements of the ships in which we served; we were ordered to do so.

My midshipman's journal, on which this book is based, had been returned to me by the Admiralty in 1946, having lain in some secret repository from 1942 until then.

This journal contained a faithful record of everything that had happened to me during my naval service in the eastern Mediterranean from 1940 to 1942. It had accompanied me all that time during which some of the fiercest fighting of the war had taken place.

Not for us the dreary swinging round a buoy in Scapa Flow waiting for the emergence of German heavy naval units. We were constantly at sea, often in action, and all this was written down by me within hours of its occurrence.

A midshipman may well be in Bligh's possibly apocryphal words 'the lowest form of animal life in the British Navy'. He certainly was little more than a schoolboy at sea, for that is how the sobriquet of snotty came to be given to him. Young boys wiped their noses on their sleeves, hence the three buttons on a midshipman's uniform to discourage this revolting practice.

We were sent to sea and to war at seventeen and a half, an age when most youths of similar years could look forward to eighteen months before going up to university.

Midshipmen might well have been striplings at sea, but they learned speedily the unpleasantness of war and how best to survive its rigours. They had feelings like anyone else but they could not confide these to their journals, for the latter were official and confidential books, inspected regularly.

Others of much higher rank than myself have recorded their experiences at this time together with their emotions. Fifty years on I felt that it was time that these events and the feelings consequent upon them should be published as from a lowly midshipman's point of view. Moreover, whilst a number of the actions about which I have written have been described by other historians, no one, so far as I know, has written an account of the attack by Italian frogmen on the battlefleet in Alexandria harbour in December 1941 as seen from the British side.

The dark and often adverse days which I have set down in the following pages are now half a century old. Our late adolescence was given over to war and not to enjoyment of parties. Nevertheless, if I have been able to bring my journal to life and to describe to the reader what it was like to be a midshipman at sea in wartime I shall have succeeded in my purpose.

1

Dartmouth

'Oh really?' said my brother Michael, and without looking up, continued the washing of his car.

In days long ago the bearer of bad tidings was as often as not summarily executed by his king or chieftain. This particular moment was centuries later, the date being 3 September 1939, the time 11.15am, and I had just brought the news to Michael that we were at war with Germany.

I was rather disappointed – my sense of a theatrical announcement had acquired all the airborne qualities of the legendary lead balloon, and yet it had been naive of me to have expected any other response. The Munich crisis of 1938 had been but a foretaste of what was to come, and ever since then, with Hitler's promises breaking like plates in a Martian pantomime, we had been living in the shadow of impending war.

There is nothing in the mass of historical material concerning the Second World War to indicate that there was any hesitation on the Führer's part. Had he quailed at the thought of Midshipman Holloway joining the fleet and being plunged into conflict against the sea-borne field-grey hordes? Was the launching of *Bismarck* and *Prinz Eugen* a year or two earlier some attempt to redress the balance in his favour? History does not relate but Walter Mitty may have something to answer for.

My naval career was almost terminated soon after it might have been said to have begun. It was May 1936 and I, in common with other blue serge suited aspirants had arrived at the Admiralty for the dreaded naval interview.

Which way did Nelson face atop his column? Which was his blind eye? What was the White Ship? What was the significance of Flores in the Azores? Had *Victory* two or three masts and how many guns? What was the number of the taxi that brought me here?

All these and other questions which I had been told might be asked of me raced through my brain.

At the end of a long corridor I was ushered into a room which contained a table and three chairs. On two of these sat two other thirteen-year-old boys like myself. I was told by an old naval pensioner to sit on the third chair. A piece of paper was placed in front of me and a pen.

'Yer writes ESS-AY at the top of the page,' said the pensioner, in a strong Liverpudlian accent. I was frightened, bewildered and apprehensive of the interview to come, but then blessed relief came. Surely I was to be entrusted, albeit at this tender age, with some esoteric naval code or cipher?

Yes, that was it and so without further ado I proudly wrote the letters S A at the top of the page and felt much better.

Later, when the essays on such piffling subjects as 'A day in the life of a penny' or 'Why I want to be like Nelson' were read, I can only conclude that my solecism had gone unnoticed. Hitler was not yet to be spared.

'Do not sit down until you are told to do so' I had been warned.

'Sit down,' said the Admiral in charge of the interview board, and I obeyed. Opposite me were a school-master, the Admiral and a Commander. I stared in fascination at the gold rings. On the wall was a map of the world.

'Point out Ceylon,' I was ordered. It was then I discovered that Philips the cartographers had omitted the names of countries and places on the map. Nothing daunted, I pointed unerringly to the right spot. Nods of approval.

'There are four brothers in a family, each of them has a sister, how many of them are there in the family?' from the schoolmaster, obviously a failed trick cyclist.

'Five, Sir,' I said smugly. Nods of approval, all was going splendidly; the old buffer had expected me to say eight.

'What is the valley called that runs from Stroud towards Cirencester?'

Horrors, what was it? 'The Chalford Valley?' I ventured.

'No, boy, the Golden Valley, because of its autumn colours.' Theirs was the wrong answer also, I was later to learn, but I felt I had failed. How stupid – it was only two miles from my home in Gloucestershire. Next a strict medical.

Three days of examination took place the next month in Russell Square, also the scene of my brother's battles with his medical examiners.

We were allowed to use Latin dictionaries which surprised me. 'Place your dictionaries quietly on the floor,' said the invigilator. The ensuing boom must have shaken the Bloomsbury avant-gardes out of their left-wing reveries.

During the examinations my prep school headmaster drove up with me from Hertfordshire each day. His name was Paul Griffith, a man I greatly revered. He had strong religious beliefs, but he never forced them upon other people. Once he took me into our school chapel, the lighting of which had just been restored.

'Rather Trocadero, don't you think?' he enquired deprecatingly.

He also loved the small boy's prayer 'Our Father which art in Heaven, Harrods be thy name...'

Each day he took me to lunch at the Savoy where, to his amusement I ordered whitebait. When, to the wonderment of all, not least myself, the Dartmouth Pass List was published in the papers, and my name was included among the successful candidates, Griffith sent me a telegram. Instead of the usual congratulations it said simply, 'Whitebait to you.'

The Royal Naval College, Dartmouth.

'At first sight,' said the Gieves booklet, 'One feels that the Royal Naval College Dartmouth is either a prison, a lunatic asylum or the house of a profiteer. '

This was not entirely reassuring to the 43 puny cadets who stood on the Mew, the GWR ferry taking us from Kingswear to Dartmouth. Surely ferries were the usual method of transport to take convicts to Parkhurst or Alcatraz?

The huge College building dominates the pretty little town of Dartmouth. If one has never seen it, you have only to cross Horse Guards Parade, look at the pink and white building to the back of the Admiralty, multiply it about six times and you have an idea of the Royal Naval College.

During the following three weeks we were to learn the discipline and customs of the College and were 'untouchable'. That word is not used in the Indian sense, but indicates that infringements of rules and customs were overlooked. After that probationary period punishments could be doled out and our bottoms were vulnerable.

Discipline was very strict but mostly fair. Presumably in order to instil respect for one's seniors, cadets had to double past the gunrooms (living quarters) of cadets senior to them; they were forbidden to talk whilst doing so, or to look inside. To speak to a cadet senior to oneself was a 'guff' offence, as was failure to double past a senior gunroom. 'Guff' offences were punishable by a beating. Cadets were divided into eleven terms, each named after an Admiral. We were the 'Blake' term, our predecessors had been known as the Bloody Blakes. We were not distinguished or ill-disciplined enough to warrant this appellation, but it was sometimes applied.

'North side will stand by to open their windows half. Stand by. Go!' It was unbelievable, a simple act like opening a dormitory window was carried out by numbers, the command being shouted by our cadet captain in stentorian tones.

'Rounds' of the dormitory were taken by the officer of the day at lights out time. Dressed in mess kit, stiff shirt and black tie, he would parade through the dormitories accompanied by his cohorts, whilst the cadets would 'lie at attention' gazing fixedly at the ceiling. Before that, at another command, 'Books away, lie down', we assumed our bed inspection postures.

At the foot of each bed was a large chest in which cadets kept their clothes. A flap let down from the top half and pants, vest, reefer jacket and shirt had to be folded neatly and displayed on top of it. Failure to satisfy the cadet captain's eagle eye as to the neatness of one's chest meant a 'chest strafe' – early to the dormitory folding and refolding one's uniform.

Quite the most barbaric of punishments was 'Official Cuts'. The wretched victim, having been previously examined by the MO, was marched into the gym guarded on either side by two burly PT instructors.

Drawn up in front of him would be his whole term, standing rigidly to attention. Opposite them would be the Captain, Commander, Term Officer and MO. In the centre, like the guillotine in the Place de la Concorde, would be a boxhorse. The cadet to be beaten would be spread-eagled on this, his trousers removed.

A third PT instructor, generally a huge Royal Marine Sergeant, would inflict on the victim the prescribed number of 'cuts' with a cane. The strength of those Royal Marine Sergeants and the terrible pain they could mete out is best left to the reader's imagination.

Needless to say this horrific and humiliating punishment was not ordered lightly. A cadet two terms senior to me received it, and naturally did not sit down for a week. I regarded him with awe and fascination at what he had undergone.

His offence? He had been caught in a somewhat amatory embrace with a farmer's daughter. Cadets were allowed to visit approved farmhouses for Devonshire teas. A blind eye was turned to their smoking but a possibly innocent excursion into the realms of sex was another matter.

Having been a magistrate for some 34 years I have often been shown round penal establishments, especially those for young offenders. I asked one inmate what he did for recreation. He replied that he fished the Usk! I reflected wryly that no one had ever invited me to do that, or anything so pleasant, and that my parents had actually paid for me to be subject to Dartmouth's discipline whilst this little tearaway was incarcerated at Her Majesty's pleasure.

'Mr Holloway, you do not seem to know whether you are in elevation or plan.' The halitosis breath of the Drawing Office instructor assailed my nostrils.

He was of course perfectly correct, but then I loathed the Drawing Office in the engineering workshops at Sandquay. I could not then and cannot now see how I could possibly have benefited from the engineering training we were all obliged to undergo. A cross-section of a crankshaft, work at the lathe, the making of screws, how did any of this make me a more efficient executive naval officer? Had we been taught the capabilities of the engine rooms to which we were later to telegraph countless revolution orders it might have made more sense. I could only conclude that it was a hangover from the days of 'Jacky' Fisher to drag the Royal Navy kicking and screaming into the twentieth century. The birthpangs had been unduly prolonged, and to my mind and many others, the big workshops had long since served their purpose.

To be appointed to the naval staff at Dartmouth was very definitely a major step on the promotion ladder. Hardly a Captain of the College failed to achieve flag rank and indeed during my first term R.V. Holt was promoted to Rear Admiral whilst still in command of the College. He was succeeded by Frederick Dalrymple-Hamilton of cherubic countenance and kindly demeanour. His wife and daughters were good enough to ask me and three other junior cadets to tea in the Captain's house. It was delightful to be in the company of a family for a while and I have always remembered how much I appreciated seeing an open fire. That was something you never saw at the College.

Our Term Officer was Lieutenant Walter Starkie, a very humane man, and one who I was sorry to see moved on with the advent of the House system. He became engaged to Admiral Cunningham's niece during the war but tragically was killed in the Mediterranean in 1941.

As Blake House Officer, we found we were to be under the command of Lieutenant Peter W. Gretton. A cadet said in later life, 'Gretton should never have been sent to Dartmouth.' This statement in no way reflected on Gretton's ability as a naval officer. When war came his rise was justifiably meteoric becoming a Captain at 38, the same age as Nelson. Retiring as a Vice Admiral, Sir Peter Gretton's ill health prevented the, till then, certainty of his promotion to First Sea Lord.

However, Gretton simply had no sense of humour and was totally unable to communicate with young cadets. During his two years at the College he was seen to smile twice and I am sure that one of those was a mistake. Conversation was non-existent, rather there were staccato barks of command at which everyone jumped and obeyed instantly.

Another officer who was never seen to smile was Captain Campbell R. Hardy, Royal Marines, later to become General Sir Campbell Hardy, Commandant General of the Corps. I am told his vocabulary on Ward Room guest nights was however quite extensive and that he was fully conversant with the sexual abilities of Eskimo Nell. This of course was a side of him that we never saw. As our PT Officer he was responsible for weighing cadets each term. We stood stark naked on the weighing machine in the gym, a gym instructor shouted out our names and weight, and Hardy, moustache bristling, would record it in his book. It never entered our heads that this seemingly unbending man might have a more human side to him. The side we saw was about as friendly as a piece of cold steel bedecked with a Sam Browne belt.

In May 1937 the rigid term system was replaced by the House system to make the College more like an ordinary public school. Terms one to five were in the junior houses, six to eleven in the senior houses. This certainly relaxed the atmosphere of awe in which we had previously held our seniors. However, at first it seemed strange to talk to a cadet quite openly whereas the previous term it would have been a beatable offence.

A typical cadet's day would start at 0625 when the College porters would shout, 'Turn out'. Cadets, who slept 40 to a dormitory, rushed to the bath place where one was given five minutes to wash and go through the cold salt water plunge. If no cadet captain (the equivalent of a prefect) was looking, a quick wetting of the head and vigorous towelling would give the impression of total immersion.

Five minutes to dress, in silence, would precede a rush to the huge Mess room where milk and hard ships-biscuits were provided. An hour's work period before breakfast was loathed equally by staff and cadets. Yawning heads cannot take in subjects well and in the dark winter months it was highly unpleasant.

Divisions were held after breakfast, cadets performed PT exercises on the parade ground before lining up in serried ranks for short prayers. We marched off to the strains of the College band which consisted of aged pensioners with brass instruments. Their repertoire was not extensive but they did add 'Roll out the Barrel' once the war had started. That fatuous song 'We're going to hang out our washing on the Siegfried Line' was not surprisingly, dispensed with after Hitler's blitzkrieg had been unleashed.

Instruction followed till lunchtime. This might take the form of ordinary subjects such as History, Navigation or Mathematics but also included Seamanship, an hour's gym, or squatting on the parquet flooring of the quarterdeck or main hall taking down semaphore or Morse. It is just as well that I never had to signal to someone in an emergency as I was hopeless at both. My mind had a mental block for some letters, whilst I never forgot others. Naval history occupied hours of our instruction, the Battle of Trafalgar even being re-enacted with models. When I had the temerity to enquire what use this was to cadets in the steam age, I was told, 'History repeats itself.' Wisely for once, I kept silent.

A Professor Callendar, who was Professor of Naval History at Greenwich, had written a tome entitled *Sea Kings of Britain*. This contained the potted lives of our wooden wall Admirals and was required reading for all cadets.

Two History masters, Hodges and Hughes, wrote *Select Naval Documents*, a small book containing extracts from letters written by Admirals in the sixteenth to eighteenth centuries. Our parents were forced to buy both these books for our education, but I doubt whether they furthered our learning. Doubtless it helped to line the pockets of their authors.

'Clear College' followed lunch. Cadets were not allowed back in for one and a half hours and during that time the place was cleaned. Exercise had to be 'Logged'. 'Logs' were divided into full and half logs. Obviously a game of rugger was a full log. A half hour's run had to be married with half an hour's squash to make a whole.

Astoundingly enough, 'shooting and haircut' counted as a whole log. I never understood why. At first, I was such a bad shot that I shot out the lights illuminating the target instead of the target itself. Gretton could not abide such inefficiency and saw to it that my shooting improved.

Instruction followed tea until Evening Quarters on the quarter-deck – a sort of 'Appel'.

Supper was followed by prep and lights out at 2125. One was usually glad to get to sleep. The latter might well be interrupted by the College clock which of course, boomed its hours in naval bell fashion.

The civilian masters were, on the whole, far more likeable and kindly than their service counterparts. They did not have the promotion ladder in front of them and were not the awe-inspiring figures which many of the super efficient officers were.

One man however, who inspired awe was the Headmaster, E.W. Kempson. A huge figure of a man with jowls like a bulldog, his robed presence struck dread into cadets. He wore a monocle and if that dropped it was a signal that thunder was imminent. Kempson had a daughter, Rachel, the famous actress, who had married Michael Redgrave shortly before our term entered Dartmouth. Twice they came to the College and performed some sketches. Little did we know how famous they were to become. Perhaps it was as well that Kempson did not live to see the left-wing antics of some of his grandchildren, he would have been horrified.

In the summer of 1937 the whole College, with the exception of the three junior terms was taken to witness the Coronation Naval Review at Spithead. We were naturally furious and disappointed but there was a small sop. As compensation, those left behind were embarked in two destroyers and taken to Devonport where we watched the launching of HMS *Gloucester* by the Duchess of *Gloucester*. Looking back it was just as well that no one could foresee the fate of this beautiful 6" gun cruiser. I was to be only miles away from her in May 1941 when she was sunk by German bombers off Crete during the hellish battle for the island.

We were constantly drilled in what would be expected of future naval officers, cadets even having to fall in outside a classroom should it be locked or occupied.

Later we progressed to Guard duties and paraded with black gaiters and bayonets fixed. The drills which I am unlikely to forget involved the unfixing of bayonets and sheathing them home in their scabbards. At the command, 'Unfix', you grasped your rifle between your knees and slipped the bayonet catch. At the command, 'Bayonets', you were supposed to carry the bayonet across your body and place it in the scabbard on your left-hand side, without looking down.

Women were conspicuous by their absence at Dartmouth. In fact, unless one was ill and reporting to Sister Cheetham in the Sick Bay you hardly ever saw one. Sister Cheetham was not exactly Marilyn Monroe either. The absence of women may have led to the fact that there was no false modesty in the huge swimming pool attached to the gym – cadets swam naked. This afforded opportunities for backsides to be inspected for signs of a beating. No cadet could keep it quiet for long that he had received this punishment; the new raw red weals turned to blue bruises later, and comments were made on the accuracy or otherwise of the cadet captain who had inflicted them.

In July 1938 one of the earliest combined operations exercises was carried out when the Ninth Infantry Brigade landed on Slapton Sands nearby. Bad weather prevented their re-embarkation and thus 1300 officers and men of the King's Own Scottish Borderers and Lincolns were housed and fed by the College. A statuette of a soldier was later presented to the College to mark the British Army's gratitude. The presenter was a then unknown Brigadier, Bernard Law Montgomery.

The start of the winter term 1938 saw the College being put on a semi war footing due to the Munich crisis. We filled sandbags and air raid precautions were exercised. Some rudimentary air raid shelters were built, the heating corridors below the College having proved unsuitable for this purpose.

Some RNVR officers appeared – we had never seen 'Wavy Navy' stripes before. Later of course their wearers vastly outnumbered the straight stripes of the Royal Navy.

Machine gun emplacements were constructed on the roof of 'D' Block. To cadets this was all heady stuff. After all, this was what our training was all about, wasn't it? We knew nothing of the realities of war and rather relished the prospect of its imminence. We practised bayoneting sandbags and hoped the enemy would not stick cold steel into our stomachs, reminiscent of Corporal Jones in the immortal *Dad's Army*: 'They don't like it up them, Sir!'

In the spring of 1939 it was evident that war would come sooner or later and the training cruiser HMS *Frobisher* was withdrawn to prepare for active service. Normally, Special Entry or 'Pubs' (eighteen-year-old) cadets and the Darts would make three cruises in her: West Indies, Mediterranean and Scandinavia. Now this had to be foregone and the 'Pubs' were sent to Dartmouth, much to their chagrin.

The two different entries of cadets had mixed in the training cruiser, but they were segregated at Dartmouth. There was nowhere else to accommodate the 'Pubs' but in the disused seamen's barracks at Sandquay. The 'Pubs' worked a separate routine and we were extremely envious of their freedom compared to ours. They could smoke, buy a pint of beer in Dartmouth, and generally behave like grown-ups whilst we were still schoolboys.

Among the 'Pubs' in the summer of 1939 was Prince Philip of Greece. On his departure from the College he was awarded the King's Dirk for the best all-round cadet.

In the summer term of 1939 three things of note occurred. The first was the making of a film by Maurice Elvey. The theme was supposed to be a fictional picture of life as a cadet at the College. Fictional it certainly was, and like the media today, what the producer and director did not know they made up. The film went by the sickening title of Sons of the Sea and the opening credits were superimposed on Dufaycolor pictures of sixteenth century men-o'-war.

An amateur cinematographer myself, I was fascinated by the film making. I had never before realised how disjointed 'shooting' a film could be. The director did actually sit in a canvas chair with his name on the back and shouted 'Cut' occasionally.

The film was shown to cadets the following term. It provoked alternate groans and laughter as scene followed scene, any resemblance to reality being totally coincidental. The final straw came when a cadet approached his House Officer and asked, 'May I borrow your car, Sir?' Since 95 per cent of cadets were prevented by law from driving due to age and cars were strictly forbidden at Dartmouth, the request had us rolling in the aisles.

The second event was the tragic sinking of the submarine *Thetis* in Liverpool Bay. The terrible drawn out saga continued for days with the entombed men tapping messages on the steel walls of their coffin.

The only comforting aspect of the disaster was the escape to the surface of Captain Oram, one of the only three survivors. His son, John Oram, was a member of my term and my House. She was a Jonah of a boat. I was later to see her in Alexandria in 1941 renamed *Thunderer*. A change of name did not prevent her being sunk by the enemy.

The third event was a private visit by their Majesties, the King and Queen, to Dartmouth at the end of the summer term. We had known about this for weeks and my term was chosen to exhibit our prowess at gymnastics before the royal visitors. I was apprehensive at the prospect. Indifferent as I was to gymnastics, I thought of them verging on the side of boredom. Moreover I had never quite mastered the art of vaulting a boxhorse.

We liked our PT instructor however, and were determined not to let him down, even when we heard that the whole performance would be in silence – our display commands would be by whistle only.

The royal yacht *Victoria and Albert* steamed majestically into Dartmouth harbour, the Royal Standard at her masthead. I had been to lunch on board her when, as a small boy, my parents and I had been invited by Paymaster Captain Louis Ricci, better known as 'Bartimeus' the author of naval books. Ricci, who was serving on board at the time had adopted his pen name by reason of the fact that he was blind in one eye.

What I could not of course foresee, would be that I should spend a week on board the royal yacht, but in less glamorous circumstances. Late in the war, in the winter of 1944, the 'V & A' was moored alongside HMS *Excellent*, the Portsmouth gunnery school at Whale Island. There she provided accommodation for officers, of which I was one, undergoing courses at the school. A very narrow gangplank was provided, and this proved fatal for some inebriated officers returning on board.

Matters of interest in the royal yacht were electrical points in the bathrooms (highly dangerous?) labelled 'Curlers', and padded loo seats to comfort cold royal posteriors.

Our gym display duly took place without a hitch, the royal party being kind enough to applaud us. If they were totally bored, since our gymnastics were not exactly of Olympic standard, they were too polite to show it. I can now with truth say that I have taken part in a Royal Command Performance.

Prince Philip was invited for tea on board during the week-end and it is said that this was the first meeting between Princess Elizabeth and her future husband. Much turbulent water was to flow under bridges between that peacetime meeting and the royal marriage after the war.

The King inspected Divisions on the Sunday and presented awards. I was not among the recipients.

In company with what seemed the whole population of Dartmouth, College and town, I was in the flotilla of boats which followed the departure of the royal yacht to the harbour mouth.

Peacetime pageantry, frock coats and swords, all this was to be swept away in the hecatomb which was to be suffered by the world. Six weeks later we were at war.

2

War

The summer leave of 1939 passed with tennis, dances and diversions galore for sixteen-year-olds. My parents had a cook, a housemaid and a gardener, beside our faithful nanny, Frances Mills. When she died, still with my parents, she had been with the family for 67 years. Faithfulness like that does not exist any more; life was enjoyable.

We returned to wartime Dartmouth in late September to find a very different College from the one we had left in peacetime. Gone were all the young, keen and super-efficient House Officers, their places taken by older 're-treads'. A subtle change was at once apparent. The 're-treads' were kindlier, because like the civilian masters, they were no longer subject to the promotion ladder. I welcomed the change.

Dalrymple-Hamilton soon left for his wartime appointment, to be relieved by Captain Cunliffe. Dalrymple-Hamilton was I hear, at Paddington Station in uniform waiting for the train to take him back to Dartmouth when war was declared. He was surprised and not a little put out to hear an old lady accost him with the words: 'Stationmaster, what time does this train leave?' Until war broke out, civilians had never seen officers in uniform, so perhaps the mistake was, almost, forgivable.

The hated blackout was rigorously enforced, but at least we now had curtains. Such luxuries had been unheard of at Dartmouth in peacetime.

Cadets carried service gas-masks everywhere. These were at least less demeaning than the dreadful civilian types in their cardboard boxes, and probably more efficient too.

Familiarity breeds contempt as always and the diverse contents of the gas-mask bags at chance inspections had to be seen to be believed. These varied from apples ('Darts') to cigarettes ('Pubs'). We felt rather juvenile – and were.

Films were shown on the quarter-deck and a special wooden projection room was set up. This was in the charge of the science master assisted by a lab technician. The science master had an accent alien to cadets' ears and the phrase, 'Stroike yer arc Green'ill,' used to echo around the assembled auditorium as the projector sparked into glowing life.

Our new House Officer was Lieutenant Commander 'Pluffy' Plowden, a charming man whose employment after retirement from the Navy had been with the BBC. He would bring his radio in to the gunroom so that we could listen to Winston Churchill's broadcasts. I remember being really thrilled and uplifted by these. For the first time one heard a politician who did not mince words and when he spoke of 'that guttersnipe Hitler' instead of the craven 'Herr Hitler' of the sycophants, one felt that here was a man with guts, a leader one could follow.

Churchill had been recalled as First Lord of the Admiralty, an appointment he had held in the First World War. On learning that the old warrior had returned to his post the Admiralty sent a signal to the fleet: 'Winston is back.'

The new First Lord wasted no time in impressing himself on the future officers of the Service, and that term he inspected us at Divisions. He affected the curious 'uniform' of First Sea Lord, a reefer jacket and cap, which many thought made him look like a chauffeur. Churchill has often been likened to a bulldog, both in looks and in bellicosity. He proved this in a rousing speech afterwards and was cheered to the echo. It made one proud to have had the honour to have actually been in his presence.

There had been little as yet to show cadets that they were at war, but soon tragedy corrected this. The venerable battleship *Royal Oak* was torpedoed in Scapa Flow on 14 October with the loss of 24 officers and 809 men. Some midshipmen who had left Dartmouth only that July were among those who perished, and that did more than anything else to bring home to us what war was all about – killing, and being killed.

We also reflected on the vulnerability of Scapa Flow, an anchorage that we, and the Admiralty, had thought to be impregnable. One has only to look back on such disasters as the Maginot Line, Singapore, Pearl Harbor and the sinking of the *Prince of Wales* and *Repulse* to realise how wrong we were.

On the plus side however, there came in December 1939 a tremendous boost to the nation's morale in general and to Dartmouth cadets in particular. The spectacular action between the 'pocket battleship' *Graf Spee* and our cruisers *Ajax*, *Exeter* and *Achilles*, led to the scuttling of the German ship at the mouth of the River Plate. It is no part of this book to relate the history of the action; the morale booster to us was a visit to Dartmouth in January 1940 by Captain Woodhouse, who had commanded *Ajax* in the battle.

It was fascinating to have the tactics explained to us by someone who had been so intimately involved in their execution. It was even more fascinating to listen to an officer who had been under heavy enemy fire, and returned home victorious. We cheered him to the echo. Little did I realise that I was to spend six weeks in that delightful cruiser, *Ajax*, when in 1942 I was ordered to return home in her from the Mediterranean.

The dark and intensely cold winter of 1940 gripped us all with profound dreariness. No one who has not endured the blackout can have any idea what it meant never to have lights blazing from uncurtained windows. Even car lights (if one had the petrol to run a car) were confined to tiny pencils of light behind which it must have been a nightmare to drive. Add therefore, cold, darkness, the onset of rationing, to 1001 wartime restrictions and the reader will have some idea of the depression thus generated.

The Easter term 1940 was our eleventh and last as Dartmouth cadets. We were real 'dogs' lording it over our juniors just as we had been subordinated to our seniors throughout our College career.

We had pockets in our trousers, our lanyard knots reached almost to our navels, and we could walk where previously we had doubled.

We had 'cabins' or studies, even though we were three to a space suitable for a small dwarf. The bliss of this was privacy; somewhere where we could retreat and play Artie Shaw records on our HMV portable gramophones. Looking back, we may not have valued it as much as we should have done. Midshipmen at sea had a total lack of privacy. One might almost have been on the lower deck in this respect.

The passing out examinations lasted a fortnight and cadets sat this in D Block, at the rear of the College. No one was allowed near and complete silence reigned. All the normal subjects were examined plus Navigation, Mechanics, Electrics, Hydrostatics and Engineering.

With History, English and Geography, I had no difficulty – I had been in the top set in these subjects all my time at the College. I was tolerably good at French, being in the middle set, and enjoyed it. But, Mathematics and anything allied to it were anathema to me and since a great deal of the examination was set on these matters, my performance in those warranted the remark 'could have done better'.

There were unexplained gaps in the Dartmouth curriculum and Shakespeare was one of them. Incredibly we were only introduced to the Bard at the passing out exam, in the shape of *Coriolanus*. I found the play uninteresting, and did not consider that Roman politics furthered my education. Contrast our lack of Shakespeare with the fact that one term was devoted solidly to learning, and acting, R.C. Sheriff's *Journey's End*. That the top English set should have been made to waste their time on this rather minor play was due to our English master. He was 'Sammy' Sampson, a delightful man but preoccupied with the last war in which he had served as an Army Officer. He thus recreated through us, his captive audience and actors, reminiscences of trench warfare. He affected the rank of Captain which has irritated me from that day to this. No army officer below the rank of Major should retain his rank. I am often inclined, when an elderly moustached gentleman is introduced as Captain Carruthers to enquire gently what ship he commanded.

The long fortnight of exams eventually came to an end. We had all passed out and next term would be Cadets, Royal Navy, not RN Cadets – a subtle distinction.

I said goodbye to the College without a backward glance. This was for two reasons, the first and foremost being that I had hated the place and was glad to get away. I had come to the conclusion when I had been at Dartmouth for a year and a half that I was 'Not quite cut out for the job.'

However, resignation was, in 1940, unthinkable, and even if allowed, would have ended in my being called up, probably as an Army Private. Horrors! If one had to fight a war I certainly was not going to do it otherwise than as an officer.

That at least opened many doors and ensured some comfort. I had no false ideas about thinking one should learn how the other half lived by practical experience. Secondly, we knew we would return to Dartmouth in May but as Frobishers not College cadets. We were growing up.

The so-called 'phoney war' ended during the Easter leave. The Führer invaded Denmark and Norway. That, though the West had no inkling of it, was but the lull before the storm.

May 1940 saw us back at Dartmouth but leading a very different life to the one we had led for three and a half years.

The Frobisher cadets were accommodated in the former seamen's barracks at Sandquay, half way down the hill from the College, going towards the engineering workshops. There, as Marie Antoinette played at being a milk maid with her courtiers, so we were playing at being on the lower deck.

Having said that I would not voluntarily wish to learn how the other half lived, here I was living the life of an ordinary seaman. There existed some important differences however. Provided we passed all our technical examinations we were certain of leaving Dartmouth as midshipmen. There was, thank heaven, no question of waiting to be made a CW (Commissioned and Warrant) candidate, of serving a year or eighteen months on the actual lower deck, with the real possibility that we might remain there. Perish the thought.

We wore blue serge trousers and sweaters, we slung and slept in hammocks (surprisingly comfortable) and we were organised as Cooks of the Mess. This fortunately did not mean that we were dependent on each other's culinary expertise. Whoever was Cook of the Mess had to fetch the meal for his messmates and clean the crockery afterwards.

If we committed a misdemeanour, we were 'in the rattle', caps off before the Commander's table. A punishment drill or stoppage of leave would result. Our bottoms were safe, beatings were left behind at the College, although as midshipmen at sea we could again be subject to a beating for a serious offence.

A cultural shock now hit the 'Darts', some will doubtless say long overdue. To those reading this now it may seem strange, but as Royal Navy cadets we had never come into contact with boys of any social class but our own. Matches were played against Downside and Blundells, both fee-paying public schools. To enter Dartmouth town was strictly forbidden, so where would we have met boys of a different strata?

We now encountered cadets from grammar schools who had entered the Navy via the Special Entry System. Accents grated on our ears and expressions were used which were anathema to us. One particular cadet was the son of an Engine Room Artificer. All credit to him, but because he was poisonous and overbearing, he was debagged a number of times *pro bono publico*.

Dominion and Empire cadets were also present; the Canadians I always liked and the Indians were charming. We were allowed to smoke and to frequent pubs, and we could wear plain clothes when 'ashore'. We felt very grown-up.

We had left schoolboy subjects behind, and concentrated instead on Gunnery, Torpedoes, Signals and Seamanship. Little did we know how soon we were to put our gunnery instruction to practical use.

There were some who were good at signals. I was not among them. Chief Yeoman of Signals Tarling would show us a flag and intone, 'Aircraft detected by RD/F [later radar] approaching the fleet.' We had no idea what RD/F was, but how glad we were of it when it came to the 'real' war!

As with Morse, I took some signals in and others I could never keep in my head. For this reason I was thankful that when I became an Officer of the Watch later in the war, the dreaded 'Officer of the Watch manoeuvres' were somewhat modified. This was something I feared. It was usually practised in the Dog Watches between 1600 and 1800. The signal to carry this out would be hoisted by the Senior Officer's ship. The correct drill would then be for everyone to clear the bridge except the wretched Officer of the Watch and the Captain. The latter was there only to take over should his ship appear to be endangered by its learner driver.

Signals indicating particular manoeuvres would then be hoisted by the flagship and the Officer of the Watch was supposed to: (a) be able to read the hoist (b) to translate it into a manoeuvre (c) turn his ship into the ordered pattern.

Horrors! The signals would have been beyond me but Richard Shelley, my Captain in the cruiser *Suffolk*, and descendant of the poet, allowed the Chief Yeoman to remain on the bridge, for which I was thankful. Possibly Shelley was anxious that his young Sub-Lieutenant should not be shown up in front of the fleet, and suffer the ignominy of the dreadful hoist, 'Signal the name of Officer of the Watch'. There, in the flags for all to see who could read, would be proof positive of the OOW's poor manoeuvre. Fortunately, I enjoyed turning the 10,000-ton cruiser, and was tolerably good at it, even on occasions meriting the accolade 'Manoeuvre well executed' from the flagship.

A signal which was not so complimentary however, was sent to Shelley; the subject matter being myself. We were in the Indian Ocean, five large troopships in convoy from Fremantle to Bombay. Our mission was to escort American and New Zealand troops to the war in Burma.

Fremantle had been a battlefield too, as the New Zealanders, rightly or wrongly thought that the Americans had been too amorous with their womenfolk back home. Leave was only allowed to separate nationalities on separate nights. This did not prevent the New Zealanders climbing down the hawsers, knives between their teeth, and beating up the Americans on shore leave. And we won the war!

I had the Middle as Officer of the Watch on the voyage back to India and had to keep station on the Commodore's ship – Something happened which taught me never, but never, to take anything for granted.

The convoy manoeuvred in Zigzag No. 10. This meant turning 10 degrees to port of the MLA or Mean Line of Advance. Then 10 minutes later, swing through 22 degrees to achieve the same effect on the starboard side. The Mediterranean fleet had used practically no other zigzag throughout the sixteen months I had served in it.

As Midshipman of the Watch in those Mediterranean days it was my responsibility to watch the clock and caution my Officer of the Watch when it was time to give the order to turn. I knew the zigzag by heart, or thought I did – this was nearly to prove a very costly mistake. Familiarity breeds contempt.

I was now Officer of the Watch on the Compass Platform, or bridge, of a 10,000-ton cruiser in the warm darkness of an Indian Ocean night; we were in the middle of a war zone.

'War is mostly waiting,' someone once said. So it is, and it can be very boring, interspersed with short periods of exciting hyper-activity. Throughout my watch I had been talking to the PCO or Principal Control Officer, a Torpedo Lieutenant who was there to control the armament in an emergency.

The huge bulk of the Commodore's troopship loomed in the semi darkness of the tropical night.

'Port 10,' I ordered down the voice pipe.

'Ten of port wheel on, Sir,' replied the helmsman, 20 feet below me.

It takes a large cruiser quite some time to answer to the wheel, my ghastly error was therefore not immediately apparent. I was saved by my good friend Charles Stephen, a paymaster midshipman who had been junior to me at Dartmouth. He was on watch in the Plot below and fortunately had his wits about him. He could see the giro compass repeater on the bulkhead, and was horrified to see it beginning to click the wrong way.

'I say Sub, aren't you going the wrong way?' came his anxious voice from below. Oh my God, I thought, it can't be, but it was. The PCO had heard Stephen's voice too, and we both swung to the left, training our binoculars on the Commodore's ship.

There was no doubt. She loomed larger in the lenses of our night glasses, a sure sign of closing range, we were turning towards each other, not together to starboard as the zigzag demanded. Commands came quickly. The PCO gave orders for increased propeller revolutions. I ordered the wheel amidships, and then 20 degrees to starboard. No time to call the Captain, asleep below in his sea cabin and blissfully unaware of the imminent danger to his ship.

Seconds ticked by; I know now what the hackneyed expression 'on leaden feet' means. We were still closing the gap, and I braced myself for the ghastly impact of two big ships. A combined tonnage of 30,000 tons at a closing speed of 36 knots made a horrific picture in my mind.

Slowly, ever so slowly, we began to heel to starboard and the terrible nearness of the Commodore's ship began to lessen. We had done it, but only just. I must admit I was shaking, and was glad of the darkness to conceal it. I gave the necessary orders to bring us back to proper station-keeping on the Commodore's ship and wished I could have had a stiff drink. (Only the MOs and the Padre drank at sea, and to be fair, they didn't consume much alcohol either.)

Then came my second error of that awful night. I did not tell the Captain that his ship had so nearly collided whilst he slept. To be fair to myself, I thought the Torpedo Lieutenant would do it, as he was the Senior Officer on the bridge at the time. Shelley slept on and was totally ignorant of what had happened.

The morning came, I was in my cabin. A knock at the door, the Captain's messenger: 'Captain wishes to see you in his sea cabin, Sir.' Butterflies, no, large moths, invaded my stomach. I knocked on the Captain's door and entered.

Richard Shelley stood there, a signal in his hand. I liked him, and he was always kind to me. His kindness was going to be sorely tried that morning.

'Read that,' he ordered, handing me the signal.

I read: 'To *Suffolk* from Commodore. Why did you commit unfriendly act last night and try to ram me?'

I had no defence. It did not need a Marshall Hall to spell out my guilt. Later, Shelley sent me a copy of the signal. I took it as having been forgiven. It taught me a lesson no other training could have done. Always, but always check your facts, however well you think you know your subject.

The German blitzkrieg in the West was launched on 10 May 1940. For a while we were unaffected in our beautiful Devonian backwater. Bland communiques were broadcast: 'The BEF is withdrawing to prepared positions.' We believed it all at the time – little did we realise, as in so many theatres of war later, that it was a euphemism for 'Retreat is in danger of becoming a bloody rout.'

Then the war hit us with a vengeance.

Readers will remember the awful scene in the film *Gone with the Wind*, where the defeated and wounded Confederate soldiers are seen lying row upon row in the blazing sun of the main square in Atlanta. A similar sight, but not quite so gruesome, met our astonished eyes on a late May morning.

I walked onto the gallery which surrounded the quarter-deck, or main hall of the College. The first thing that struck me was the smell. Smells are pleasant and unpleasant, most are evocative. A boys' prep school very often smells – of small boys naturally, a melange of chalk and urine.

A dining room after a dinner party smells rich; it is the brandy fumes and the cigar smoke that does it. One's beloved smells of scent, probably given to her by her lover. A prison (and I have visited a few, as a magistrate) smells strongly of disinfectant.

The odour which arose from the quarter-deck was one I had not encountered before but was to come to know very well during the war years. It was of unwashed human bodies, particularly feet – those of troops. It had a rancidity in it which one old Indian Army Colonel was to describe as 'hot rickshaw coolie'.

The quarter-deck was covered with men's bodies, men in khaki uniform, mostly still sleeping, dirty, dishevelled and unshaven. Their kit, or what was left of it, lay beside them. There seemed to be very few rifles or weapons of any kind.

I realised with a sense of deep shock that I was looking down on some of the remnants of a defeated army. Soldiers of the British Expeditionary Force lay below me. A once much vaunted body of men, they now lay like the Confederate troops, driven from the Continent by a ruthless and vastly better equipped enemy.

Later, I was to see Italian troops in like case as prisoners in Egypt. Our own soldiers, defeated and evacuated from Crete. But this was my first real sight of war, and I did not like it.

Events followed thick and fast as the German mastery over France and the Low Countries took effect. The troops on our quarter-deck had been evacuated from France as the German trap closed tight around the Allied forces.

The next day we awoke to find the harbour choked with Belgian, Dutch and French trawlers. Their skippers had fled the enemy onslaught and made good their escape whilst a route was open to them.

Here again, they looked haggard, as well they might. They had brought their families and possessions with them and chosen freedom in England instead of subservience to an alien master.

The German guttersnipe was dancing beside the Voiture-restaurant in Compiègne forest. France, Belgium and Holland lay prostrate at his feet. This sudden influx of foreigners must have caused a headache for Captain Cunliffe, now Naval Officer in Charge, Dartmouth, beside being Captain of the RN College.

Ever since the German attack in the West, rumour had been of the fifth columnists impeding the fighting capacity of our forces. Nuns were seen who later produced machine pistols from their habits. Parachutists were dropped behind the Allied lines in British or French uniforms and played havoc with the signposts.

The Germans were poisoning the water etc., etc. Rumour feeds upon rumour, and in the harried retreat of our forces to the Channel Coast some credence was bound to be put upon this falsehood.

It was against this background that Cunliffe decided to use the Frobisher cadets to patrol the streets of Dartmouth. Although we resented being cast in the role of soldiers, this was nevertheless an exciting event for us when we received the order. We were actually to be made part of the war machine.

That classic television series *Dad's Army* would not be broadcast for 30 years. Had we had a preview of it in 1940, we might have felt that there was a dreadful resemblance to our own posturings in spite of our youth. The Wehrmacht and Luftwaffe would have made mincemeat of us and the Home Guard, had it not been for the RAF. Fortunately for us, ignorance was bliss, and we relished our new role as defenders of Dartmouth.

The *Dad's Army* image was further enhanced by our orders, or lack of them, as to what we were actually to do. We were ordered to act as sentries on Dartmouth's darkened streets, rifles on our shoulders, bayonets fixed – what else? No one really knew – there had not been a curfew in the UK for centuries, and none was ordered then.

The only image we had of a Frenchman was Breton jersey and beret, onions dangling from his bicycle. Suppose the crafty Kraut fifth columnists infiltrated us without the onions. Should we challenge them? And what about the Belgians and the Dutch? Did they usually sport clogs and how were we to recognise them if they didn't?

Fraser in *Dad's Army* had nothing on us. Fraser was afraid of the dark. One of our cadets was so frightened in the still of that night in 1940 that he shouted out the challenge, 'Halt. There he goes', instead of the customary, 'Who goes there?'

Chief Yeoman of Signals Tarling emerged from the shadows and was lucky not to receive some cold steel in his belly as a reward for doing his rounds.

Whilst I was doing my bit to repel the Fuhrer's military ambitions, my future wife, unknown to me at the time, was doing hers. She lived near Porthcawl in South Wales, and when an invasion seemed imminent, offered her services, together with a school friend. The two young women were ordered to proceed to the end of Porthcawl pier. There, fortified with thermos flasks, and comforted with pillows and blankets, they were to keep watch.

'Report at once by telephone any sign of enemy forces trying to land,' was their order. It was not until three days had passed that they discovered that the elementary precaution of connecting the telephone to HQ had been overlooked. And we won the war.

The hours of night sentry patrols were not taken into account when it came to our technical work by day. This was a foretaste for us all of what it would be like at sea: four hours on, four hours off, and in your waking hours you were expected to study as well. I like my sleep and never got used to it.

The threat of invasion came ever closer in those midsummer months and frantic precautions were taken using every available weapon to fortify our coastline.

To our sentry duties therefore was now added another obligation. Some ordnance authority had unearthed from its cache a 6" calibre gun. By whom had it been manufactured? By the Japanese! This gun was hastily installed on the headland beyond Dartmouth Castle opposite Kingswear.

We were given orders to man it. We had only that term been introduced to the theory of gunnery. Far earlier than expected therefore, we were now to put theory into practice. For those readers whose knowledge of gunnery is scanty, let me say that a 6" gun would be fitted as the main armament of a light cruiser such as *Ajax*, of River Plate fame, or the secondary armament of a battleship such as *Warspite*. Our weapon therefore was certainly no pop gun, and had an invasion taken place it could have wreaked havoc among the enemy forces.

With the benefit of hindsight however, our vulnerability was virtually 100 per cent. We had no cover whatsoever, no armour plating as in a warship, and the projectiles were stored under a piece of canvas. A flight of three Stuka dive bombers could have wiped us out in seconds, as they did the radar tower on the Isle of Wight in the Battle of Britain.

Our Petty Officer Gunners Mates were of course in charge and we soon found ourselves loading and unloading, laying and training, and fetching ammunition from our highly vulnerable makeshift 'magazine'.

We thoroughly enjoyed it in the halcyon weather of that summer. We slept under canvas by the gun, and lived a marvellous outdoor life with Cornish pasties from the College galley as our staple diet. What our reactions would have been had it been cold and pelting with rain can well be imagined.

The defence of Dartmouth harbour was further strengthened by a torpedo tube which was installed near Kingswear Castle on the opposite side of the harbour mouth. The idea of this needs no explanation, but in those days of lack of weaponry, was this not in retrospect a tragic waste? Dartmouth harbour is very narrow at its mouth, no invasion force would have dreamed of landing there; they would have made for Slapton Sands, an ideal landing site and later to be a training ground for the Normandy landings.

Neither the gun nor the torpedo tube were ever put to use, even in exercise. Doubtless the terrible shortage of every kind of weapon and ammunition then was responsible for this, but it made one wonder if the 6" gun and the torpedo tube would ever have proved their effectiveness.

July 1940 came and we had three immediate and pressing tasks with which to occupy ourselves. We had to patrol Dartmouth's streets, we had to man the gun, and we had to take our passing out exams. Which had priority?

I think we all took the long term view that the defence of the realm was best left to our seniors, those who had more experience. If we did not pass our exams we would not go to sea, and of what use would we be to His Majesty's Naval Service then? Accordingly, we addressed ourselves to our studies, and in spite of the lack of sleep occasioned by our extra-mural duties, sat and passed our exams.

I had left Dartmouth three months ago, but knew that I was to return for one more term, albeit as a Frobisher. This time I was to leave it and would not return until we had beaten the Italians, the Germans, and finally, the Japanese.

When war was declared in 1914, all the cadets at Dartmouth were sent to join the fleet, leaving only the juniors at Osborne. It was monstrous; the youngest sent to war were aged only fifteen and a half, little more than children. The eldest were only seventeen and a half.

We too were seventeen and a half, three and a half years away from our majorities, and entitlement to vote. We could fight, but not elect those who would send us to war.

The leave train from Dartmouth was always a happy one. Cadets would blow whistles, shout and cheer, lavatory rolls would stream behind, soon to be blackened by the engine smoke.

We left Dartmouth in high spirits. The blitzkrieg had forced our army from the Continent, and we faced the might of Germany on our own. The Battle of Britain was about to begin, but we were oblivious to it all.

Who would man the gun when we had gone? 'Dad's Army?' We neither knew, nor I fear cared. We were to spend our last leave with our families before our sea appointments. In my case I would be separated from parents and home for nineteen months. I would be lucky to return – some of us never did.

3

To the Mediterranean

My last home leave in the hot months of August and early September 1940 was a very happy one. Nothing had really changed in my parents' household, we still had servants, a cook, a housemaid and a gardener.

My faithful old nanny lived with us – she had been my mother's nanny and had come to 'settle her in' after my parents' wedding in 1910. I adored her. They don't make them like that today.

There were tennis parties, dances, picnics and treasure hunts, teenage romances and riding with a girlfriend. I drew a parallel with *Gone with the Wind* in the previous chapter. This was another parallel: Tara – before the war between the States had touched the Deep South. The men were anxious to fight, their girlfriends looked their prettiest and if their boyfriends were in uniform, so much the better.

My promotion to Midshipman RN. came through and I proudly put up the white patches on my lapels. White was for Royal Navy, blue for Royal Naval Reserve, and red for RNVR. I discarded the white twist of an RN cadet and felt all the manlier for it.

Before we left Dartmouth we had filled in forms which showed our preferences for our sea-going appointments. The Navy always tried to be helpful in this way which surprised me, cynic that I am. Later it was to stand me in good stead. In 1942 I had been appointed to a perfectly ghastly clapped out 1917 vintage ex-US destroyer; I hated it from the word 'go'. My mother entreated with an Admiral friend, a word went to NA2SL (office of Naval Assistant to the Second Sea Lord, where all appointments were made) and I was speedily transferred to the cruiser *Suffolk*. If you can pull strings, why not?

When I qualified as a Fighter Direction Officer, I visited Queen Anne's Mansions where NA2SL was situated. There, my appointment to a fleet carrier was carried out by none other than Michael (later Sir Michael) Hordern, the famous actor.

A Dartmouth friend, John Cardew and I elected to ask for the 8" gun cruiser *Kent*. We did this (a) because we had heard the County class cruisers were very comfortable ships, and (b) because we believed she was in the Mediterranean, though, due to wartime secrecy, the whereabouts of warships was not exactly common knowledge. We did not want to join the Home Fleet and die of boredom swinging round a buoy in Scapa Flow.

My large trunk was packed, my tin trunk (for the tropics) was packed, my white tropical gear purchased, and I awaited my summons to oppose Hitler. The latter had just been joined by Benito Mussolini, who, jackal that he was, hoped that Italy could feed on the carcass of France, recently killed by the Germans.

The Mediterranean was never to be 'Mare Nostrum' as he boasted. his ignominious end was to be hanged upside down together with his mistress, Clara Petacci, on the shores of Lake Garda.

A kind and rich uncle gave me a beautiful pair of Zeiss night binoculars. It was a splendid present. They were immensely useful and much better than the Admiralty issue Barr and Stroud variety. I was always afraid of losing them but I have them still.

Sir, I am commanded by my Lords Commissioners of the Admiralty to appoint you as Midshipman Royal Navy to His Majesty's ship *Kent*.

You are to proceed to your appointment in accordance with the enclosed instructions.

I have the honour to be, Sir,
Your Obedient Servant,
O. Murray
Secretary to the Board

In this delightfully old fashioned way I found that my choice and John Cardew's had been accepted by my Lords Commissioners. My poor parents, particularly my mother, must have dreaded this missive arriving on our hall mat. For me, sad though I was to leave home, my sadness was tempered by excitement. I was only seventeen and a half, more and more people were appearing in uniform, and I might as well get on with it.

The instructions which accompanied my appointment ordered me to report to the Liver Building, Liverpool, on 8 September 1940. My parents of course, were coming to see me off, and booked rooms at the Adelphi Hotel. I had never heard of it, but when I walked into this prestigious LMS establishment I was impressed.

I was not so impressed by Liverpool – I thought it an awful place. This may have been due to my only visits to that grey northern city having been occasions of sadness. My leaving home for war now and later in 1942 when I was serving my brief period in HMS *Richmond*, the old four-stacker.

During that latter time I shared digs in Birkenhead with the First Lieutenant and two young civilian chemists from Lever Brothers' works at Port Sunlight. Liverpool had been heavily bombed, it was a cold, dark November, there was little heat and the war outlook to say nothing of the view from the window was bleak and cheerless. I have never been back. I never want to.

The Liver Building with its two enormous Liver birds stands guard over the dismal Mersey. I found the place depressing also, many rooms had been subdivided with plywood. Uniformed personnel scurried back and forth together with civilian messengers and typists. This was before the building would have been full of pretty Wrens, their pert, serge-skirted bottoms undulating through the corridors.

The David Langdon cartoon comes to mind. A huge plotting room filled with officers and ratings, a gigantic map of the Western Approaches covering the wall.

A busty Wren with long gorgeous legs is standing on tiptoe at the top of a high ladder moving a convoy to its nearest known position. All the men are more interested in the Wren than the convoy.

'Second Officer,' says the Captain in charge.

'Sir?'

'Either we move that convoy further south or you put that Wren in trousers!'

A chance encounter brought temporary joy to our faces. Down the impersonal corridors of the Liver Building came the figure of a small man in the uniform of a Commodore RNR, three rows of medal ribbons adorning his reefer jacket. 'Peter!' my mother exclaimed, and kissed him fondly. Peter was none other than Rear-Admiral Kenelm Creighton (later Sir Kenelm), a life-long friend of my parents. He was always called Peter, never Kenelm.

Peter Creighton had been brought out of retirement to serve as a Commodore of Convoys. These senior officers did wonderful work during the war by acting as commanders of important convoys. They made the necessary tactical dispositions so as to prevent attack and, if that occurred, to defend the convoy. Creighton wrote an account of his experiences in a book entitled *Convoy Commodore*.

To our great delight Peter Creighton told us that he had been appointed Commodore of the convoy in which I was to sail. Obviously it comforted my parents to know that a great friend would be 'in loco parentis', whilst it comforted me, too, to know that 'Uncle' Peter would be with me even if we could not speak to each other.

Our delight was further fuelled by Peter Creighton telling us that due to suspected aerial mines having been dropped in the Mersey no ships could leave harbour, and we could go away for the week-end.

My parents had great friends called Norem, who lived in Knutsford. Nils Norem was Norwegian Consul in Manchester. They had two boys; Robin was my brother Michael's contemporary, Max was my age.

Max had a train room at the top of the house. A fabulous layout had been bought for him from Bassett Lowke, which ran round the room at waist level. He and I spent many a happy hour there in our prep school days. Accordingly we entrained for Knutsford. Max and I renewed acquaintance. I never saw him again, his bomber was shot down over Germany. Doubly tragic for his mother Freda, who was German. Her countrymen had killed her son.

The Battle of Britain was now at its height and we listened enthralled to the news bulletin accounts on the wireless of the huge numbers of German aircraft shot down. That these figures were found after the war to have been greatly exaggerated, matters not. The RAF was gallant – they saved Britain and our morale.

Winston Churchill was growling his magnificent defiance at the 'Narzi guttersnipe', and we loved him for his spirit. There was never any question among us but that we would win, great as were the odds stacked against us.

In the light of what we were to see in the Mediterranean, and particularly Crete, the Navy would never have prevented an invasion. Air power was paramount, a lesson badly and belatedly learned in Whitehall. Fortunately we were in ignorance of this and imagined ourselves safer than we were.

The week-end went by all too quickly, Monday came and we entrained once again for dreary Liverpool. John Cardew and I, together with eight other 'exDarts' were to sail from the Gladstone Dock. Our ship was to be the Shaw Savill liner *Dominion Monarch*. A magnificent new ship, this was to be only her fifth voyage. She loomed above us as we walked to the gangway. My luggage was taken away. I was an inexperienced traveller then and it never occurred to me to see it hoisted aboard. Three days out at sea, the thought came to mind, and sick with apprehension I hurried to the baggage hold. Thankfully I beheld my two trunks. Someone else was not so lucky, the stevedores had forgotten his.

That wonderful film *The Lady Vanishes* recounts a similar situation: Basil Radford and Naunton Wayne, the two archetypal pre-war Englishmen, stand in the corridor of a train discussing the Test Match. They are in a clearing in a German forest.

Basil Radford looks out of the window, then exclaims, 'I say Caldicote, the rear half of the train has been shunted away.' Naunton Wayne does not bother to look up from lighting his pipe. 'Oh no, old boy, quite impossible, our luggage was in it.' I said goodbye to my parents, my mother tearful, my father trying to hide his concern. I was not to see them for nineteen months.

John Cardew and I shared a single cabin. This was luxury compared to US troops embarked later in the war in the 'Queen' liners. They 'slept hot' which meant you had eight hours in your bunk, then relinquished it to two other occupants before getting your head down again.

It was really very like a luxury cruise in our troopship. We were summoned to meals by the playing of *In a Monastery Garden* over the tannoy. Our steward was a pleasant Canadian called Brazil. Every breakfast time he would say, 'Well now boys, what'll it be today, the old toemayto juice?' I rather felt he should have called us Sir, but let it go as colonial familiarity. We were not crowded in the lounges and I was introduced to 'Housey Housey' as the British Army calls it, Tombola to the Navy and Bingo to civilians.

The Army manned some light AA guns, we midshipmen were ordered to do look-out duty on the bridge. I mounted the ladder and wondered if I should salute the Captain. I didn't know the drill, after all, he was Merchant Navy and I was Royal Navy. Fortunately, I didn't go so far as to think that he should salute me, so I gave him a smart hand to cap which he acknowledged perfunctorily.

It was all dull work, but after it I always had sympathy for ratings doing the same job. I never saw a periscope, all I saw was the coast of Northern Ireland. I have never seen it since.

My sea-going experience at that time amounted to one Channel crossing, and our trip to watch *Gloucester's* launching, recounted in Chapter One. I was now to undertake a voyage of some 12,000 miles, to Suez via the Cape. We were one of the WS series or 'Winston's Specials'. These were run monthly round the Cape to build up our armies in the Middle East and India. We had never been so close to invasion since the Napoleonic wars, yet the Prime Minister denuded the British Isles of men and equipment sensing the threat to the

Suez Canal. For this courageous enterprise, he was in possession of information to which few others were made privy: the Enigma decrypts. It is history now that we were reading top secret German cypher signals and this must have had an incalculable effect on our chances of winning the war.

Churchill knew when the Germans had abandoned Operation *Sealion* (the invasion of England), and could therefore reinforce the Middle East with less apprehension. I hasten to add that this is no denigration of a very valiant, and correct decision. I shall touch upon Enigma as it affected Greece and Crete in a later chapter.

There were some odd episodes in life on board *Dominion Monarch*. Being an all male ship, we used the male and female lavatories indiscriminately. Rather naturally I had never before been in a ladies' loo.

At first our protection against raiders was the cruiser *Sheffield*. In company were six destroyers, our reassurance against submarine attack. They turned back at the supposed edge of the U-boat zone, having insufficient fuel for the journey to Africa. *Sheffield* left soon after, and we were then protected by the battleship *Ramillies*, ancient, but mounting 15" guns. Admiral Sir James Somerville later described the 'R' class battleships as 'dear old ladies who couldn't hold their water' – a reference to the inescapable fact that their evaporators could never distil sufficient fresh water for their aged boilers.

The protection afforded us illustrated the importance of the convoy. Eleven huge liners, crammed with troops and equipment would have been a wonderful target for the enemy. Equipment could soon be replaced but it would have taken eighteen years to replace the men.

The convoy consisted of *Britannic*, a Cunard liner in which Peter Creighton flew his Commodore's flag – in company were ourselves, the veteran four-funnelled *Aquitania*, the luxury Royal Mail liner *Andes*, *Athlone Castle*, several Union Castle liners and four 'Star' ships carrying guns, tanks and munitions. How lucky that our enemy was one whose sea power in no way matched that of Japan. The latter's vast and formidable navy would have sent us all to the bottom in double quick time.

An extraordinary coincidence concerned *Andes* and my friend John Kane. He had been in my term at Dartmouth, and like me was destined for the cruiser *Kent*. On board *Andes* was a seventeen-year-old girl called Patricia. Her parents, living in the Middle East, had discovered that their daughter had joined the WAAF by falsifying her age. They moved swiftly, Patricia was discharged and sent on board *Andes* to join them. *Andes* parted company with us at the Horn of Africa and proceeded up the Persian Gulf, thus reuniting the errant Patricia with her parents.

Many years later, Patricia and John met; she is now Mrs John Kane.

We were extremely lucky that *Dominion Monarch*, having been built for the New Zealand run, was for us at least, a cool ship. Not so the Cunarders, built for the colder Atlantic run and without any forced draught ventilation. I talk of the officers' accommodation, for the troops it was not so good. I made my first visit to one of the troop decks to hear a concert. Instantly I was struck by a wave of heat and that awful fetid smell which I had first encountered on the College quarter-deck the previous May. God, I thought, how awful to have to endure this all the voyage. The fans could not cope with the overcrowded troop decks, and I was glad to escape to cooler 'officer country'.

Not for the first time I thanked my lucky stars that I never had to undergo a period on the lower deck. My wife, who was a Wren rating before being commissioned, teases me about this and avers that I didn't know I was born. She has a point.

Lovely, warm, balmy days, flying fish and a change from 'blues' into tropical whites brought me to my first sight of another continent. We dropped anchor in Freetown harbour, and were immediately surrounded by blacks in wooden dugout canoes offering to dive for a 'Liverpool sixpence'. This was the 'white man's grave' I had heard so much about, but it looked lush, green and rather beautiful.

We were only there to refuel and take on water, no one was allowed ashore. Later, in 1943, I was invited to play tennis there on the Governor's court with Richard Shelley, my Captain. It was the hottest game of tennis I have ever played, and I have never forgotten the wonderfully cool fresh limes which we drank afterwards – sheer nectar in that enervating heat.

Water for some of the ships in the convoy, not constructed for the South Africa run, caused grave problems. The need to conserve water in ships at sea is constant, but in HM ships it is much easier. The difference between the high performance requirements of warships and the commercial need for economy is evidenced by the fact that warships make their own water. This, as I have pointed out previously, is distilled from sea water by evaporators, but it consumes much extra fuel.

This does not mean that water can be used ad lib. The sight of naked officers standing under dry showers in a fleet aircraft carrier, shouting at an engineer officer to 'open your bloody cocks!' illustrates my point.

Conversely in *Dominion Monarch*, we had warm baths with no restrictions but it was salt water! Across the bath was a soap rack and on it stood a tin tub of warm fresh water for soaping. I never quite got used to it.

Britannic's tanks were dry, and the naval authorities protested that the small water boats they had could not cope with her requirements in time for the convoy' s departure. The problem was solved by a Royal Fleet Auxiliary tanker. She had just discharged her oil fuel and her tanks were filled with fresh water. No time to clear the tanks and *Britannic* received her water heavily tainted with oil fuel. Yuck! Peter Creighton told me later that the troops substituted oil-gripe for seasickness. It must have been highly unpleasant but the convoy left on time.

The Equator was reached and my first Crossing the Line ceremony. *Neptune* came on board, held his 'court', demanded to know who had not crossed the Line before, and sent his 'policemen' to search for them. Willing victims were placed in a chair beside the pool, 'shaved' with a huge paint brush and unceremoniously tipped backwards into the water. There they were ducked by the 'bears' before being allowed to climb out and watch the antics of others.

I have crossed the Line many times since then – on one occasion in the Indian Ocean in 1943 we carried out a zigzag which on one leg took us south of the Equator, and on the other to the north. What a shame that air travel has consigned this delightful ceremony to history.

Soon after leaving Freetown I was handed a signal. It read: 'To Midshipman Holloway from Commodore. I hope you are enjoying the trip.' I felt very important at receiving this and basked in the reflected glory of knowing the great man.

A midshipman whom I disliked and who knew of my poor signalling abilities came to me and said that I ought to semaphore the reply myself as it was forbidden for junior officers to ask the Merchant Navy to send messages. I asked one of the signallers nicely and within minutes my reply was translated into a flag-waven response. Honour had been preserved.

The wonderful effortless flight of a solitary albatross was our first indication that we were really in the South Atlantic. These great birds are never seen north of the Equator, and I felt thrilled as I watched it wheel astern of us.

The approach to Table Bay by sea is one of the most spectacular that can be enjoyed. It is comparable to seeing New York City from Long Island Sound, or entering the harbour of Rio de Janeiro. Air travel has again turned this wonderful landfall into a screeching of tyres near the Cape Flats.

I fell in love with South Africa as soon as I saw it and this affection has not diminished over the years. To those who foam at the mouth when the Republic is mentioned, it means nothing that we would have lost the war without South Africa's incalculable help. The loss of the Cape route to the Middle East would have meant that no men and materials could round it. With the Western Mediterranean closed, the Suez Canal would soon have belonged to the German guttersnipe, together with the vast oil supplies of the Persian Gulf. Russia could have been rolled up from the south.

John Cardew and I could not wait to get ashore. Three weeks is a long time to be cooped up in a ship. First we called on Commodore Creighton, whose ship was just ahead of ours along the quayside. He greeted us warmly, gave us a drink, and advised us what to see.

We went up Table Mountain by cable car and to Groote Schuur to see the Prime Minister's residence, a wonderful example of Cape Dutch architecture. The buses all had signs, 'nie rook nie' (do not smoke) and 'moenie spoeg nie' (do not spit). The fact that they are the only words in Afrikaans that I know is hardly a linguistic achievement.

But oh, it was the lights, the lights, and again the lights at which we just stared in wonderment, like children around a Christmas tree. There was no blackout in Cape Town and we stood in Adderley Street, for a short time, as if drunk with coruscation.

Jeanette Macdonald and Nelson Eddy were starring in Blue Moon, their names blazing in the warm spring night. It was sheer heaven. The kind South Africans entertained huge parties of young men – some lucky midshipmen met the beautiful Tockie Hellawell, and returned entranced.

The joys of heaven, if vouchsafed at all, do not last long in wartime and within 24 hours we had left our beautiful, scintillating port, en route for Durban.

Later, in 1943, I was to spend three months in Durban when Suffolk was in dock. We were only second to Renown in length of stay; it was said of her Captain that she stayed so long he was next in line for Mayor.

In 1940 however, we only spent a night there, and with no shore leave I had to wait three years to get to know what was then a beautiful city. Sadly, now as in England, the 'planners' and the developers have turned its sea front into a mirror image of Blackpool.

Italy having entered the war, we had to be wary of Italian Somaliland, now of course enemy territory. An uneventful passage to the west of the island of Socotra brought us to a rendezvous with the 8" gun cruiser *Shropshire*, sister ship to *Kent* for which I was destined. She escorted us through the dangerous Perim Strait, and we entered the Red Sea.

Suddenly, about 0900 without any warning, there was a most unpleasant 'whooshing' sound; a sound with which we were then mercifully unfamiliar. We were, like the smell of men's rancid bodies, to become hideously familiar with it later on.

A three-engined Italian plane, probably a Savoia, was just visible at a great height having unleashed its bombs between the ships of the convoy. I had not witnessed any of the Battle of Britain fighting, this was my first glimpse of the enemy, and the first of his attempts to kill me.

The Italians, with honourable exceptions, had little stomach for war, and they rarely bombed except from a great height. *Shropshire* did not even bother to open fire. We had however been summarily introduced to war even before we had arrived at our destination.

I have mentioned smells before in this book. Readers may be forgiven for thinking that my olfactory senses were working overtime. Suez smelt. We smelt it before we could see it – it smelt of unwashed 'gyppo' and oil fuel, each vying with the other to produce a malodorous pot-pourri, for ever to be associated with a Middle Eastern oil port.

Anyone who thinks of the Middle East as glamorous needs gentle correction. It is not. It is hot, dusty, often dirty, noisy and smelly. However, we were excited at the sight of a strange country and though disappointed with our first view of the land of the Pharaohs, we nursed the hope that exotic vistas would soon be unveiled before our eyes.

Not for us the Suez Canal, boring though I later found it to be. We landed at Port Tewfik, the lesser known name for the southern end of the Canal and entrained early in the morning for Alexandria.

Six to a compartment, we set off into the Egyptian countryside. As in English trains then, photographs of the region looked down on us from above each seat. There, to my excitement, was a photograph of the legendary Shepheard's Hotel. I was at the time a devotee of the books of Dennis Wheatley. One of his books, an espionage thriller, described Shepheard's in fictionally glamorous tones.

Here I was in Egypt – what exciting scenes would I witness? Not much that day. We travelled slowly, first inland towards Cairo – were we to see the fabled capital city? No, the nearest we got to it was within 20 miles, the flyblown junction of Zagazig, where we changed trains.

Miles and miles we travelled, our journey soon palling into the tedium of the fellaheen tilling their fields or sailing their feluccas down the Nile. All that can be said for it was that it looked authentically biblical.

A midshipman called Michael Stanley had suggested to those in his compartment that they should wear their pyjamas the whole of the journey in case the dirt and dust of the train should spoil their immaculate white uniforms! Looking like well-fed concentration camp inmates, they astonished the native travellers on Zagazig's platforms. Stanley's idea to arrive on board spotless was basically sound, but defeated by our arrival in Alexandria in an air raid, and the blackout!

Picket boats took us to our ships. I protested that we had been deposited on the wrong ship, we were climbing the gangway of the battleship *Valiant*.

'Oh no, you're not,' said an officer. '*Kent* has been torpedoed, you are now a *Valiant* midshipman.'

An enemy torpedo had altered my life at that early stage. I count myself lucky that it did.

4

Valiant

'If you behave like officers and gentlemen, you will be treated as officers and gentlemen. If you behave like schoolboys, you will treated as schoolboys.' So spake Commander Peter Reid, executive officer of the 32,000-ton battleship *Valiant*, to which I had so suddenly found myself appointed. All the newly arrived midshipmen were lined up on the quarter-deck. It was pitch dark, trying to rain, we had had a tedious and tiring journey and longed for something to eat; somewhere to lay our heads. I don't remember feeling much like an officer then, much more like a schoolboy, thousands of miles from home, in a foreign country, surrounded by strangers in a huge and unfamiliar battleship in wartime.

No wonder that at seventeen and a half, when most boys would indeed be still at school, that inwardly one felt miserably isolated, not a little frightened and with the excitement of earlier anticipations completely evaporated. Of course we couldn't admit it – it was like being under fire or being bombed, you had to put a brave face on it, even though you felt scared as hell.

The Commander spoke some further words of welcome and we were dismissed. Later to rise to the rank of Admiral and a knighthood, Peter Reed was a delightful man, very efficient and as far as a good officer can be, humane and kind. I did not know it then, but *Valiant* was a very happy ship indeed, mainly due to Reed and his Captain, H.B. Rawlings. They had hand picked the officers and many of the senior ratings when the ship commissioned at Devonport.

Everyone knew his job and did it efficiently because they were well led. Napoleon's maxim of 'there are no bad soldiers, only bad officers' had long since been a tenet of the Navy's, and Rawlings and Reed had heeded it.

Perhaps, as I was to hear later, the one person they had not chosen was the Padre. I was told that at the time of the fall of France, the ship's company assembled for Sunday prayers on the quarter-deck. The Padre, recounting the recent tragic events, said, 'And now there is nothing left for us to do but pray, and put our trust in Almighty God.'

The service ended, and as the sailors were about to disperse, Rawlings jumped up and said, 'Sit down, all of you.' They obeyed, wondering what was coming next.

'Don't listen to a word the Padre has said,' exclaimed the Captain. 'Of course there is more to do than pray. We shall fight and fight and fight again, and we shall emerge victorious.'

The ship's company, forgetting they were supposed to be at prayer, stood up, cheered and waved their caps. The Padre slunk away, so, as a later film showed, did Canon Collins when he tried to reprove Air Chief Marshal Sir Arthur Harris for having bombed Dresden.

From the quarter-deck, David Peck led us below. He had been a term senior to us at Dartmouth, a charming junior midshipman. He had less than a year to live – a German bomber was to sink his destroyer *Wryneck* during the evacuation from Greece the following April.

I have touched on the smells which came to my nostrils. An HM ship does not smell, sailors are very clean and always doing their 'dhobeying' (washing their clothes).

'And now I must away, for duty calls, but (hand cupped to mouth) psst, really 'tis to dhobey smalls' sang the large false-bosomed Good Fairy in the ship's pantomime.

It is noise which assails the ears in a warship, never ending, unremitting noise. It may vary from the crash and bang beloved of Gunners' Mates as their gun crews heft the metal-encased fixed ammunition on to steel decks, to the gentle humming of a nearby pump. Indeed, as I shall show in a later chapter, it was the humming of a pump which guided the Italian frogmen to us, thus enabling them to blow us up.

The nails in our shoes clattered on steel ladders, the steel decks of the gangways reflected

Valiant's gunroom ready for breakfast. (Author's collection)

sound, steel doors clamped shut with the clang of a prison cell. The only place in a big ship which is relatively quiet is the quarter-deck, for that is made of wood. Officers taking a constitutional in the Dog Watches are said to be 'pounding the teak'.

Peck led us through this unfamiliar cacophony of sound. We ducked our heads and lifted our legs over the steel cills of the watertight doors. We further ducked under ratings' hammocks, slung in the gangways, such was wartime overcrowding. No doubt they were muttering the time honoured lower deck expletive as some of us bumped heads on their bottoms. (Officers were known as 'pigs' by the sailors. An uncomplimentary allusion, it reflected their view of our living accommodation.)

Bright electric lights protected by steel guards, blazed from the deckheads. A green curtain was drawn across a doorway. Peck pushed it aside and ushered us into the Gunroom. This was to be our home for as long as we were on board.

'Here you are,' he said triumphantly. We looked around. A large mahogany table set for supper, stretched from a small hatch three-quarters of the length of the compartment. At the far end were four or five armchairs. Running the length of the ship's side was a banquette seat, facing chairs at the table. A portable gramophone stood at the armchair end.

From the hatch peered the face of a man. A devotee of Popeye, I thought he looked just like him, toothless and bald. He only lacked the pipe.

'Evenin' Sorrs,' said Popeye.

Petty Officer Cook Hancock looked after our stomachs. I hoped he knew his job. Clad in a singlet, his nether regions out of sight, he did not appear to be a reincarnation of Escoffier. From what might be termed the senior end, two figures rose. The first, slighter and not so tall as the second, wore the single gold stripe of a Sub-Lieutenant.

This was Sub-Lieutenant the Honourable Terence G.T. Stopford, son of the Earl of Courtown. An old Etonian, it was he who would be our lord and master so long as we were snotties in his domain. He smiled a somewhat toothy smile and bade us welcome.

I heaved a sigh of relief for he appeared to be, and indeed was, so nice. The Sub of the Gunroom could make or mar a midshipman's life. He was responsible for the 'Young gentlemen's' discipline and terrible stories used to be noised abroad of bullying by sadistic Subs, aided and abetted by the senior midshipmen.

'Breadcrumbs' it was said they shouted on guest nights. Junior midshipmen obediently put their fingers in their ears. They must not listen to what their seniors were saying. Those who removed the fingers from their ears were soundly beaten when the command 'Belay Breadcrumbs' was given. It was evident from their obedience that they had been listening and so on.

None of that nonsense obtained with Stopford. He ruled the roost yes, in company with senior midshipmen, but it was a very benevolent autocracy for which we were thankful.

The other figure was tall, dark and well built. Sean Connery had yet to make his name as a film star; the young man wearing rather faded white patches on his reefer jacket was the Senior Midshipman, another Terence, Terry Lewin.

Terry Lewin was destined to have a brilliant naval career. Its climax came when, as Chief of the Defence Staff, he master-minded the superlative Falklands campaign. As

Admiral of the Fleet the Lord Lewin, he would never retire, for officers of that rank do not. I heard him speak to the Chatham Club on *Trident*. He spoke for 30 minutes without a note. [Baron Lewin KG GCB LVO DSC passed away on 23 January 1999.]

1 said to Terry Lewin that peacetime evening how grateful we were that Stopford, he and the senior midshipmen did not indulge in the unpleasantness which we feared.

'I stopped all that,' he said forthrightly. 'In any case, such practices have no place at sea in wartime. Also,' he added laughingly, 'there weren't any guestnights.' Even had there been, I know that Stopford and Lewin would have made them enjoyable occasions for us all, senior or junior.

Lewin welcomed us as well, and we settled down to a much needed meal in company with some fifteen others.

The full complement of *Valiant's* gunroom would be about 33, comprising twelve sub-lieutenants, and the remainder midshipmen.

Later, we were shown to the Admiral's flat. This was not an apartment block occupied by a Flag Officer, but a large space in the stern leading to the Admiral's quarters. *Valiant* was not a flagship, so the Captain used this accommodation in harbour.

Never let it be said that the sleeping accommodation of midshipmen at that time was luxurious! We slept twelve or fifteen, on camp beds if we were lucky, in the Admiral's flat. Our clothes were kept in sea chests; the privacy of a cabin was never ours. People came in

Midshipman (later Captain) B.H. Kent and the author beneath *Valiant's* crane. (Author's collection)

and out, voices were heard at all times, occasionally someone would stumble over us in the darkened flat. We didn't care, we were exhausted – and young. We slept at once.

Morning – Reveille is sounded by a Royal Marine bugler over the broadcast system. 'Oh God, what do we do, where do we go?' We soon knew.

'Come on, all midshipmen, PT on the quarter-deck,' came the order. Bleary-eyed with sleep we tumbled up the ladder into a Mediterranean dawn. Press-ups before breakfast, ghastly – even at Dartmouth we did PT after our morning meal!

At that time the decks are swabbed down so everyone is either bare footed or in 'half sea boots'. Sailors cast amused glances at the junior officers exerting themselves. I never saw sailors having to exercise as we did – it seemed unfair and somewhat humiliating.

PT over, we could look around Alexandria harbour. There lay His Majesty's Mediterranean fleet, the battleship *Warspite*, flagship of the C-in-C, the redoubtable Admiral Sir Andrew Browne Cunningham. *Barham* was there, and ourselves, comprising the First Battle Squadron. All however, First World War ships, modernised of course, but nothing as new as what confronted us across the Mediterranean in Italian harbours.

Valiant was the most modern of the three, having very recently had a major refit. Apart from her massive guns she possessed a priceless asset which no one else had – RD/F or Radio Direction Finding (Radar). This was to prove invaluable as the war progressed.

The modern carrier *Illustrious* and the elderly carrier *Eagle* were there, together with cruisers, destroyers and submarines. It was a magnificent sight, but my gaze returned time and time again to the warships, one old, but most of them modern and with sleek lines, made fast to the Mole.

This was the Eastern Mediterranean Fleet of our former ally France, crushed under the heel of her German conquerors. These ships were now interned in Alexandria, their breech blocks removed so that they could not fire their guns, fuel denied to them except for light and heat. The old battleship *Lorraine* was about 1912 vintage and pretty useless. However, the beautiful cruisers *Duguay-Truin*, *Toulon* and *Trouville* were modern, plus the destroyers.

Their Admiral Godfroy had, after prolonged negotiations, agreed to their internment, and there they rotted throughout the war. What a tragic waste, and how valuable they would have been to the Allied cause.

Later, on shore leave in the city, I used to meet hordes of French sailors, their red pom-poms distinctive among the British sailors' white caps. They seemed cheerful enough and seemed to have money – who paid them? I hoped we did not.

It is no part of this book to dilate upon this military and political disaster. Suffice it to say that we felt bitter at the French. When it came to actually having to fight them in Syria (see Chapter Fourteen) our bitterness was mixed with anger.

The new midshipmen were speedily introduced to the routine of a battleship in wartime. First, we were introduced to our 'snotties' nurse', Lieutenant Commander Penton or 'Nuts'. The latter appellation was not an Americanism for his mental abilities, but because he was the Navigating Officer – 'Nuts' was a naval phonetic for the letter 'N'.

A reflective pipe smoker, he seldom smiled, but when he did, he showed a hidden warmth. I was rather in awe of him, but like many people with gruff exteriors, he improved vastly on acquaintance. He was responsible for our welfare and training, and discharged these duties well.

The first priority was to get to know one's way around the huge ship. I thought I would never do it, and of course there were compartments into which I never went, so complex was the honeycomb. Up and down ladders we went, through bulkhead after bulkhead, mess deck and gun turret, W/T office and engine room, bridge and double bottom, there was no end to it.

We were ordered to draw up plans of each deck. This took ages but was very effective in teaching us our way round.

Another mentor of ours was someone we had all known at Dartmouth. The senior 'schoolie', Instructor Commander Sidney B. Taylor, had been on the staff there teaching us navigation. Schoolmaster officers were carried aboard the big ships; the senior ones to continue the midshipmen's practice of the celestial arts, whilst the junior ones taught literacy and numeracy to ratings who would never pass the eleven plus.

Sidney B. Taylor was a hard taskmaster. 'I don't care if you are propping up your eyelids with matchsticks,' he said. 'You will fix the position of the ship every day when we are at sea.'

This was really very hard. At sea we were on watch four hours on four hours off throughout the 24. When you consider that this was interspersed with dawn action stations, false alarms and real alarms and that it took about three quarters of an hour to take and work out a sight, our eyelids were indeed not a little droopy. Furthermore, our journals, on which this book is based, had to be written up each day as well, so life at sea was not a luxury cruise.

Nowadays, you press a button and a satellite tells you where you are to a few yards. Not so in 1940.

When in harbour we all kept watch on the quarter-deck, acting as dogsbodies to the Officer of the Watch. Telescope under my arm as my badge of office, I felt very important. We received visiting officers at the gangway, ran the routine following the Commander's orders and ordered the bugler to blow the 'Attention' if an Admiral should pass in his barge. The latter kept one alert – you were punished if the Flag Officer passed by unnoticed.

The punishment? Well, midshipmen, like cadets could be beaten by the Sub-Lieutenant, but Stopford never did this, nor was he ordered to by 'Nuts' Penton. Stoppage of shore leave was adequate but a 'mast heading' did occur.

Our Commanding Officer was Captain Charles Morgan (later to become Rear Admiral Sir Charles) and a descendant of the famous pirate Henry Morgan. A midshipman –we will call him L – was on watch on the bridge. On the bridge stands the chart table. Its primary use is obvious, but some officers would use it to light cigarettes under its canvas flap, the use of which was to prevent light escaping.

L espied a bottom sticking out from under the flap. For some reason L thought the posterior belonged to a fellow midshipman who had been needling him. Without bothering to check, he swung his right leg and delivered a sharp kick in the arse.

Midshipman (later Captain) B.H. Kent, Sub-Lieutenant (A.)J.F. Begley, RNVR (OOW), Paymaster Midshipman (later Rear-Admiral) B.C. Perowne, before Sunday Divisions on board *Valiant*. (Author's collection)

A muffled roar like that of a wounded elephant erupted from the depths of the table, and the owner of the bottom so temptingly exposed emerged. 'How dare you!' shouted Captain Charles Morgan to the now terrified L. 'G-g-get off my bridge.'

L turned up in the gunroom looking somewhat the worse for wear, and recounted the story. It was not all loss on his side, Catch 22 had not then been invented, but Morgan was in it if ever anyone was. He would wish to punish L, but could not say that he had had a boot up the backside from a junior midshipman without losing, shall we say face, or rear.

L was Catch 22 also perhaps; you needed to be mad to be a midshipman in wartime. You needed to be even madder to give your commanding officer, a fourstripe Captain, Royal Navy, a kick where it hurt most.

Morgan solved the problem by 'mastheading' L for inefficiency. The hapless kicker had to climb to the top of the mast and stand there until allowed to descend, the object of the sailors' ridicule. He never quite lived it down.

L was, I am afraid, the butt of some maliciousness both from his peers and others more senior who should have known better. He had been rescued from a ship which had been sunk by German bombers and sent to us. As a result he was 'twitchy', but we were only senior school boys, and they can often be cruel. I would see L walking along a passageway trailed by a fellow midshipman. The latter would imitate faithfully the terrible whistling sound of a bomb falling from a Stuka dive bomber. It was these which had sunk L's ship and he jumped a mile.

L fell foul of Lieutenant Commander Torbuck, one of the Officers of the Watch at sea. As L would emerge on to the bridge for his watch, Torbuck would raise his eyes to heaven and in supplication say, 'Ah, here cometh the Crown of Thorns.' For some reason L did not like him.

When it came to drinking in the gunroom, an ironical situation arose. Because our new batch of midshipmen was under eighteen, we were not allowed to drink spirits. We could smoke, yes, go ashore, and if minded bed a woman, yes, be shot at by the enemy, yes, but gin and whisky? No! I did not mind that too much except that strangely for the grandson of a brewer, I did not much like beer ... however, the point that stuck was that beer was about five times as expensive as gin. The latter was only one old penny, per tot, at duty free prices. A further snag was that our wine bill limit was two pounds per month so those over eighteen could drink for that amount but we could only raise our elbows occasionally.

Running the ship's boats was an essential part of every midshipman's training, and we were no exception. *Valiant* possessed two picket boats, both very modern and capable of great speed. Originally they were fitted with a Rolls-Royce Merlin engine, producing a speed of some 25 knots. This of course was criminally wasteful, when it became obvious that the RAF needed these marvellous engines much more than the Navy. The Merlins were exchanged for Ford V8s which did not seem to detract too much from the boats' performance.

The picket boats had black hulls round which ran a thick white stripe – our ship's insignia. To be in command of one of these magnificent boats was the greatest fun. They carried a crew of four, coxswain, bowman, stern-sheetman, and stoker, but the midshipman was in charge. Standing in the cockpit you would slowly open the Bendix Gear throttle and glide away from the gangway with a muted growl. More power, the growl became a powerful roar, the bows lifted and the screws bit deeply.

It was thrilling, but thrills had to be tempered with caution. There were numerous traffic problems in a crowded harbour. Furthermore, some midshipmen were less adept at boat handling than others – too much power trying to show off and bang! You hit the gangway. Boat is hoisted in, shipwrights get busy, officers who would be taken ashore in it are furious, midshipman's leave is stopped. Expensive crash.

The launch was *Valiant's* maid of all work, and the boat I came to know best. Forty-five feet long, she was utilitarian built, and very sturdy. She could accommodate numbers of liberty men, or sacks of potatoes or other stores. Her coxswain was Leading Seaman Jones. He had one of the ugliest faces I had ever seen but this did not prevent us becoming firm friends, and in the close confines of this boat I called him Jonesey like everyone else.

The relationship between a midshipman in charge of a boat, and his coxswain requires illustration. The midshipman is an officer, the coxswain a rating, but try explaining that to a drunken liberty man at Number Ten gate waiting to get back on board late at night.

It is useless to order him to do anything. Such a command from a very raw teenage officer is most likely to result in a stream of invective plus a lunge towards the midshipman standing in the stern sheets.

Now here is where the coxswain must defend his midshipman and protect the drunken liberty man. It is the latter who must be kept at bay. Why? Because for a rating to strike an officer is one of the most serious offences there can be. Sozzled with drink, and aggressive with it, A.B. Jenkins must be prevented from hitting the officer and the latter must not provoke him.

It is then that the coxswain, not the midshipman, gives the order to the drunk to calm down. If he does not, a smart blow with a belaying pin or a push over the side should cool him down. I have seen officers running round the barbette or base of Y turret, hotly pursued by a drunken sailor. The officer does not fear that he might be in some danger, it is the court martial of the sailor that he is trying to prevent.

Running a boat was one of the finest character forming duties a midshipman could perform, and I loved it. Drunken liberty men would shout and sing on their return to the ship, but it was forbidden to take them alongside in that condition. Those singers of 'Bless 'em all' for which of course the copulative verb was substituted, soon learned that an extra cruise around the ship would keep them from their hammocks. Muted admonishments to their shipmates: 'Shut up or the pig will take us round again,' had their effect and made me smile in the dark of an Alexandrian night.

The launch had the most wonderful gear for propulsion and evolution. It was called the 'kitchen rudder'; I have never seen one before or since. Behind the propeller were two flanged pieces of metal, or 'buckets'. The launch's engine never went astern, all you had to do was to close the buckets and the thrust of the water thus imprisoned took your way off and you went astern. At the same time you spun the wheel to the side to which you wanted to move your stern, and in she would go. This seemingly ungainly boat was therefore most marvellously manoeuvrable; You pointed your bow at an angle of 45 degrees to the quay, closed the buckets and spun the wheel. The launch would manoeuvre in her own length, literally 'standing on her tail'. Power steering makes it easier to park a car, but this was child's play.

Whenever the launch was called away, the midshipman in charge had to go with it, whether he was eating his lunch or asleep at night. Sometimes the boat had to be manned by climbing on to the boom and down a rope ladder. I thought of the ignominy of a fall into the 'drink', but gravity never asserted itself. Once, when I was in a hurry to get back on board I had myself hoisted inboard by clinging to the crane's swivel. Somewhat undignified, but speedier!

I often thought that the paymaster midshipmen had a boring time. Preoccupied with naval stores, their most exciting moments being the deciphering of signals, they kept long hours in their offices.

One showed me a marvellously archaic list of essential requirements. It ran:

1. Chamber pots, china, crested, Flag Officers for the use of.
2. Chamber pots, china, uncrested, Officers for the use of.
3. Chamber pots, wooden, ratings.
4. Chamber pots, rubber, lunatics.

Had the enemy captured this gem, he might have suspected some esoteric code.

Terry Lewin and others of his seniority, would help us with our seamanship. Roddy Macdonald (now Vice Admiral Sir Roderick and a well-known marine artist) was one. Another was Henry Kirkwood. He later turned his collar round and was put in charge of a Bristol parish.

On reflection, I have always been glad that I opted for the Mediterranean fleet. First and foremost, the weather was almost uniformly fine and hot. Although this could be oppressive at times, we had off-shore breezes. It was infinitely preferable to swinging endlessly round a buoy in Scapa Flow or Hvaalfjord, Iceland. Those who endured this tell me that it was sheer hell. Some of the foulest weather in the world swirled round the hapless ships. If you were unlucky enough to be sunk your chances of survival lasted about three minutes.

When it came to April and May, and ships were plunging to the bottom, victims of the Luftwaffe, a great many survived in the warmer waters. Unless the bastards machine-gunned them as they clung, choking with oil fuel, to their upturned lifeboats.

5

The Taranto Raid

As will be seen from the photograph of my journal's frontispiece (below), the objects of keeping the journal were to train midshipmen in: (a) The power of observation (b) The power of expression (c) The habit of orderliness.

Apart from purely naval matters, we were also required to comment on current affairs world-wide. This presented no great difficulty, but we had only two disparate sources of information: the BBC World News and the English-language *Egyptian Mail*.

The objects so simply stated above were probably written by some Admiralty civil servant, safe in his nine to five job. The draft may even have had tea stains on it. The civil servant could not contemplate how difficult it was in wartime, often in action, desperate for sleep, for the wretched midshipman to write up his journal. No excuses were allowed, and the journals were inspected regularly by 'Nuts' Penton and Captain Morgan.

We were not issued with our journals until early November 1940. My account begins with our having put to sea, on an enterprise which was to be applauded in the free world, and the lessons from it to be well learned by at least one Axis power. This was Japan, whose naval hierarchy lost no time in translating our success at Taranto into crippling destruction for the US Pacific fleet in Pearl Harbor.

Midshipmens' Action and cruising stations were varied to provide experience. At this time I was midshipman of the Middle Watch on the bridge. The scene is one portrayed often in naval films. The bridge is open to the sky, so you are unprotected from the elements. However, this has the advantage that a captain can more easily 'con' his ship when trying to avoid falling bombs. Once more, I was glad I was not in a North Atlantic gale, peering through the murk, whilst trying to shield myself from biting sleet.

In the centre is the dimly illuminated binnacle behind which stands the Officer of the Watch. He has charge of the whole ship, but in wartime is concerned chiefly with maintaining good station on the nearby ships and in zigzagging. The PCO or Principal Control Officer perambulates the bridge, ready to bring the armament to bear at any alarm. The Chief Yeoman of Signals leans against the steel bulkhead, ready for any orders coming by lamp or flag. I don't think these men ever slept at sea, they always seemed to be in the background. Two lookouts complete the picture, constantly training their glasses for anything which might threaten the ship. The Captain only appears occasionally. He, like

Journal for the use of Midshipmen.

1. The Journal is to be kept during the whole of a Midshipman's sea time. A second volume may be issued if required.

2. The **Officer** detailed to supervise instruction of Midshipmen will see that the Journals are kept in accordance with the instructions hereunder. He will initial the Journals at least once a month, and will see that they are written up from time to time during the month, not only immediately before they are called in for inspection.

3. The **Captain** will have the Journals produced for his inspection from time to time and on a **Midshipman** leaving the ship, and will initial them at each inspection.

4. The following remarks indicate the main lines to be followed in keeping the Journal :—

(i.) The objects of keeping the Journal are to train Midshipmen in
   (a) the power of observation.
   (b) the power of expression.
   (c) the habit of orderliness.

(ii.) Midshipmen are to record in their own language their observations about all matters of interest or importance in the work that is carried on, on their stations, in their Fleet, or in their Ship.

(iii.) They may insert descriptions of places visited and of the people with whom they come in contact, and of harbours, anchorages and fortifications.

(iv.) They may write notes on fuelling facilities, landing places, abnormal weather, prevailing winds and currents, salvage operations, foreign ships encountered and the manner in which foreign fleets are handled, gunnery and other practices, action in manœuvres, remarks on tactical exercises.
   On the ship making a passage of sufficient interest they should note weather and noon positions.

(v.) Separate entries need not necessarily be made for each day, full accounts should be given of any event of interest.

(vi.) The letterpress should be illustrated with plans and sketches pasted into the pages of the Journal, namely :—

   (a) **Track Charts.**

   (b) **Plans of Anchorages** (these should show the berths occupied by the Squadron or Ship, and if a Fleet was anchored the courses steered by the Fleet up to the anchorage).

   (c) **Sketches** of places visited, of coast line, of headlands, of leading marks into harbours, of ships (British or Foreign), of Ports or fittings of ships, or any other object of interest.

5. The Journal is to be produced at the examination in Seamanship for the rank of Lieutenant, when marks to a maximum of 50 will be awarded for it.

Drake, is in his sea cabin down below trying desperately to get some much-needed sleep. For deep sleep is what he can never attain; every alteration of course has to be reported to him, together with any untoward arrivals or departure of ships in company.

It does not help the Captain if, when as a friend of mine relates, he is jolted into scalding consciousness by hot cocoa being poured down the voice-pipe and landing on his face. My friend, wanting to play a trick on a fellow midshipman, mistook the voicepipe in the dark with dire consequences!

My duties were to stand unobtrusively near the back of the bridge, to warn the Officer of the Watch when to zigzag and which way, and to make cocoa. The latter was supplied in blocks which had to be chipped off and then boiling water poured on them. Known as 'pusser' s kai' it was warm and sweet. It bore as much resemblance to Cadbury's 'Bournville' as a Rolls to a 3-wheeler Reliant Robin.

The battlefleet had put to sea from Alexandria on 6 November 1940, our ostensible duty to escort convoys to and from Malta. As soon as a warship leaves harbour, any executive officer worth his salt will inform the ship's company of the nature of the mission. Security is

Midshipman John Cardew taking a sight. (Author's collection)

not breached and everyone is left with his own thoughts on the matter. Will it be dangerous? Probably, most wartime operations are, and some peacetime ones too in inexperienced hands. What opposition are we likely to meet? Are we stronger than they are? Here I should add that any operation against the Italian Navy was regarded as a 'doddle', likewise an encounter with the Regia Aeronautica, whose high-level bombing was inaccurate and their dive-bombing non-existent. The Germans were yet to appear in the Mediterranean. The literal impact which they made is recorded in a later chapter.

This time, Commander Reid gave out that the Italian fleet (and I quote from my journal) 'was, as per usual, holed up in Taranto, except for a few destroyers and a cruiser in Brindisi'. The innocents in Taranto.

That evening I attended my first burial at sea. The dead man was Stoker William Shields who died of suffocation in a gas filled compartment. I was fascinated and horrified to watch the coffin, draped in the Union Jack, suspended at 45 degrees on the quarter-deck rail. I was reminded of The burial of Sir John Moore at Corunna 'his corpse to the ramparts we hurried', and could not help reflecting that this was probably the nearest Stoker Shields had ever been to that holy of holies, the quarter-deck, in all his naval career.

The Padre intoned the burial service in the half gloom, the Royal Marine guard shouldered their rifles and fired a last salute. At a nod from a petty officer, the Chief Shipwright removed a blocking pin and the mortal remains of Bill Shields slid forward, hitting the sea with a ghastly thud. In a moment he had gone, to be no more than an entry in the ship's log. Later, his messmates would hold an auction of his belongings, paying inflated prices, the proceeds of which would go to his widow.

Any burial is emotional, those at sea seemingly more so and akin to 'The Flying Dutchman' in the pathos of having no last resting place for remembrance.

Long after the war, the lighter side of a burial at sea was recounted to me by a Dartmouth term mate. A petty officer died in the Royal Naval Hospital at Haslar, near Portsmouth, and in his will desired to be buried at sea, as was his right. My friend commanded the duty destroyer and was ordered to carry out the man's last wishes. A filthy day, gusting winds and overcast. The Solent looked uninviting. The keening relatives came aboard. The coffin was saluted and placed on the after deck. My friend was dubious about the whole operation, but as the relatives and deceased were there, he thought he must go through with it.

All except those required to 'con' the ship proceeded aft. The ceremony was enacted, the coffin hit the sea with the usual leaden splash. Now came the moment of truth. The undertakers had been civilians, unused to burials at sea; it never occurred to them that the coffin should have been weighted. Instead, therefore, of disappearing beneath the waves to join the Mary Rose and the Royal George on the seabed, the coffin bobbed up and down like a spent torpedo. My friend took quick action. The keening relatives were despatched to the other side, there to gain additional knowledge of the contours of Horse Sand Fort. Meanwhile, in the half gale now blowing, the seaboat was lowered on the coffin side. The shipwrights were embarked with chains, and whilst the relatives were suitably diverted, the errant coffin was secured and sent on its final plunge.

'There is nothing that the Navy cannot do!'

Back to 1940 and our operations, as in the story above, the weather started to worsen, there were brilliant flashes of lightning and rainsqualls lashed those on deck. I learned soon enough that the Mediterranean cannot be trusted in winter despite what the travel agents will tell you. It may not be as cold as the Atlantic, but it can be very unpleasant and very rough.

Our aircraft carrier, *Illustrious*, was soon plunging into the waves, the flight deck wet and pitching. As a result, two Swordfish aircraft crashed into the sea, their crews being picked up by destroyers.

In the morning of 10 November we sighted the battleship *Barham* accompanied by cruisers and destroyers. Malta was plainly visible on the starboard beam. I longed to visit somewhere new but it was not to be. The destroyer *Hotspur* had just rammed a U-boat and was to be taken in to Malta for repairs. This form of warfare was forbidden later on as it meant ships were out of action for far too long.

What did one feel, knowing that a submarine had been in the vicinity and would undoubtedly have tried to torpedo us had she been in a position to do so? Initial relief, at the fact that there was one less adversary with which we had to deal. Beyond that, what can one do? The threat of U boat attack is with sailors as soon as they leave harbour. It is not confined to the open sea, as the attack on *Royal Oak* at Scapa Flow and later ourselves in Alexandria, can testify. You just have to live with it, and put any thoughts of being sunk right to the back of your mind. It is not bravery, but the behaviour of an ostrich, otherwise you would go mad with worry. Soldiers and airmen have only the anxiety about their enemies on land and in the air. For sailors, the menace lurks underneath them as well.

From the depths to the air – at 1400 a stick of bombs was dropped between ourselves and the flagship. Four Cant S.79s had suddenly appeared overhead and surprised the fleet. They were chased away by fighters from *Illustrious*, nevertheless they should never have got as near as they did. Fighter direction was virtually non-existent at that period of the war, hence our being caught with our trousers down in spite of the presence of a fleet carrier.

We and *Illustrious* were fitted with the latest aircraft seeking radar but no one really knew how to make the best use of it. A midshipman would sit at a horizontal ground glass table on the Air Defence Position near the bridge. An umbilical cord connected his headphones to the radar operator scanning the green rays of his set. The Air Defence Officer, Lieutenant G. Pooley, paces the deck, eying the glass table. The midshipman reaches forward and marks in a cross on the perimeter of his glass table. Officers peer at the cross as though it is some harbinger of evil, which well it may be. On the other hand, it could be the return of a friendly fighter.

The hand moves again, the crosses move nearer the centre. Sometimes they veer away, sometimes they close the fleet too uncomfortably. It is then that the dreaded bugle call of 'Repel Aircraft' – dah, dah, deedee, dah, dah, dee ('There's an aircraft overhead') is sounded over the broadcast system and everyone doubles to his action station.

Later in 1944, when I was to qualify as a Fighter Direction Officer, I was to contrast the incredible primitiveness of our so-called air defence in 1940 with the sophisticated Air Direction Rooms with which the fleet was later equipped. Excellent radar (although estimation of height was still mostly guesswork), huge personal radar screens, improved R/T communications, all contributed to a highly efficient response to air attack. This was all, or mostly due to US Navy influence.

The battles of the Coral Sea and Midway (the only fleet action where the opposing fleets never saw each other) were aircraft carrier actions, not those between battleships. Added to this, the majority of American senior officers were pilots. Not until Caspar John, son of Augustus John, the painter, was promoted to Flag rank, did any British admiral wear wings on his sleeve. This was not only quite disgraceful, it was criminally negligent, and led to many thousands of British lives being lost at sea unnecessarily.

A small illustration can be provided by the experience of Captain Reginald Whinney, DSC who recounted in a book his ill-fated application to become a naval pilot. The time was the mid 1930s; he was a Sub-Lieutenant and keen to transfer to the Fleet Air Arm. Whinney submitted his application to his Captain who was none other than Andrew Browne Cunningham, by now my Commander-in-Chief. Reaction was swift. Whinney was summoned to his Captain's cabin, ordered to appear in frock coat and sword. This was court-martial uniform, but what crime had he committed? He was soon to find out.

Standing rigidly to attention before his Captain, Whinney perceived a sheet of paper on the table. Cunningham picked it up and in a voice of cold rage asked Whinney, 'What is this?'

'My application to become a pilot, Sir,' answered Whinney. 'What did you join the Navy for?' queried Cunningham.

Whinney knew the stock answer to this one. 'To serve at sea, Sir,' he said.

Cunningham nodded, tore Whinney's application into shreds and curtly dismissed him. This is deeply illustrative of the attitude of mind of the senior British naval hierarchy at that time. Gunnery officers were God and the Holy Trinity, any suggestions that surface ships could not fight off the tiresome gnats which might attack them from the air was unthinkable.

I often wonder if our Commander-in-Chief Admiral Sir Andrew Cunningham, with his almost paranoid dislike of the Fleet Air Arm, ever gave a thought to the fact that had it not been for a brave naval pilot, his victory at Matapan might never have taken place. For it was an aerial torpedo which crippled the Italian cruiser *Pola*. This led to Admiral Iachino to despatch *Fiume* and *Zara* to her aid, thus enabling us to fall upon them and send them to the bottom.

Like the British Army's lack of preparedness for panzer warfare, the Admiralty was quite unprepared for air defence at sea, their only major contribution being armoured flight decks in the newer carriers. We were to pay a ghastly price for this criminal attitude in Crete. Those, like Terry Lewin, who suffered as very junior officers from this neglect, were later to make sure that air support was available in the Falklands, and that the vital carriers were kept out of range of enemy aircraft. A lesson that had taken 40 years to be learned.

The debit side of what I have just written concerning naval air warfare has to be set against the credit side of the Taranto raid. This brilliant operation was first mooted in 1935. Planned in the peace and quiet of pre-war London, it was finally to be carried out on the night of Monday, 11 November 1940. The C-in-C made a signal that morning that he 'intended to act offensively off Greece'.

Great speculation was cast upon the form that the offensiveness was to take. Why Cunningham should have said Greece and not Italy has never been made clear. Perhaps he was afraid that a pilot from *Illustrious* would make a forced landing and be indiscreet in advance of the operation. If so, why signal any intention at all? By now, in the extraordinary way that 'buzzes' or rumours, go around a ship, we were certain that the fleet's target was Taranto, the Italian equivalent of Portsmouth. There, we were told, were six battleships and fourteen cruisers. *Illustrious* and her attendant destroyers left us at 1800 whilst light forces under Admiral Pridham-Wippell also made off, their mission a foray into the Strait of Otranto.

It is no part of this book to recount further details of the raid on Taranto. Firstly, the author did not fly on the mission, secondly, a number of accounts have been written describing it in detail. Lastly, there is an excellent working model in the Fleet Air Arm Museum at the Royal Naval Air Station at Yeovilton. This shows the air defences which our aviators had to avoid in order to hit their targets.

Complete success was, however, to be ours – the new *Littorio* and two of the older *Guilio Cesare* battleships were sunk at their moorings, all for the loss of two aircraft. Pridham-Wippell's forces met a convoy bound for Brindisi and destroyed three of its four ships. We intercepted many SOS messages during that night from Italian ships in that area, and my journal records that 'our cruisers are not wasting their time'.

Our surface forces had sailed right into the Gulf of Taranto, something we would never have dared to do had our opposition been German. Thus was British maritime power reasserted in the central basin of the Mediterranean in no uncertain fashion.

A certain Commander Genda of the Imperial Japanese Navy was naval attaché in London at that time. My father always called attaches 'accredited spies'. He was right in Genda's case, who, an aviator himself, took an intense interest in the Taranto raid. Little did those who planned our attack realise what a terrible harvest would be reaped by the Japanese in their copy book attack on Pearl Harbor a year later.

The next morning, 12 November, *Illustrious* rejoined us; an hour later the island of Zante off the Greek coast, was plainly visible. Again, had this been a year later, we would have been bombed out of the water. That day in 1940, apart from the Italian planes shot down by fighters from *Illustrious*, it was uneventful. The alarm caused by the proximity of the enemy planes interrupted our lunch, but as anyone on active service will know, that was par for the course.

Later that evening we received a signal ordering us to cancel all previous orders and return to Alexandria at high speed. We immediately put on 260 revolutions which gave us 26 knots. It was a spin-off on the credit side from our lack of sleep which resulted in our sleeping like babes in arms when the opportunity presented itself. Even our tiredness though, had difficulty in fighting the terrible vibration which our high speed engendered in the Admiral's flat. We were right above the propellers, and those, combined with the servo motor of the steering gear bade fair to keep us from the arms of Morpheus.

Our only contact with the United Kingdom, apart from letters, was the BBC Overseas Service. This was always the best of the Corporation's channels and bore little resemblance to the left-wing biased reporting familiar to us today. The SRE or Sound Reproduction Equipment (the Navy could not demean itself to use the word loudspeaker) was switched on every day at newstime. The news on 13 November was full of the Taranto raid, Winston Churchill having given it the greatest prominence in the House.

We carried on board at that time an American war correspondent called Larry Allen who worked for United Press. That evening he gave out over the loudspeakers the draft of the despatch written for his newspaper chain. In it he described the Taranto raid as 'Mussolini's biggest naval headache of the war'. We felt we were ten feet tall and agreed with him wholeheartedly.

One of the Ancient Wonders of the World was the Pharos at Alexandria. This great lighthouse beckoned to Mediterranean sailors, and guided them to safety in the harbour. Centuries had passed since it stood duty, and modern sailors had to make do with the doubtless more powerful but less romantic Ras-el-Tin light at the end of the Mole. This we sighted at 0430 and after some very poor ship handling on the part of our tug's captain, our stern was swung round and we secured fore and aft.

What was all the rush to get us back to Alexandria? No one knew, but rumour quickly went round the ship that 'the French were getting obstreperous'. 'Gad, Carruthers, the natives are restless tonight.' No tomtoms sounded, not even the ghastly accordion music always associated with Edith Piaf floated across the harbour from the immobilised French fleet. How would the French have 'become obstreperous' as my journal records? What could they have done and with what would they have done it?

It is almost always impossible to find out who starts a 'buzz' or rumour, but those on board ship generally had some basis in truth. One which comes to mind doing the rounds in 1941 was that our navigating officer was to be appointed NOIC (Naval Officer in Charge) Tripoli. This was perfectly correct as far as it went, although there was one rather large snag – the large Libyan port of Tripoli, through which most of the supplies for the Afrika Korps came, was still in enemy hands. The Eighth Army was miles east of the place. Never mind, the rumour was, naturally enough, that a British offensive was imminent, and the appointment of NOIC Tripoli was merely good forward planning.

Sadly, the Libyan Tripoli was not to fall into Allied hands until Monty entered in triumph in 1943. It was the Lebanese port of Tripoli to which an NOIC had been appointed; a sinecure adjacent to the Turkish border! Perhaps some reports had been carelessly left lying about in the C-in-C's office ashore, perhaps some writer in the Captain's Office had seen a cipher message not intended for his eyes – we never knew.

The record is in my journal but how the Vichy French, interned in Alexandria were to have caused trouble is probably in the files of the Public Record Office at Kew. There it will doubtless have the infuriating classification 'Not for release to the public until 2115'. Why ever not? My researches for this book have taken me to Kew on a number of occasions. This classification was thrown up by the computer there regarding Japanese atrocities against Allied Naval personnel. I had entered this enquiry in the computer in error but was astounded at the reply. As Lord Russell of Liverpool said of the Japanese, 'To call their actions bestial is an insult to the animal kingdom.' Why then conceal their ghastly crimes for 70 years? No doubt the Vichy French have the same extraordinary protection.

On 14 November 1940 my attack and action stations were changed. An explanation of attack stations is required, action stations are obvious. Attack stations is the position occupied in the ship by everyone when at sea. Organised in watches, the idea is that the ship should not be 'caught napping' by a sudden attack, and that there are trained personnel to cope with this should it arise. When Action Stations is sounded, there is a mad rush to close up into those positions assigned for fighting the ship.

From an attack station of Midshipman of the Watch, I was made an Assistant Air Defence Officer. It sounds grand but in reality consisted of being on the ADP or Air Defence Position and assisting in directing the secondary armament of 4.5" guns on to hostile aircraft. Orders to open fire were transmitted by telephone line to the High Angle Director Positions perched high in the superstructure. These were in the charge of Sub-Lieutenants, prominent among whom was my gunroom companion the Hon. Jocelyn Parker, son of the Earl of Macclesfield.

Perched in his eyrie, he would train the director tower on to the aircraft's bearing. The bearing and angle of sight would be transmitted automatically to the High Angle Control Positions deep in the bowels of the ship. These HACPs were commanded by midshipmen, and I was to spend much of my time shut away down there.

Imagine a compartment twelve foot square, crammed with machinery, dials and consoles. It is situated well below the waterline. Access is gained by a vertical steel ladder. On top of this is a four inch thick steel spring-loaded hatch which is closed tightly in action. It resembles the conning tower hatch of a submarine. In this Black Hole of Calcutta are the midshipman, a leading gunnery rating, a torpedoman and three other ratings. Should the steel hatch jam, as it did in the January dive bomber attack, those in the compartment would be trapped like the proverbial rats. It was inadvisable to be too imaginative whilst spending four hours on, four hours off, down there the whole time the ship was at sea.

The function of the HACP was to be the forerunner of the modem computer, to calculate range, bearing and elevation, and to transmit this information to the gun batteries. Millions of pounds must have gone into the development of this anti-aircraft gunnery system. I suppose that to an attacking enemy pilot the barrage must have been formidable. Not lethal though I fear, for it never succeeded in bringing down any of our assailants.

After a spell as AADO. and in charge of our HACP, my action station was changed from the Port Fore HACP to 'B' turret. *Valiant* had four turrets housing her main armament, the huge 15" guns. Three were manned by sailors,

'X' turret was manned by Royal Marines. There was great rivalry between the sailors and the 'bootnecks' as to who could be the most efficient!

A 15" gun turret could be likened to a Martian operating theatre. Polished steel gleams everywhere, the 'theatre staff' are, like their medical counterparts, clad in anti-flash gear so that their arms are gloved up to their elbows and their faces peer through their white masks. Here, the medical resemblance ends, for a gun turret is a noisy place. Commands are shouted in stentorian tones by gunners' mates, their voices echoes of many a gun drill at Whale Island, the gunnery school. They compete with, but never win against the cacophony of sound created by the loading machinery.

In the centre of the turret is a deep well or barbette. Up through this barbette travels the steel container with its shell weighing one ton. Behind the shell is the cloth wrapped cordite charge looking for all the world like a huge lethal suppository. This is the propellant, which when ignited electrically will blast the shell on its way towards the target.

The great breech of the gun opens, the steel cage arrives with a clang of metal. The ramrod thrust pushes shell and charge into the gun, the ramrod withdraws, the breech slams shut and locks, the cage sinks into the well. 'Gun Ready' lights flash and remain illuminated. The firing bell gives two rings and you wait tensely. High above the bridge the director layer presses his trigger. Inside the turret the guns give a mighty boom and recoil. A steel lever is pulled, the breech opens and air rushes in under pressure to clear the smoke. It is all tremendously exciting, and never ceased to move me with the visible evidence of immense firepower.

'Ammunition is perfectly safe until you forget that it is dangerous' – so runs the mnemonic on the lecture room wall at Whale Island. Perfectly true, and supposing you get a blow back? This is illustrated by the old question, 'What is the wait of a misfired gun?' Note the spelling; wait does not refer to tonnage. It refers to the half an hour which must elapse, if a gun fails to go off, before the breech is opened. The reason for this interval is that the cordite which failed to explode might still be burning in the gun. Opening the breech too soon would result in the incoming air fanning the smouldering charge and killing all the turret's crew.

I had personal experience of this in the cruiser *Suffolk*. When I was turret officer of 'B' turret, one of my 8" guns misfired. I ordered all the turret's crew out and we waited for half an hour. I then ordered Petty Officer Ward, the gunner's mate, to re-enter the turret with me. Trying not to show my fear I ordered him to open the breech. That was one of the longest moments of my life had I given the order which would kill us both?

It seemed an age before the mechanism worked, the breech swung open, we were alive! We peered into the gun barrel. Somehow, inexplicably, the cordite charge was missing, the loading cage had failed to deliver it. 'I suspected it all along,' said the Gunnery Officer cheerfully as I made my report. He could have told me earlier!

The officer in charge of 'B' turret was Lieutenant Henry P. de Horton Barnes. He resembled the actor Robert Morley in generous proportion and loved his food. When in harbour Henry Barnes would call for Horton, the Ward Room Steward, asking to see the dinner menu. If he did not consider it came up to standard he would dine ashore in Pastroudi's, an excellent Alexandrian restaurant. Rumour had it that he had two wealthy aunts who doted on him. Lucky Henry, he never seemed short of cash.

Petty Officer Colville was the gunner's mate, in overall command of the turret's ratings. A tall, gaunt reticent man, he was good at his job. He was to show his mettle on my next birthday.

The huge guns were named Darby and Joan. Little did we guess what havoc they were to wreak upon the Italian fleet at Matapan. Their names suggested an old married couple living in connubial bliss. The connubial bliss of many Italian households was brought to an abrupt end by those guns on that night.

My contribution to fighting Il Duce whilst in 'B' turret could truthfully be said to have been a minor one. I was really there for training and took no active part in the running of the turret, unlike my other action stations. In those I gave orders and like to think I was useful. In 'B' turret everyone had their allotted tasks and knew them well – I sat by Henry Barnes who didn't seem to do much either. It was Colville who appeared to run the turret, but had there been a crisis doubtless Henry B. would have asserted himself. My time in 'B' turret was not to be uneventful.

6

Action Stations

The 'young gentlemen' were allowed shore leave in Alexandria when duties permitted. This had its compensations. For a start, it was incomparably better than the shore leave available to our contemporaries in the Home Fleet. Swinging round a buoy at Scapa Flow, battered by wind and rain, their shore leaves tended to be sheer monotony. We, for our part, had wonderful African weather, and the facilities of an international seaport. The Home Fleet had sheep and sleet, we had sunshine and blue skies.

Our war in the Mediterranean was about to intensify, but in harbour it had its compensations. Alexandria was centuries old, with Greek and French influence beside Egyptian. The streets had French names such as the Rue Fuad and Rue Saad Zaghloul. There were fine squares, and good hotels. There was the Union Club (senior officers only) and the Sporting Club. The latter was what I liked best – tennis and swimming in the hot sun, followed by tea and sticky cakes served by Egyptian waiters in immaculate white robes with wide red sashes. Oh yes, better than Flotta in a rainstorm – you could keep the Old Man of Hoy.

My parents were very kind and generous, making me an allowance of £50 per quarter. How it was managed in wartime I do not know, but this sum always arrived at the Bank of Egypt on time. It was a lifesaver, and I had no financial worries as a result. Those subsisting on a midshipman's pay of five shillings per day (25p) were forced to count the pennies.

After lunch, those off duty would be taken ashore in one of *Valiant's* fast picket boats, landing at No. 6 Gate; the officers' gate. Officers and ratings had separate dockyard gates in case drunkenness should cause incidents as described earlier. There a gharri awaited us, or a taxi if we were in funds. The gharri was an open horse-drawn carriage, the poor beast usually looking ill-fed and in need of care. To take a gharri through the narrow streets which led from the dockyard area to the centre of the city was quite safe by day. By night it was another matter. Our Surgeon-Commander was pulled from his gharri by what would now be described as muggers. It was not advisable to travel alone.

Muggers were out for money, but other predators would have political motives. The Egyptians were no great lovers of the Allies and one's reception en route would quite often depend on whether or not the 8th Army was advancing in the desert. Doubtless the gyppos would have been kicked by any victorious Germans but the latter never had the chance to chastise the natives.

On foot, other gyppos waited. 'Eh, Captain, clean your shoes?' '*Imshi*' (Arabic swear word) was the unwise reply, for that resulted in the little guttersnipe flinging horse manure on to one's immaculate white tropical shoes.

These delights of foreign travel surrounded us, but it was incomparably better than the Orkneys. There were cinemas which surprisingly showed quite modern films, all in English with Arabic sub-titles. I was in love with Deanna Durbin and saw all her films. My journal records that on 14 November 1940 the film show was stopped after half an hour due to an air raid. It re-started, and then a quarter of an hour later it stopped again and everyone was asked to leave as the Egyptian Prime Minister had died! That respect was never shown in England when Churchill finally expired.

Later in the evening there were the Carlton and the Monseigneur, both good nightclubs where a decent meal and cabaret could be enjoyed at a very reasonable price. Sometimes we met army officers there who had travelled out with us in the *Dominion Monarch*. Pastroudi's, the haunt of Hemy Barnes, was a restaurant run and owned by a Greek, but with an international cuisine. There, I drank my Liebfraumilch, whilst musing on the fact that it was fortunate that the countrymen of its pays d' origine were not sitting here sipping their wine.

All this may seem very fine and large and we were lucky in what we had. Nevertheless, we were thousands of miles from home; mail was sporadic (letters often took six weeks if you were lucky), we could not telephone loved ones and we often longed for a family atmosphere. In this respect, John Cardew and I were unlucky. Practically all the English families had fled Alexandria for South Africa – the French and Greek communities kept to themselves. There was literally no one to visit in Alexandria, unlike Durban or Cape Town where hospitality was organised on a vast scale. How unlucky we were I did not know, until after the war when I met Joan Tubbs. Her maiden name was Finney. Her family was a wealthy and old-established one, drawing its wealth from cotton. They had lived in Alexandria for many years and, unlike others had chosen to remain when war came. Their lovely house kept an ever-open door for English officers. There was no rank consciousness in that a midshipman might find himself at a dinner party where the most prominent guest was the Commander-in-Chief himself. Another guest was Midshipman HRH Prince Philip.

In 1940, Joan Finney was a very pretty redhead in her early teens. Growing up quickly she joined Gabriella Barker's concert party and received many a wolf whistle from her all-male audiences. Lucky indeed were the midshipmen who knew Joan and her family then, but sadly I was not among them. Now Joan lives with her husband Vincent in a beautiful Cotswold house only five miles from us. I regret very much that I never had an introduction in those far-off days.

So, our shore leave would come to an end and officers would congregate at No. 6 Gate to be taken back to their ships. The powerful battleships' picket boats would jockey for position alongside the quay together with fussy little motor boats from the destroyers. Shouts of *Valiant*, *Warspite*, would mingle with *Nubian*, *Orian*, *Gloucester*, all names steeped in naval history, many of the ships soon to lie at the bottom of the Mediterranean. Some officers (Warrant I suspect) could be heard calling in tipsy voices for *Scharnharst* and *Gneisenau*!

One Egyptian boy at No. 6 Gate had a sense of humour. He approached a certain Sub-Lieutenant and offered to sell him a copy of the *Egyptian Mail*. The Sub-Lieutenant declined. For some reason this refusal annoyed the boy and he strode up and down the quay, hand on head in perplexity and frustration, muttering, 'Oh, how you say, how you say?' The Sub-Lieutenant, an old Harrovian of long lineage and great rectitude, took no notice. He was about to board his picket boat, senior officers stood all around. Suddenly the Egyptian boy ceased his pacing, and, like Archimedes shouting 'Eureka' in his bath, pointed an accusatory finger at the Sub-Lieutenant. 'I have it, I have it,' he cried. 'Your a*se!' The senior officers were incredulous, the Sub-Lieutenant was decidedly embarrassed. As they used to say in *Punch* – 'Collapse of stout party.'

On 16 November we put to sea at 0320. Wartime sailings were of course, kept secret from everyone until about two hours beforehand. The only people in the know would be the Captain, Commander, Navigator and Engineer Officer. It took two hours to flash up the boilers. Steam had to be raised to work the huge capstan, and the Navigator rather naturally had to know where we were going and make sure he had the correct charts.

We were to proceed to Suda Bay in Crete, escorting a convoy bound for Greece. We dropped anchor in Suda Bay at 0900 the next day. My journal says, 'The town of Suda looks quite nice, but there is not a great deal of it. I hear that the place's claim to fame (or notoriety?) lies in its cream cheese.'

Less than six months later I was to be in the last HM ship to escape from the port, the sound of German machine guns only three miles away being plainly heard. It was just as well that one could not read the crystal ball. As it was, the bay was still, there were no air raids, everything seemed to be at peace.

Our return to Alexandria was uneventful, the whole operation being like a pre-war exercise. Six days later we embarked commandos for Greece. This was the first time that we had seen troops trained especially in hand to hand fighting and they looked fearsome enough. They came armed with picks, swords, tommy guns and villainous looking knuckle dusters. The latter had knife blades attached to them, the object being to knock your enemy senseless and then slit his throat!

The commandos disembarked in Crete. One wonders what happened to our passengers. Did they survive Greece only to be killed in Crete next May? Perhaps it was best to be left in ignorance. After Crete we proceeded towards Malta. As Midshipman of the Watch I kept 'the middle' (midnight to 0400) during which it pelted with thunderous rain. Standing there exposed, I longed for a covered bridge. That night, the aircraft carrier *Illustrious* pulled right out of station to starboard, and then realising her mistake, turned back to port. *Valiant's* helm was put hard-a-port and we only just avoided a collision.

I have already dilated on bad station-keeping at sea, but the reader will, I trust, bear with me if I reiterate just how difficult it was to zigzag at ten minute intervals in huge ships displacing some 30,000 tons each, all of it in pitch darkness and often in poor visibility. No surface radar then to assist, you just used your eyes as best you could and hoped that the image of the ship next to you would not grow too large in your night binoculars.

Later on we warned the cruiser *York* of *Illustrious'* notoriously bad station keeping. She replied that after two months she had come to realise this as well!

The 28 November had its moments. We could see fingers of light probing the sky at midnight and knew that we were watching Malta enduring an air raid. The island was plainly visible at dawn. Later in the morning we had many aircraft scares and the cruiser *Glasgow* brought down one plane by pom-pom fire. Later two parachutes were seen dropping into the sea but where they came from, no one knew.

We were joined by the 3rd Cruiser Squadron. *Southampton* flashed us the news of the action she had had with units of the Italian fleet. In company with the battle cruiser *Renown*, *Ark Royal* and the old battleship *Ramillies*, the engagement had taken place with four *Zara* class cruisers. The latter immediately turned tail and fled under a smoke screen accompanied by two Cavour class battleships. There were recorded gunfire hits on the battleship and two cruisers while *Ark Royal* claimed two direct hits on one cruiser by her aircraft. It was the *Zara* class cruisers which, four months later, we were literally to blow out of the water at Matapan.

Later we heard on the radio that the cruiser *Berwick* sustained two gunfire hits fired by the Italians, one officer and twelve ratings being killed. This action, known as the Battle of Cape Spartivento, greatly excited and encouraged those like myself who were waiting to see action. We were young and stupid; later we were to get plenty of it, a great deal being on the receiving end.

Sunday 1 December was literally a red letter day for me. I received my first mail from home, my first news of my parents since leaving Liverpool in early September. As soon as I arrived on board *Valiant*, I had cabled my parents of my change of ship and these letters were properly addressed. Mail addressed to the torpedoed *Kent* did not arrive until much later, so I was glad I had been able to get a message through. I cannot stress too strongly what a morale booster it was to receive these letters. The 'Postie' was a rather large and jolly Corporal of Royal Marines. He was always first ashore when we entered harbour and I used to watch eagerly for the return of his boat. How the powers that be managed to organise the mail to all quarters of the globe in conditions of war I do not know but within the severe limitations imposed upon them they performed a most wonderful service.

In the early stages of the war, mail was sent by sea in letter form as it had been sent for centuries. Later, an 'aerogramme' form was introduced. The writer wrote on a special form which was then photographed and much reduced in size. Flown to West Africa and then to Egypt, the aerogrammes were then enlarged to half the size of the original. Although quicker, I did not like them; they were so impersonal, unlike the earlier letters which had actually been in the hand of the writer.

Another form of 'air mail' designed for brevity and therefore weighing less was used. Various messages had designated numbers. No. 1 would be 'Am well, do not worry' and so on. One disconcerted mother received a message from her 20-year-old son. Someone had typed in the wrong number and the message read: 'Twins born, please send money.' The son, on receiving an anguished letter from his mother told his Captain. The latter said, 'I will deal with this,' and replied: 'Give the boy a chance, he's only been out here three months!'

Letters written by us were censored by either the Padre or one of the 'Schoolies'. We were not considered sufficiently responsible to be entrusted with the secrets of our movements. Many had their own code of course, which they used to tell their loved ones the odd bit of personal news. When I became more senior, I had to indulge in the distasteful task of censoring and it was an eye-opener to see how appallingly ill-educated many of the ratings were.

Their letters often ended with 'well now dear, I must close' as though their letter was some sort of gate. The two 'codes' which they often wrote on the backs of their envelopes were SWALK ('signed with a loving kiss') and NORWICH. They were hardly esoteric but perhaps some particularly Teutonic intelligence officer wasted time on them. On reflection I think perhaps not.

Three days later we put to sea for gunnery trials. Sadly, the gunnery was not at all accurate. Enough books to fill many libraries have been written about the merits and demerits of naval gunnery, and many comparisons have been made between that of the British and German navies.

The German navy's gunnery was horribly and frighteningly accurate – initially. One has only to cite the sinking of *Hood* by *Bismarck*. The beautiful British battle cruiser blew up after only a few salvoes had been fired at her.

Perhaps German naval gunnery had always operated on the 'blitzkrieg' principle: make the first four salvoes deadly accurate and you have won the battle. Later, if there was a later, their superb optical instruments were more affected than ours should they take any hits themselves. This naturally caused a fall-off in subsequent performance.

Our shells at Jutland were so badly constructed that many of the armour-piercing variety failed to explode. As ship after ship succumbed to the German fire, Beatty made the famous remark: 'There's something wrong with our bloody ships today.' His ghost was perhaps gliding in and out of *Valiant's* turrets that day, shaking its head at the poor gunnery and the inefficiency of the turret machinery. My turret – 'B' – held up the performance for 20 minutes. The flash doors jammed when the cage was at the breech, hence the cage could not be lowered again. Ordnance Artificers and the turret's crew worked madly to free it and later succeeded.

The OAs were clever ratings who knew all there was to know about turret machinery; there were few problems they could not solve. As the Japanese cannot pronounce our letter 'R', so the lower deck could never pronounce the word Artificer. They invariably pronounced it Artissifer. Had I needed to separate friend from foe in the Far East and in the dark, and had I suspected the password might be compromised, I would have chosen Artificer. The Germans would undoubtedly have pronounced it correctly.

Eventually the huge 15" guns were ready, the 'Ready' lights flashed on, the firing gong ting-tinged, and moments later there were two huge explosions as the enormous guns fired and recoiled. Breeches opened, air rushed in, cages clanged and all was ready again.

It was my first experience of a 15" gun firing, and I found myself with a splitting headache afterwards. The Navy at that time had no cissy ideas about men going deaf through gunfire. Earmuffs? Certainly not, it'll make men of them to hear proper gunfire! Funnily enough, the smaller guns had more of an effect on one's eardrums than their larger sisters. The noise of a 4.5 ' gun, with its awful whiplash crack as it fired, was far worse than the 'Big Berthas'. Later, ratings employed on Asdic duties reported that their hearing was being impaired by gunfire. As it was essential for the proper performance of their duties that they should be able to hear a 'ping' on a submarine, their Lordships issued an AFO (Admiralty Fleet Order) on the matter. This laid down that no Asdic rating should be exposed to the sound of gunfire. This did not stop those who had the temerity to invoke the spirit of the AFO from being labelled poofy sea-lawyers.

All the shots went over the target and to the right of it. The Gunnery Officer, Lieutenant-Commander Unwin, normally a pleasant man even for a Gunnery Officer, went about with a thundercloud on his face. I was glad my participation in the shoot had been 'for training only'.

To cap it all, as we were about to enter harbour, the destroyer *Havock* collided with us. Destroyers have been known to have been literally cut in two by larger ships, but this was fortunately a glancing blow and did neither ship any damage. *Havock* had a commanding officer who was not only an audacious destroyer commander, but one who was brave enough to take on his Commander-in-Chief. Cunningham was standing on the quarter-deck of his flagship. Sweeping Alexandria harbour with his telescope, he espied *Havock* passing his bows, about to put to sea. As was customary, the ship's company were fallen in for leaving harbour, salutes were exchanged. Then suddenly Cunningham stiffened, 'Flags,' he commanded. His Flag Lieutenant saluted, signal pad in hand. 'Make to *Havock* from C-in-C. Why was the captain of *Havock* smoking a cigarette when his ship was leaving harbour?' ordered the C-in-C. Signal lamps flashed, Yeomen and Chief Yeomen of Signals recorded the messages. They nearly dropped their signal pads. The reply read: 'To C-in-C from *Havock*. Because he can't afford cigars!' Fortunately for *Havock's* Captain and his chances of promotion, Cunningham loved it and took no further action. A former destroyer captain himself, he knew what a strain they were having to bear in the confined waters of the Mediterranean. A little light relief was permissible, even if only occasionally.

On 10 December 1940 General Sir Archibald Wavell, C-in-C Middle East Land Forces, commenced his offensive against the Italians in the Western Desert. The first day's 'bag' comprised two generals and some 400 prisoners.

We had put to sea the previous afternoon in company with the ageing battleship *Barham*, *Illustrious* for our air cover, and the destroyers *Vampire*, *Vendetta*, *Hyperion* and *Hasty*. We had the honour of having on board a Times war correspondent, one David Lyle. We expected to be ordered to support the army by bombardment of the town of Bardia and its approach roads. Our targets would have been the hairpin bends of the coast road along which the Italians were expected to retreat, together with the ammunition dump near the town. I say 'would have been', but things are seldom if ever straightforward in war. We should have commenced firing at 0800 but were not in the correct position for action, consequently we did not go to Action Stations until 0930.

'Firing will commence at 1000,' I was told when I arrived in 'B' turret. The appointed time came and went. We did nothing. Soon afterwards we heard that the whole operation had been cancelled. Very strong off-shore winds were blowing the desert sands right on to us, reducing visibility to 400 yards. Bombardment was hopeless.

Our Swordfish aircraft was catapulted off at 0930 to 'spot' the fall of shot. The pilot, Hughie Davenport, was a short, dapper Lieutenant in the Fleet Air Arm with a tendency to grow his luxuriant black hair as long as he dared. When acting as Officer of the Watch at sea he would get the duty midshipman to light his cigarettes from under the chart table flap. Many a Chesterfield have I lighted for him in that way. When ordered to fly, he would enter the Ward Room and announce dramatically, 'Gentlemen, I am off to dice with death!'

On that occasion, our plane radioed that they were being attacked by enemy aircraft. It was not pressed home however, and as our slow Swordfish turned away, so did the Italian fighter! The latter probably had a speed advantage over the Stringbag (Swordfish) of at least 150 knots but its pilot decided it was better to fight another day.

Later the cruiser *Gloucester* threw up some anti aircraft fire but fortunately soon desisted. The 'enemy' had British markings! HM ships were 'trigger happy' throughout the war, with good reason. More often than not, an aircraft was hostile, and 'shoot first and ask questions afterwards' was a fairly sensible policy. Our own pilots too, were not without fault, and required more instruction in ship recognition. It was by no means unknown for friendly planes to bomb their own ships. The German surface ships would have large swastikas painted on their foc'sles, presumably acting on the principle that the Luftwaffe would find it hard to believe that they were at sea.

Soon, Sidi Barani was ours, together with 20,000 prisoners. I never think of this North African town without remembering the inimitable Kenneth Home as the Wing Commander in *Much Binding in the Marsh* – 'When I was in Sidi Barani!'

Back in Alexandria, an unpleasant incident occurred. The Gunroom Wine Store was broken into and fourteen bottles of rye whisky were stolen, beside liqueurs. Theft is a mean crime anywhere; when such an offence is committed by one or more of one's shipmates it becomes all the more odious. The culprit, although he must have been very drunk on his ill-gotten gains, was never found. The brotherhood of the lower deck protected him, and a Mafia 'silenzia' descended like an impenetrable cloud.

No rest for the wicked, and midnight on 16 December 1940 saw us putting to sea, heading for Crete. We did not know it at the time, but the operation for which our very powerful force was intended was potentially a very dangerous one. Perhaps because of this, although neither he nor most of us were aware of it, we embarked a *Daily Mail* war correspondent, Desmond Hartin. These war correspondents wore a khaki coloured suit resembling uniform, with War Correspondent written on their shoulder flashes. They were all extremely nice men, and on the rare occasions when I spoke to them, very friendly. To me, as a seventeen-year-old junior midshipman, they were, in spite of their civilian status, Ward Room material, and therefore way above my station. Looking back as I write after 70 years have elapsed, I can quite see that they might well have welcomed the chance to obtain a snotty's view of things, but I was too conscious then of seniority to do anything other than keep my distance.

In company with us were the C-in-C flying his flag in *Warspite*, out fleet carrier *Illustrious*, and the Third Cruiser Squadron. That morning, two Fulmar fighters crashed whilst attempting a landing on the carrier, but both pilots were saved. The next day at 0400 *Illustrious* flew off twelve aircraft, six to bomb the island of Rhodes, and six to bomb the island of Stampadia. Like so many events in wartime, ignorance was our lot concerning this operation, and no one ever heard if it was a success or not.

We anchored in Suda Bay, Crete, at 0900 to let the destroyers take on oil fuel. The snow-capped mountains looked magnificent in the weak winter sunshine, and I longed to stretch my legs on shore. However this was not a pleasure cruise, courtesy of 'Grey Funnel Line' (the Royal Navy's name, usually for those taking passage in HM ships), but a wartime operation, and we stayed but a couple of hours.

As always, if ships' companies were to be told anything at all about what they were to undertake, and to be fair, they nearly always were, such information would be imparted at sea. Short of dropping bottles overboard with messages inside, or a 'bent' W/T operator, security would therefore be literally watertight. The news that Captain Morgan broadcast to us that evening aroused varying emotions according to how brave you were – we were to bombard the Albanian port of Valona.

Now, if you will take your school atlas and look at a position 40°2T'N and 19°30'E you will have found our objective. Alternatively, if you have not received the advantages of an education in navigation, let me say that Valona lies some 60 miles to the north of Corfu, and 100 miles to the east of the Italian port of Brindisi. A further study of the map will reveal that we would, when in position for bombardment, be well up in the Strait of Otranto, and thus deep into enemy waters. It was therefore with mixed, but private, feelings that we received the Captain's news. When he added that 'this might well be a very dangerous operation, and that we may well come under fire ourselves from the shore,' we wondered if this was not a re-run of the Charge of the Light Brigade.

'Ours not to reason why' – we did not fear so much the Italian Navy, but heavy shore batteries were a different kettle of fish, and what about aircraft? We would only be 30 minutes' flying time from the Italian mainland. Highly unpleasant! What was the reason for risking heavy units of the British fleet in such dangerous waters? The reason was, support for the Greeks in their heroic struggle against the Italians. The latter were using Valona as a replenishment port into which to pour men and war material. By throwing bombardment shells into the port we were supposed to put a stop, even if only temporary, to their game.

At 1230 on 18 December we went to Attack Stations; only one degree less than Action Stations. We were getting near the danger area. During the afternoon however, the weather deteriorated considerably, with a high sea running. This made it hopeless for flying and our Swordfish, which was airborne before the weather worsened, tried to land on *Illustrious* seven times before succeeding.

At 1600 Cunningham signalled that although he did not expect the bombardment to take place (cheers from the faint-hearted), he intended to take us up to a line in search of enemy warships (groans from the faint-hearted). Reports had been received from our

Naval Attache in Athens that two Italian heavy cruisers and four destroyers had been bombarding the Albanian coast; we were to look for them. 'Our man in Athens' was evidently doing his job.

At 2100 we went to Action Stations which involved me in an unpleasant gymnastics exercise. When a capital ship is at sea in wartime, the turrets of the main armament are kept trained at 45 degrees to the bow and stern. The reason is obvious when you consider the tremendous weight of the 15" guns in their turrets; they can only train (turn to the enemy's bearing) very slowly, and by being in these positions they have at least a greater chance of bearing on the target more quickly. 'B' turret – my Action Station – was no exception.

The question arose, how was I to get in? The manhole below the turret itself was now quite out of reach; it jutted over the side! There was only one way in: to climb all the way up the barbette, the huge steel trunking which extended from the turret itself right down to the shell rooms and magazine, deep in the bowels of the ship.

Now, to proceed between decks in a large warship closed up at Action Stations is in itself a tedious and laborious business. It is an impossibility in a small ship such as a destroyer; there simply are no doors through which to pass each bulkhead. This created problems in the Battle of Crete. Each bulkhead or cross-section of a large warship has in it a huge steel door. These are called the X and Y doors, and all are clamped shut in action. There are eight clamps to a door. Before I even reached the barbette, therefore, I had to unclamp and re-clamp six doors. It does not take a Senior Wrangler to calculate that I had to clamp and re-clamp 96 times for a start.

I hurried between decks, getting hotter in my haste, and due to the fact that I was wearing a scarf and duffel coat. The Adriatic in winter is not a warm place.

At last I arrived at the bottom of the barbette and realised the Herculean task still before me. I opened yet another steel door in the trunking and gazed upwards in horror. Above me, seeming to stretch right up into the sky, was a steel ladder clamped to the side of the barbette. To get into the turret I must climb up the whole way.

I waited for a moment to get my breath, and to cool down – both were impossible. Then I was struck by an awful thought. Supposing we started firing and I was not at my post? Dreadful thoughts of my court-martial flashed through my brain. I had seen a film at Dartmouth of the hapless Dreyfus being stripped of his badges of rank before his assembled regiment.

Did they do that in the Royal Navy? Would a Gieves minion be summoned to cut off my white patches before the whole ship's company? I decided not to put the matter to the test and began my climb.

What I had not realised was that the steel rungs of the ladder would be oily. My hands and my feet slipped occasionally, it was awful, like climbing the greasy pole. I was hot, sweating profusely, and, with all my winter clothing on, in danger of getting stuck in the steel tube. I felt like Alice when she grew too large. It was frightening.

Halfway up I did what you should never do when climbing – I looked down. The bottom seemed miles away, the top out of reach. I longed for someone to help me. I was terrified of falling down the tube, and ending up with two broken legs.

At last I made it to the top after what seemed an eternity and crawled into the huge turret. I practically collapsed at the feet of Petty Officer Colville. I was hot, exhausted, oily and out of breath and for moments lay there like a stranded whale. I hoped Lieutenant Barnes had not seen my unceremonious arrival. He was not there. Where was he? It was then that I heard his voice outside the turret.

'Petty Officer Colville.'

'Sir?'

'Train the turret fore and aft.'

'Aye, aye, Sir.'

I simply could not believe it. No one gave orders as to where the turret was to be trained during Action Stations except the Director Tower.

The powerful machinery slowly moved the immense turret so that its guns pointed forward. The entrance manhole was thus easily accessible. Henry Barnes crawled through it, a white scarf around his neck, an immaculate British Warm covering his large body. He would never have made it up my torture chamber. For my part, I would never have dared to give such an order and thus take our turret off its appointed bearing. Henry B. did and I had to admire him for it. It was a long time though, before I was able to forgive him for taking the easy way in.

The heat which I had generated during my passage through the ship and up the barbette soon evaporated. It was very cold inside the turret, only 42 degrees Fahrenheit. We tried to make the best of a bad job, and get some sleep, but it was not easy . We slept on three machine gun ammunition boxes with a board between them. We waited...

At half past midnight we were told that the bombardment would take place after all. The pompous entry in my journal reads: 'Naturally everyone was very pleased!' Well, yes, we were going to see some action, and that was what we had come for. Twenty minutes later the flagship opened fire. Within our thick steel walls the sound was muted, so that it seemed like her 6" secondary armament, not the huge 15" guns. We opened fire five minutes later, 'Darby and Joan' firing eleven rounds. I was in action against the enemy at last!

The Director Control Tower kept its trigger permanently pressed. This meant that as soon as our guns came to the 'Ready', they fired. This gave us shocks as no one knew when they were going to go off!

The Italian enemy appeared to have been taken completely by surprise. The only action they took was to fire a few starshell well astern of us. Surely the dreaded shore batteries could have fired at our gun flashes? We could not see the results of our bombardment owing to the fact that we were firing over a hill. Our own targets were, we were told, an ammunition dump and great quantities of stores and army trucks. Due to the bad weather no aircraft could 'spot' for us so we were firing blind. Altogether we fired 52 rounds; if this was added to *Warspite's* firing, 100 15" shells must have fallen on Valona.

After the bombardment we made off to the southward. Had this been German held territory we would have been bombed out of the water. As it was, the Italians left us quite alone.

The bridge was extremely cold, and that night we endured a very severe hail and snow storm. The compass became covered in snow, making it impossible to read. I was kept warm by having to rush up and down ladders, making and fetching cocoa. This had unfortunate consequences, as I was due to wake the Captain at 0630. No need. I tripped outside his sea cabin, dropping a cup of hot cocoa with an almighty crash. A call became superfluous.

Calling the Captain or the Navigator was part of a midshipman's duty. It had been impressed on me that almost the most heinous crime in a snotty's book was to dare to shake a senior officer awake. This was tantamount to assaulting him, and if anything was a beatable offence, that was. A knock on the door, the words repeated, 'Captain, Sir, it' s o-six-three-o' should suffice, but never a shake.

The Navigator would growl, 'Any stars?' but fortunately never asked which ones were visible, as my recognition of heavenly bodies was virtually nil.

The Commander, Peter Reid, was marvellous. He would just answer quietly, 'Thank you Holloway.' He recognised one's voice even though he had just been woken up. I admired that.

On 21 December, the BBC broadcast the news of our Albanian bombardment. The news reader said that this gave the lie to Mussolini's boast of the Mediterranean being 'Mare Nostrum', and that he should be wondering about the Adriatic now.

The afternoon found us off Malta. Aircraft from *Illustrious* flew off to attack an enemy convoy. This sadly resulted in our ship's first casualty in action since my joining. Our observer, Lieutenant Vereker, had also doubled as Signals Officer. Lent to our carrier whilst in Crete, Vereker had been the first to spot the convoy. Our aircraft sank three merchantmen with torpedoes, but sadly Vereker did not return. Fuel for their revenge was added the next day when *Illustrious'* aircraft attacked Tripoli in the early morning.

They reported the city to have been 'well plastered'. This attack on enemy supplies was doubtless not lost on the Germans. The presence of aircraft carriers had been amply demonstrated by Taranto and now this. They were soon to take a savage revenge. With the euphoric feeling of operations against the enemy having been well carried out, we steamed eastwards towards Alexandria at 20 knots. Tomorrow would be Christmas Eve.

7

The Dive-Bomber Attack

Any Christmas spent thousands of miles away from one's loved ones is bound to be a melancholy affair. We were only 1500 miles from England by direct route, but 12000 miles round the Cape. This was the only route open to us, had we been able to travel at all. With no telephone link, and these vast distances separating us from all those at home, we were indeed isolated.

We had anchored in Alexandria harbour at 1500 on Christmas Eve. The next day would be my first Christmas away from home, and I longed for the first time in my life, for it to be over. I had always adored Christmas, I still do, and make no bones about it. I love the 'jingle-bellsery', and if there is snow to make it more Dickensian, so much the better.

For me, the contrast between Christmas 1939 and that of 1940 could not have been more marked. A thick blanket of snow covered Minchinhampton Common in 1939, giving it a fairytale appearance. The road past our house was blocked, so we walked a mile to church. Rationing had made little or no impact, the table groaned with Christmas fare, there were presents galore. My parents had just bought a beautiful Ferguson wireless set. I spent many happy hours on its shortwave bands logging the faraway stations.

On Boxing Day, we walked two miles to a friend's house, over the snow-covered common to Amberley. Lunch and tea there, and I smoked du Maurier cigarettes, feeling very grown up. I was sixteen.

Now, I was in North Africa, in a Muslim country. No church bells rang out on this very Christian day. The plaintive wailing of the muezzins atop the minarets of their mosques was a forceful reminder that this would certainly not be a Dickensian Christmas. In this country snow was unknown, our sledges, left at home, would not be used for many a year. I was seventeen, wishing that some genie would appear from his lamp and transport me instantly to our Gloucestershire fireside. It was not to be.

I have, I am glad to say, never spent Christmas in prison. I do however, imagine that it bears some resemblance to the festive season in one of HM ships in wartime. Some pitiful paper chains are hung up. There is a ghastly air of enforced jollity as everyone tries to persuade himself that he is having a good time, and fails miserably. The entry in my journal for Christmas Day 1940 begins: 'Today might well have been vulgarly described as 'The Great Booze'!' Sadly, it was just that.

The day started with Divisions on the quarter-deck. A short Carol Service was conducted by the Chaplain. We were much nearer Bethlehem than being at home in Gloucestershire, but somehow it added to the incongruity and melancholia.

At 1000 the petty officers and some Royal Marines were invited into the Gunroom, and as my entry shows, 'Beer flowed freely.' We were not meant to entertain ratings, but I found out that an able seaman who lived only a quarter of a mile from my parents' house, was serving on board. He was duly summoned to the Gunroom and we wished each other a happy Christmas. Both of us wished we were back in Minchinhampton. I could only offer him a bottle of beer in the Gunroom Pantry – the segregation rules for ratings as junior as he were very strict.

After our entertainment of the POs we were all invited into the Ward Room where, as befitted our better paid seniors, champagne as well as gin was on offer. At home, my father never drank spirits, my mother never drank. This was in spite of, or perhaps because of the fact that my grandfather had owned a brewery; too many of the family had become addicted to alcohol, supposedly rather disgraceful in those days. I had therefore little or no experience of 'the hard stuff', and after my glass had been refilled half a dozen times I began to feel distinctly 'woozy'.

The 'young gentlemen' of the Gunroom then entertained the Ward Room officers with yet more champagne. It would be a general charge on our wine bills, and on five shillings a day (25p), I wondered if I could afford our generosity. At seventeen, I was not supposed to drink anything harder than beer anyway!

Finally, those who were able to walk went over to the Warrant Officers' Mess and drank some more there. The afternoon was spent in sleeping off the effects of the morning's debauch, thus missing the King's speech.

Well, better a Christmas spent in harbour in a big ship I suppose, rather than in a cold foxhole in the Western Desert. Not for the first time was I glad that I was serving in the Royal Navy.

My life just after Christmas and into the New Year of 1941 was fairly uneventful; that is to say when compared with wartime life in general and that on active service in particular. Although we were in harbour, New Year's Eve came and went without celebration. It was perhaps fortunate that we were not in the inebriated state of Christmas Day, for at 0400 on New Year's Day an air raid warning was sounded and I made my way to the Air Defence Position. A false alarm, but our sleep had been rudely disturbed.

Bardia was proving a tough nut to crack, and we were soon to assist as the nutcrackers. Two huge troopships arrived in Alexandria, the P&O liner Strathaird and Empress of Canada, crammed full of Australian troops. Doubtless they were to assist in Wavell's desert campaign. Meanwhile, I played squash ashore and complained to my journal of the inability of Alexandrian taxi men to find their way even to the most well-known parts of the city. Compared to their London counterparts they were, what that wonderful comedian Terry Thomas would have called, 'an absolute shower!'

On 2 January, and a midshipman came into the Gunroom. 'I say Stopford,' he said to the Sub-Lieutenant, 'I hear Prince Philip is joining the Gunroom.'

Stopford looked up from the after end of the Gunroom where the gramophone was playing Judy Garland's 'I'm just an in-between'. This happened to be Terry Lewin's favourite. It was fortunate I liked it as well since it was seldom off the turntable. 'Well,' said Stopford, 'What about it? What do you expect me to do?'

The midshipman who had got so excited now looked rather foolish and crestfallen. 'Well,' he said rather lamely, 'I thought you would be meeting him at the gangway.'

'Certainly not!' Stopford replied sharply. 'He's no different from any other mid. Doubtless I shall see him when he's settled in.'

Of course Stopford was quite right. His Royal Highness Prince Philip of Greece and Denmark had no claim to a more privileged position than any of us, his fellow midshipmen, nor, I am sure, would he have wished for it. Later to marry our future Queen, and to become Duke of Edinburgh, HRH was at that time comparatively unknown, serving as a midshipman in the Mediterranean fleet.

Philip, as he was called, joined us without ceremony from the County class cruiser Shropshire. Seated eating his meal at the Gunroom table, those who had been inclined to have been in awe of him found him to be quite mortal. If Philip noticed the covert looks in his direction, he gave no sign. Lunch was much more interesting.

Bardia awaited our attention and at 1800 we sailed, accompanied by Warspite and Barham. Our faithful aircraft carrier Illustrious joined us at 2300. It was fortunate that those on board her were blissfully unaware of the terrible events which were to overtake them in eight days' time.

Before dawn broke we were off the Cyrenaica coast and approaching our target. Precious little sleep when we were at sea, 'watch on, watch off', meaning we were on watch every other four hours. I had the First (2000–0000) and Morning (0400–0800) on the Air Defence Position. I had the grand title of Assistant Air Defence Officer, and was mainly concerned with relaying commands to the Air Director Towers which controlled our anti-aircraft weapons.

At 0540 I was told to go and have some breakfast. At 0615 we went to Action Stations. Without being ordered, the Chief Yeoman of Signals hoisted our battle ensigns, the largest White Ensigns he could find. From gaff and truck our colours flapped proudly. 'Mare Nostrum?' More likely 'Mare Britannica' we thought. Not for long.

My Action Station in 'B' turret provided me with a grandstand view of the proceedings. From time to time Henry Barnes, Petty Officer Colville and myself climbed up through the manhole on to the top of the turret to have what the gyppos call 'a shufti'. There was no great bravery we thought in this – we did not appear then to be in any danger. Later we were to appear somewhat mistaken and foolhardy.

We looked towards Bardia, and could see a good many bombs bursting. The RAF was softening up the enemy before our projectiles arrived. The town itself could not be seen due to all the spouts of sand being thrown up. Flashes of gunfire could plainly be seen. These were the visible signs of the Australians attacking Bardia, where they penetrated the first line of defences. I wondered if they were the ones we had seen sailing so recently into Alexandria, if so, their baptism of fire had not long been delayed.

HMS *Valiant* in 1939. (Author's collection)

Our intrepid aviators in their 'Stringbags' (Swordfish), were catapulted off at 0730 in order to spot for us. I could see it cruising over the target, unmolested.

Orders came through the 'phones to load with high explosive, the huge breeches yawned open, the projectiles and cordite went in, breeches clanged shut, and precisely at 0800 the fire gongs 'ting-tinged'.

All was now action. Watching now more prudently through the turret periscope, I could see our shell bursts making mountains of sand where previously the bombs had created hillocks. The land was temporarily obscured. I wondered what the enemy on the receiving end of all this was thinking, if he was alive to think at all. Later, I was to have a graphic description of our bombardment from an Army officer. 'Imagine,' he said, 'the noise a tube train makes when it is hurtling through the tunnel.' It is a never to be forgotten sound and I told him so. 'Exactly,' he said. 'Well, that's what your 15" shells sound like as they travel overhead. And when the crump comes, you just thank God that the shells are ours, and hope that the shooting will continue to be accurate!'

Huge gouts of yellow smoke came from the turrets of the three battleships as we steamed majestically in line ahead. At the risk of a cliché, it was an awe-inspiring sight.

After 45 minutes, and when we had exhausted nearly all our shells, we ceased firing, and turned away. It was now that the Italians had the impertinence to return our fire, and that, of course, was not nearly so funny as dishing it out. The enemy, who must have had gun emplacements in the rocky cliffs, was firing at us with uncomfortable accuracy, some of their shells falling very close to us and to the flagship. They were not stupid, concentrating their fire on the turning point.

I reflected that in my short active service career, I had now been bombed and shelled. Doubtless had I been in the US Navy my chest would already have had a considerable array of medals to demonstrate my bravery to the world at large. The Royal Navy does things differently and my bosom remained bare of decoration.

Bardia fell to the Eighth Army on 6 January. Our efforts had not been in vain, and some 61,000 prisoners were taken. Enemy radio propaganda recorded in my journal makes interesting reading. From Germany the *Deutsche Nachrichten Dienst* proclaimed that the war in Africa did not matter – the final decision would be reached in the invasion of Britain. Quite.

The Italians called the British offensive in Africa a fiasco. My journal comment was: 'I am beginning to wonder how the enemy describes their own fighting.'

Three days in Alexandria harbour was our small respite before we were ordered to sea once more. Off Bardia we had been cocky, facing an enemy who we knew we could beat. We were shortly to have the rudest shock of our lives and to face the onslaught of an implacable and deadly foe.

Tuesday, 7 January 1941 saw me on watch at 0200 in the Air Defence Position. At four o'clock we put to sea, and due to the difference between sea and harbour watches I was forced to keep a six hour watch instead of four. I was not best pleased. Commander Reid told us that this was 'just an ordinary convoy job' – we were to escort an eastbound convoy which was being passed through the Strait of Pantelleria, south of Sicily. Nobody seemed to think much about it; if we drew out the Italian Navy we would get the better of them, we felt sure. The Regia Aeronautica was no threat, did we not have our fleet aircraft carrier *Illustrious* with us? Her fighters would protect us, and so on.

A state of euphoria enveloped us. Tobruk aerodrome had been captured. The army was well on the way to taking the town. What harm could befall us? We were stupid innocents.

The morning of 8 January dawned and with it the mountains of Crete hove into view. The snow had gone from most of the mountain tops and the island looked greener than on previous visits. The destroyers refuelled, and within 90 minutes we were on our way again. As we entered Suda Bay four cruisers passed us outward bound. Little did they know their future fates as well. *Orion* was to sustain severe damage and 500 casualties in the Battle of Crete the following May. *York* was to be attacked by Italian frogmen in Suda Bay, later to be beached, abandoned and bombed to destruction. The Australian cruiser *Perth* was to be sunk by the Japanese in the Battle of the Java Sea in early 1942. Only *Ajax* was to survive, and in her I was to take passage home to UK in February of that year. All fine, beautiful ships, they sailed proudly out of the bay later to meet tragic ends.

We sailed westwards towards Malta; it might have been the peacetime Mediterranean fleet on exercises. Commander Reid broadcast that the next day we would be twelve miles from the island of Pantelleria, the spot appointed for us to pick up the eastbound convoy. The next day would be 10 January. It was nice to spend my last day as a seventeen year old in comparative peace. I would soon be longing for my birthday to end, something I had never done before.

As with previous Christmases, about which I wrote in the last chapter, so with my previous birthdays. Unlike many unfortunates at boarding school, my birthday on 10 January always fell in the holidays. It was sufficiently far away from Christmas for relations not to give me a combined present. I should have been extremely put out if they had. A party was always given for me on my birthday. It was a day I had always enjoyed to the full. This practice was to come to a rude and abrupt halt in 1941.

There are no birthday parties at sea in wartime. I suppose I told one or two friends that I would be eighteen, not that they cared much. For members of my term, we would nearly all be Capricornians, so we were literally all in the same boat.

My journal entry for 10 January 1941 begins: 'Today is my eighteenth birthday, and I think it was quite the weirdest and most fully-occupied birthday that I have ever had.' Looking back, I think that I would cross out the word weirdest and substitute the word harrowing. After all, if, instead of a teenager's birthday party, a collection of people who you have never met, are going to do their best to kill you, and you are going to try to do the same to them, it really is somewhat different, isn't it?

My birthday, like all birthdays, began at midnight. I kept the Middle Watch on the Air Defence Position and also the Forenoon, from 0800 to noon. Our invaluable radar tracked many groups of aircraft, but none came closer than eight miles. The cats were playing with the mice.

Not content with loss of sleep through keeping watches four hours on, four hours off, Dawn and Dusk Action Stations were interposed. Today's was at 0720; there was purpose in this one.

'Gunfire on the starboard bow,' came a report. Up through the turret manhole we scrambled, eager to see what was going on. It is not always easy to make out events when they occur some way from you at sea. However, this we could discover, and it was indeed surface gunfire. The Commander's voice came over the loudspeaker: 'Bonaventure is engaging an enemy destroyer.' Bonaventure was a very new 6" gun cruiser which had just come through to us from the Western Mediterranean. She was being 'blooded' at an early stage. The birthday boy gave a sigh of relief. At least they were smaller than we were!

We watched, fascinated, here was the surface enemy at last. I was wearing headphones connected to the Director Control Tower in the highest part of the ship, and therefore commanding a much better view. Through the 'phones I heard an excited gasp, 'My God, the destroyer's blown up.' One moment there had been a shape on the horizon, and the next moment there was nothing but a pall of black smoke to show where hundreds of Italian sailors had died.

A great deal of sentimental and hypocritical rubbish is put about in the media today as to how people react when your enemy is killed before your eyes. American films depict combatants shedding copious tears and requiring psychological treatment afterwards. As far as those of us on board Valiant were concerned, those feelings existed only in the minds of writers and producers. Reality was a great cheer, and thankfulness that an enemy pawn had been removed from the board.

There had been two Italian destroyers, but one slipped away whilst Bonaventure dealt with her sister ship. Rather infra dig I thought, comparable with one of our destroyers sneaking into Portsmouth whilst her compatriots were being sent to the bottom off the Isle of Wight.

Meanwhile, the eastbound convoy which was our main concern, passed us, and

Bonaventure, her killing mission accomplished, joined the fleet. By this time, we had practically passed through the Strait of Pantelleria, and so the order came to turn around and head east towards our home base, Alexandria.

No sooner had this episode been concluded, than another occurred. I was climbing the ladder to start my watch in the Air Defence Position. I had just reached the Flag Deck and saw at once a number of officers and ratings staring over the starboard side at a cloud of smoke on the water. I asked someone what it was. He replied that it was one of the planes from *Illustrious* which had crashed in the sea. Pointing to a large object in the water, he said, 'Look, there's the tail-plane.'

I have often marvelled at the human tendency to make something up when they lack actual knowledge of their subject. Newspaper and radio reporters are great sufferers from this syndrome. The smoke cleared away, and it was clear that no aeroplane had crashed – it was much worse than that.

One of our accompanying destroyers, *Gallant*, had struck a mine, and the supposed 'tail-plane' was none other than the ship's bows which had been cut clean away. White smoke began to pour from her funnels and she began to settle slightly by the bow. Two other destroyers, *Griffin* and *Mohawk*, went to assist the crippled ship, which was later escorted into Malta.

There are a variety of ways in which as a sailor, you can find your life abruptly brought to an end. You can be bombed, shelled or torpedoed, all of which happened to me at one time or another, but a mine, no, that had never entered my head before. Now, reality stared at me from a very close distance. It was not a pretty sight, and one that made me think.

War is often a game of snakes and ladders; only minutes ago we had been on the ladder, cheering at the dispatch of the Italian destroyer. Now, we were on the snake, and thinking of those who must have been trapped in the bow section. They would not have known much about it. One of our pawns had been taken, the score was fifteen all. The enemy was soon to take out more than a pawn.

I made my way slowly towards the Gunroom. The scene was as usual, two Sub-Lieutenants lounged in the armchairs by the electric fire, four or five midshipmen were seated at the long table, journals or the working of sights before them. I decided to leave the writing of my journal until the afternoon. Somehow I did not feel like work, and anyway, a steward was about to lay the table for lunch. There would be nowhere to work.

We sat down to lunch, everyone chattering excitedly about the day's events, and recounting them to those who had been on watch below at the time. Soup was served, Brown Windsor. I remember thinking that Popeye was not really trying. The time was 1223.

Suddenly, there was a click and the ship's loudspeakers blared with the chilling bugle call – 'Repel Aircraft.' In a flash we were all making for the door and our Action Stations. The ship was full of men running as hard as they could. Steel ladders clanged under foot, steel doors began to shut in order to isolate watertight compartments. As I rushed towards 'B' turret, I kept wondering what had gone wrong with our radar. Why had we not been given the usual 'Yellow Warning'? This was much more urgent and frightening.

Mounted on the top of each huge turret were two 0.5" machine guns. These were manned during an aircraft attack, and it was up to these I scrambled through the turret top manhole. Henry Barnes was just behind me. PO Colville's gaunt figure was already there, ratings were at the guns. Necklaces of machine gun ammunition littered the turret top.

An aircraft swooped low on our port bow, a torpedo slid away from its underside and made towards us. It jumped out of the water, fell back, and disappeared. Moments later we could see its track, now thankfully keeping parallel with us. Some torpedoes can be set to imitate the letter 'W'. If that had been done, it would in all probability have exploded against our side just below where I was standing. The din was horrendous. The awful crack of the 4.5" anti-aircraft guns was accompanied by the thumping of the pom-poms and the crackle of our own machine guns.

'Cease firing,' yelled Henry Barnes to the machine-gunners who were cheerfully wasting valuable ammunition by firing at the torpedo bombers, now well out of range.

Suddenly, one of the starboard machine-gun crew, who had been gazing skyward, shouted, 'There they are,' and pointed to the starboard quarter. There, astern of us, at a height of about 10,000 feet, was a cluster of aircraft. They seemed to hang motionless for a while, outlined against the cloudless blue Mediterranean sky. We counted them – seventeen – waiting up there like hawks over a prospective kill. Looked at dispassionately, that is just about what we were. Stomach muscles contracted. This was not going to be a picnic by any manner of means; we were on a very large snake.

Then the attack started in earnest. At first, we thought the convoy was their main target, but we were very wrong. One or two of the enemy planes did attack the merchant ships, but it was His Majesty's Eastern Mediterranean Fleet, and in particular our beloved aircraft carrier *Illustrious* which it soon became apparent they wanted to eliminate.

My journal entry reads: 'The first plane that came for us came from the port bow. It was the first time that I (or many others) had ever been dive-bombed. I could not help looking up as the plane came down to 2000 feet, and the bomb slowly swung out from underneath the fuselage. The nose of the bomb looked very oval as it came towards us, and then we were all flattening ourselves on the turret top as the machine screamed overhead. When we looked up, a cloud of spray was beginning to subside on the port bow, much too near for comfort.'

That was the journal entry. What I did not record in it, because I knew it would be read by senior officers and I would be adjudged on it, was how absolutely petrifying the experience had been. The scream of the aircraft as it made its dive and the infernal whistle of the bomb itself was quite terrifying. Coupled with this the horrendous din of our own guns, and you have a pretty fair picture of hell. If anyone tells you that in those circumstances he was not frightened I would say he was either a monumental liar or very, very brave. You couldn't of course show that you were frightened. Like Charles I at his execution, if you shivered, it was due to the cold and nothing else!

The planes continued their attack, mostly now from astern. We felt somehow safer on 'B' turret because of this, but it was ostrich thinking. The bombs launched from this angle were potentially just as deadly. I was convinced that one was going to land on the forecastle just below us, but a huge crump and showers of spray were evidence of our being spared again.

At each swoop, Henry Barnes would yell, 'Down,' and we flattened ourselves. As one aircraft came very near, Henry shouted, I fell and he fell on top of me, causing more physical damage to me than the enemy. He was porcine, of Henry VIII proportions, and I lay momentarily winded. The thought then occurred to me that the ratings would think I was frightened (which I was, very). So I struggled to my feet to face the next onslaught.

Suddenly someone yelled, '*Illustrious* has been hit!' Forgetting our own troubles for a moment, we looked round, and saw our carrier, brown smoke pouring from her and hanging over her like a pall. A large bomb had landed on her after lift and then exploded in the hangar. It was obvious now that she was the main objective of the attack, daring swoops being made on her, some enemy planes coming as low as 200 feet. *Illustrious* was now out of control and began to swing around in a large circle. She came right across our bows, and then went astern of us, blazing furiously. We were all very much afraid at the time that if the fire got to her aviation spirit she would go up like a Roman Candle. Fortunately, her fire drill had been well exercised, thus saving many lives.

She was a pitiful sight. The after part of the flight deck was buckled right up where the lift had been, with two aircraft blazing on deck. She was red-hot between decks, and we could plainly see wounded men being carried below.

The planes continued their attack, and as one came particularly low over where we were crouching, I looked up and saw black crosses on the wing tips. Evidently Hitler had decided that Italy's conduct of the war in the Mediterranean was disastrous and had sent in the Luftwaffe. There was no mistaking the deadly V-shaped wing, we were being attacked by Junkers 87B, the Stukas which had spearheaded the German blitzkrieg in France.

During a lull, Henry Barnes remarked to me, 'I can't think why they don't machine-gun us.' That's all I need I thought. It had not entered my mind, I was too busy trying to make

A painting of the Stuka attack which took place on the author's eighteenth birthday, 10 January 1941, as it would have been seen from the cockpit of a 'Stringbag' (Swordfish). (Vice-Admiral Sir Roderick Macdonald)

myself as inconspicuous as possible so that I would not be killed. Henry's remark only added to my problems. Just as well we had been somewhat in ignorance. We found out afterwards that this was precisely what they had been doing, spraying the pom-poms and the top of 'X' turret with an accurate fire. So much so, that an able seaman died of his wounds, whilst two others were wounded on 'X' turret. The pom-pom crews had casualties too. The dead and wounded were the machine-gun crew on top of their turret. Had the attacks from the bow continued, the casualties would have been from 'B' turret.

At last we were left alone, the Stukas returning to their Sicilian bases. Their bombs had all been dropped on us, but we all guessed, with an unspoken dread, that they would be back after re-arming. We had no carrier now to protect us, and Malta's aircraft were hard-pressed. The raid had actually only lasted for fifteen minutes, but it had seemed like an eternity. It was therefore only 1245 and there were far too many hours of daylight before we could hide ourselves from our attackers.

Everyone was kept closed up at Action Stations until 1400 when we returned to a very littered Gunroom for our interrupted and now cold lunch. My journal: 'The soup was not at the top of its form.' We rested and discussed the raid. Half an hour afterwards, the Gunroom door opened and in walked John Kane. He had had a very nasty experience indeed. His 'Repel Aircraft' station had been in the Port Fore High Angle Control Position or HACP. The cramped conditions in this tiny compartment deep in the bowels of the ship have been described earlier. What was so horrifying was that when John and his crew heard the 'Secure' ('All Clear'), they tried to open the armoured steel hatch which was their only access and exit. It was jammed. For half an hour they had to wait like the crew of the ill-fated submarine *Thetis*, entombed in what for all they knew, could be their steel-lined coffin. Had the ship been damaged and/or sunk they would literally have been caught like the proverbial rats in a trap. We did not like to think of it, and it was not until later that I wondered which of us was in the most danger? I was being bombed and machine-gunned on deck. John was protected but could do nothing to save himself in an emergency. Fortunately we both survived.

At tea-time our attackers returned. This time we had good warning, and the enemy did not swoop on us for 20 minutes. The waiting time was awful, almost worse than the raids themselves. We knew what to expect now, and could do nothing about it except scan the sky. No friendly CAP (Combat Air Patrol) flew overhead. The Germans had the air to themselves and would doubtless make the most of the opportunity. A curtain raiser was the sight of *Illustrious*, now on the horizon, making for Malta. She was under attack, and firing at her tormentors. Our turn would undoubtedly come.

My problem was that when action came, I had nothing to do. Nominally I was second-in-command of the machine-gun crew should Henry Barnes be killed. But we had not been in action against aircraft before, and no one had thought of instructing me in machine-gun firing, so any one of the ratings was more valuable than me. (Privately I doubted whether Henry knew much about it either, but wisely kept my doubts to myself.)

However, as an officer I had to stand there on top of the turret, get shot at and be bombed whilst appearing not to have a care in the world. I would have been better off and perhaps more use, even if only feeding ammunition, – if I had been inside the turret, but I could hardly voice such a 'chicken' opinion.

The first phase of the second attack was made by high-level bombers. This had been entrusted to the Regia Aeronautica and was not commendable for its accuracy. Mere dots in the sky, a long way from our AA fire, they opened their bomb doors and then legged it for home. If the Regia Aeronautica and the Luftwaffe shared a mess in Sicily, I was glad not to be an Italian pilot.

Then the Stukas arrived centre stage, and all hell broke loose once again. *Warspite* and *Valiant* received the attention of five planes each, their screaming dives resounding in one's ears, the evil bomb looking for all the world like the birth of a pterodactyl as the claws of its parent were released. The sky was brown with AA bursts and the sea boiled as 1000lb bombs fell perilously close to us.

Inexperience, doubtless coupled with fear, made our machine guns ineffective. The gunners opened fire far too soon when the enemy plane was high up and out of range. Consequently, when it was at the end of its dive and we might have hit it, the guns ran out of ammunition. Nobody seemed to have heard of the famous maxim, 'Wait till you see the whites of their eyes', but how right it was. Could it have been the German goggles which distracted our gunners? I think not.

During the infernal din, no one could make himself heard. Henry Barnes, seeing the tragic waste of ammunition, tried to make the port machine gun cease firing by hitting the gunner on the shoulder. While he was engaged thus, he nearly fell a victim to the starboard machine gun which was pumping lead as fast as it could go three inches from his duffel coat! Every time there was a lull, men came up on to the turret top festooned with 'necklaces' of ammunition, whilst we literally waded about amongst the spent shells.

After what seemed an eternity, but in reality cannot have been, like the morning's attack, more than a quarter of an hour, the Germans left us. We were immensely cheered to see them being attacked in the far distance by Hurricanes from Malta. The attack had taken place well within sight of the island – why the hell, we thought, hadn't they come to our aid sooner? Splendid though, the Stukas were no match for our fighters, and six were shot down.

We had to remain on the turret top till 1800 by which time shivers of cold alternated (dare one say it?) with shivers of apprehension. Darkness saved us, and thankful to relax after a fashion, we trooped back to our quarters talking excitedly.

There is seldom drinking among officers at sea, but today's events made an exception. Kind Henry Barnes invited me into the august Ward Room precincts, and stood me a birthday drink. Whilst there, some of the machine-gun bullets which the Stukas had fired at us were brought in. They were found to be dumdums, ghastly things which penetrated your flesh and then exploded. They had been forbidden under the Geneva Convention, like poison gas, as being too horrific.

8

Crete and Malta Convoys

The events recounted in the last chapter have faded into history. Suffice it to say that *Illustrious* had 126 men killed and 91 wounded. She limped into Malta for temporary repairs and there was subjected to more aircraft attack. Only her armoured flight deck saved her.

With the benefit of hindsight and the events of the Falklands War, the question should be posed as to why Cunningham placed our only modern aircraft carrier in such jeopardy. For by placing her in such jeopardy, he also endangered his fleet. Down in the Falklands, the carriers' role had been learned and they were kept out of range of enemy aircraft whilst at the same time providing a CAP for the rest of the Task Force. Cunningham, a brilliant surface admiral, knew nothing of the air, and like so many of his contemporaries looked down on the Fleet Air Arm as a rather common necessity forced upon him.

Agreed, the Mediterranean is in no way comparable to the South Atlantic. The former is landlocked, the latter wide open. But even if Cunningham had anticipated an attack by Italian capital ships he should still have kept *Illustrious* separate from the main body. He could have interposed the battlefleet between her position and the Italian mainland from which an enemy sortie might come. Perhaps he had been lulled into a false sense of security by only having the Italians with which to deal. The arrival of Fliegerkorps X and their aircraft changed the whole ball game.

The Fliegerkorps had been specially trained to attack shipping. We could unfortunately, bear witness as to the efficacy of their training.

The Mediterranean fleet now had only the old and slow aircraft carrier *Eagle* at a time when air fighter cover was desperately needed during the hours of daylight. We could do nothing but rely on our own AA guns putting up an effective barrage. After two attacks the day before, during which the said secondary armament inflicted no damage on the enemy, I was less than sanguine at the prospect.

The air raids had one amusing side however. Commander Reid happened to be passing Midshipman Prince Philip. 'Philip,' he said, 'how many are there between you and the Greek throne?'

Philip looked perplexed and then replied, 'Nine, sir, I think.'

'Yes,' said Reid, 'I see. Well, I still think you'd better wear your tin hat.'

Saturday, 11 January 1941 found us heading eastward towards Alexandria for which I for one, was profoundly grateful. It was not however, politic to say so!

At 0740, just after Dawn Action, our pom-poms opened fire and sank a mine. Those vile machines could and did inflict enormous damage. That we ourselves did not suffer the terrible fate of the cruiser *Neptune* when we bombarded Tripoli later in the year will always be a source of wonderment to me.

At 1600 we received a signal to the effect that the beautiful new cruiser *Southampton* had, like us, been attacked by German dive-bombers and very seriously damaged by three direct hits. We were ordered to turn westward again and escort her whilst she was being towed by *Gloucester*. The latter had also been attacked, one bomb landing right on top of the Director Control Tower and then penetrating down through three decks. *Gloucester* was spared that time, the bomb did not explode. Four months later off Crete, *Gloucester* was not so lucky.

The next day, Commander Reid broadcast the news that the damage to *Southampton* was so severe that *Gloucester* had been forced to pump three torpedoes into her and sink her. We learned later that the Germans had tied six incendiary bombs to their high explosive bombs. This caused the ship to become a raging inferno, and as there was no prospect of controlling the fires near X magazine, the order was given to abandon ship. In all, 27 officers were killed, including four midshipmen, one from my term. I began to count my blessings that I was still alive, something I was to do often in the next twelve months.

My journal records a news item: 'Today the Italians have scored a notable success just to keep up with the triumphs of their Axis partner. A large Italian force landed on a Greek island. They left again four hours later. The vanquished population, which consisted of two shepherds, was then left to get on with the work in hand.'

We arrived back in Alexandria in the early morning of 13 January. The harbour looked empty with both aircraft carriers absent. The interned French were still there of course, and I wondered what their thoughts were when they saw us sail and return after fighting what had been our common enemy until only seven months ago. Perhaps there were a few who felt some guilt, but in the main I expect it was the French equivalent of 'I'm all right Jack.' The British naval synonym would have been, "I'm in the boat, shove off.'

Later that day I went ashore to dine at Pastroudi's with friends. There we met a term mate who had been rescued from the stricken *Southampton*. He was still pretty shaken, telling us that he got away in a pair of serge trousers, a silk shirt and reefer jacket – nothing else.

As the war progressed, I used to find survivors reacting differently. Some were 'twitchy', even after some considerable time had elapsed. Others were proud of it, as was Captain (later Admiral) Tennant of *Prince of Wales*. Sunk by the Japanese, he was picked up and was later to command the Third Cruiser Squadron in the East Indies, in which I served. When inspecting sailors he would stop in front of a man and demand in a menacing tone: 'Ever had to swim for it?' The wretched man would be made to feel quite guilty that his ship had not been sunk under him!

One survivor incident made me feel awful. I was greeted by a Lieutenant (E) (Engineer) who asked, 'Don't you remember me?' I didn't speak for a moment and then fortunately recovered myself and assented hurriedly. His face was a terrible red mess of scarred tissue, and although I pretended to know him I just could not recognise him. Torpedoed whilst on duty in the engine room, he had been dreadfully scalded by the escape of superheated steam. I felt so sorry for him, and hope that in later days plastic surgery was able to help.

Mundane harbour tasks followed, I ran my beloved launch in the warm Egyptian sunshine. The horrors of my birthday began to fade a little. On one trip we collected spuds. I wished to get on board as quickly as possible on our return to *Valiant*. The spuds were being hoisted in by the port crane in a rope net, so I grabbed hold of the net and was speedily hoisted inboard!

The overseas service of the BBC reported the Admiralty communique of our bombing the week before. It omitted the sinking of *Southampton*, but did say she was hit and that casualties had been sustained. The same reference was made to *Illustrious*, and the damage to *Gallant* was also reported, together with the sinking of the Italian destroyer. It is strange to hear details broadcast of an operation in which you have taken part, and interesting to divine what has been omitted. This latter was to have unpleasant consequences after Matapan.

Stable doors were now being closed after the horses had bolted. Three days after our return to Alexandria a dive-bombing exercise was carried out and I was, at long last, initiated into the fairly simple mechanism of the 0.5" machine gun. I wanted to learn how to use it, our lives might depend on it one day, but I had great difficulty in containing my laughter whilst my instruction continued.

The reason for my mirth was that our 'dive-bomber' was our own venerable and much loved Swordfish aircraft. This is not in any way to denigrate these wonderful machines built by Fairey and used to great effect during the war. It was just that the comparison between our biplane 'Stringbag' which might manage 80 knots in a headwind, and the lethal manoeuvring Stuka, its swept back wings full of menace, was too great. I tried to imagine it was the attacker of my birthday, but as I laid and trained the gun on the slow bumbling aircraft, I felt it was sheer pantomime. Private Pike of *Dad's Army* with the cacker-cacker, rat-tat-tat of his submachine gun, 'hosepiping' wildly, would have done as well. 'Stupid boy!'

A Gunroom rugger match was played between *Warspite* and *Valiant*, which we won 15–3. They would have had to have been in extremis to have chosen me, but I was glad not to be in the team, rugger was never my forte, and I was delighted to volunteer for an extra watch on board.

I had now finished my time in 'B' turret and said good-bye to Henry Barnes, PO Colville and the ratings with some regret. I suppose that there was something between an Evelyn Waugh character and one created by Noel Coward when it comes to describing Henry B., as he was known in the Gunroom. Basil Seal in *Put Out More Flags* was: 'regarded by his seniors as an enfant terrible and by his juniors as a rather dilapidated Bulldog Drummond.' There was undoubtedly more of Coward about Henry B. than Waugh. One could picture him in a decorative silk dressing gown, glass and cigar in hand, pirouetting on the stage like a sleek, well-dressed seal. (This is not intended as a pun with Basil aforementioned.) I never saw Henry B. ruffled, or a hair out of place. His uniform was always immaculate and well pressed. Although Royal Navy, I do not think he rose to high rank. Probably the rich aunts saw to it that he resigned his commission after the war, and gracefully accepted some lucrative directorships in the City. I was fond of Henry B. and wish him well.

The HACP or High Angle Control Position which was now my Action Station, has already been described. The hours and hours of waiting in it during watches at sea and in harbour could not exactly be called time spent in the enhancement of one's cultural knowledge. There was no kindred spirit to talk to like Henry B. I even missed the gruff, rather staccato conversation of PO Colville. Instead, in the cramped confines of our steel box, there were six ratings and myself.

The senior rating was Leading Seaman Beechey, a 'Scouse' of limited outlook and conversation. At frequent intervals, rather as my old nanny used to say, 'There now,' he would say, 'Roll on my twelve,' an allusion to the length of time for which he had signed on in His Majesty's Naval Service. It was hardly politic to remind him that the war would take precedence over his contractual service should the latter predate the former. Beechey's conversation was confined to basics; discussions with Henry B. of the previous night's menu at Pastroudi's were now a thing of the past.

Behind the ground glass screen of the height finder sat Torpedoman Pike. Somewhat rotund, he was of higher intelligence than Beechey, but his utterances were few. Perhaps he felt he was casting pearls. The other ratings are not worthy of mention. They tended their instruments and made desultory conversation with Beechey, usually about Liverpool, their home city.

As the reader is aware, I felt that a flattening of Liverpool by German bombers would not come amiss, but wisely decided not to express my opinion. Because *Valiant* was a 'Guz' ship (one manned from Devonport), her ratings were drawn either from the West Country or the north-west of England. The Westcountrymen were delightful, with their Devonian burr. I was not so enamoured of the Liverpudlians.

On 22 January we were ordered to sea to escort the wounded *Illustrious* back into Alexandria. We expected torpedo-bombing attacks when we were only 60 miles from the Italian-held port of Derna. However, nothing occurred beyond our opening fire at two Cant shadowers. They sheered off as soon as we opened fire. Their nationality was not therefore in doubt.

At lunchtime on the 24th I went up to the Flag Deck to take a sight. My navigational expertise was not of a high order. I could never properly bring the sun down to the horizon, the damned sextant would never keep still. A friend had to stand by with the deck watch which had been set that day by the ship's chronometer. When the sun hit the horizon, I would say, 'Now!', he would call out the time in minutes and seconds and then I had half an hour's battle with log tables to fix our position. I never took a star sight, it was quite incomprehensible to me which star was which. I stuck to the sun and the moon. They were much more predictable, and I had some idea of their position in the sky.

Illustrious appeared, accompanied by the destroyers. I looked at her through my glasses but could not make out any signs of the terrible damage which we had seen inflicted on my birthday. Steaming at 24 knots, she belched forth clouds of black smoke, a give-away of her position for miles around. Fortunately, no enemy aircraft accepted what was virtually an open invitation to bomb. The journey back to Alexandria was accomplished without incident, and *Illustrious* entered harbour to the sound of the cheers of assembled ships' companies. Although mindful of the ordeal through which she had been, we were also mindful of the fact that she would now undergo extensive repair and refitting in some delightful watering-hole, probably the US or South Africa. Midshipmen were not allowed to enjoy the fleshpots of a prolonged refit however, and would inevitably have been transferred to other, more operational ships. As a reward for our baptism by bombing, all night leave was granted to alternate watches of our ship's company, a most unusual occurrence where the virtual instant readiness of the battlefleet to put to sea is considered.

Air raid alarms, false and real, dogged our nights, and it was rare to get one's ration of sleep. We thought it was a bit much really, to be in constant danger from attack when at sea, and not to be immune when in harbour. You had the ridiculous feeling that as in a game of 'Sorry' or 'Halma' you had achieved home base and you deserved to be safe there! Not for us the huge, completely bomb-proof U-boat pens at L'Orient. We were out in the open and had to add our gunfire to the land-based AA barrage during a raid. Later I was to become so tired that not even the sound of our own guns would wake me.

Once having just come off watch, I was caught literally with my trousers down, or rather not on at all. Starkers, in the bath, the air raid alarm sounded. Grabbing a blue sweater, grey trousers and sandals I arrived at my action station looking like a bombed-out evacuee. What was worse was that it proved to be a false alarm.

My journal is full of eulogies to the Greek nation locked at that time in their gallant fight against a nation superior in numbers but not in courage. It was not until Hitler decided that the Balkan question, together with the Jewish, required a final solution, that they gave in. This was to have deadly consequences for the Mediterranean fleet.

On 1 February we sailed from Alexandria and were told that we were at sea in order to create a diversion for the operation of Force 'H' in the Western Mediterranean. We were shadowed by enemy aircraft but our sortie was uneventful, and after three days we returned to Alexandria. A week later the papers were full of the bombardment of Genoa by Force 'H'. Planes from *Ark Royal* bombed the Ansaldo electric works, whilst 15" shells from the capital ships created havoc in the port. Rome radio said the bombardment was carried out under the cover of fog, giving this as the reasons for the slow response of their shore batteries! Would it not have applied to both sides? It was nice to know 'our journey had not been unnecessary'.

The following day, 11 February, the British fleet was dressed overall in honour of King Farouk's birthday, whilst the Royal Marine band played the Gilbertian Egyptian National Anthem at Divisions. Stories were circulating even then of the excesses being practised by Egypt's ruler in Cairo. Some of the more lecherous may even have been wishing that they were taking part! The sailors had, with typical irreverence, put words to His Egyptian Majesty's National Anthem. Whilst it was hardly Coward or Novello, it amused the troops, if not the King.

Farouk had the reputation of being pro-Axis, and his alleged dislike of the British cannot have been diminished when our tanks surrounded Abdin Palace on the orders of our Ambassador, Sir Miles Lampson. Farouk surrendered to *force majeure* and got rid of his Prime Minister who was a Nazi sympathiser. Whilst we had not sent a gunboat up the Nile, Lampson's actions had the same effect.

In Scapa Flow they had mist and fog. In Alexandria we had sandstorms. The sand blanketed the harbour, swirling round and round for hours. It was impossible to see even ships moored nearby, and the melancholy sound of their bells rang out across the harbour. I wondered what it was like for the army in the Western Desert in such conditions. Patrolling would cease I imagined, and one might well find oneself too close to the enemy for comfort when the sand had cleared! How would aircraft land? Once again, I was glad to be in the Navy.

Benghazi fell on 7 February. Our forces seemed invincible. Besides the capture of this major port, the Eighth Army had taken prisoner ten out of the fifteen divisions in Libya. Wavell's praises were shouted from the roof tops, and all seemed well. Alas, what the world did not know was that it was all being done on a shoestring, lines of communication were sorely stretched, and comparatively few had heard of a young German general named Erwin Rommel. The Italians had been put to flight; next stop Tripoli? Sadly, not for another eighteen months.

Harbour routine was carried out as usual. Boats ran, divisions were inspected, exercises were carried out, and the Gunroom settled into the life of a battleship in wartime. Terry Lewin played Judy Garland's 'I'm just an in-between' on the gramophone incessantly. I loved her voice, which was just as well. At that time Deanna Durbin occupied my thoughts and when her films were showing in Alexandria I went to every one. Cinema shows for the officers were held on the quarter-deck, weather permitting. The ratings had theirs on the foc'sle. Charts were corrected from Notices to Mariners, the gunnery department made as much noise as it could in order to impress, whilst the Royal Marines were noisily efficient.

19 February came and the battlefleet sailed westwards to protect our cruisers. The latter had been ordered to Malta, there to disembark two infantry battalions. The thought of invasion of the island must have been ever-present in the minds of the high command. These troops were to be landed in order to discourage such thinking on the part of the enemy. Why invasion was never attempted has always seemed a miracle to me.

The usual aircraft alarms were sounded; in one we were just about to open fire when the 'enemy aircraft' dropped two red flares – the recognition signal! We had *Eagle* in company, and her fighters drove off some Heinkel bombers, shooting one down and damaging another. As dusk approached, *Eagle* landed her fighters for the night. It was then that five groups of enemy aircraft was reported, closing us on the radar. If they caught us now, with no fighter protection, we would be sitting ducks once more. The events of my recent birthday loomed vividly. All the indicator lamps which could be seen from above were obscured. The rest of the fleet was told of the approaching menace by short range W/T. thus obviating any likelihood of Aldis signal lamps giving away our position. The bombers came so close that they could be heard by those on the bridge. Darkness saved us and we breathed again.

Commander Reid told us that all was well with the cruisers in Malta, we were now to turn eastwards so that *Eagle*'s aircraft could bomb Rhodes. We steered north towards enemy country and pondered our fate. Apart from my watches, I spent the night outside the officers' cabins in order to be near my action station. I was temporarily Searchlight Control Officer, and had there been a sudden night action it would have been my duty to direct the searchlights where ordered. The enemy must have got wind of who had this important post, as they never put in an appearance. A month later at Matapan, Prince Philip was doing this same duty.

Morning came and with it bad weather, so bad in fact that no aircraft could take off to attack Rhodes. During the night we had been ordered to alter course to the south and return to Alexandria. This had unfortunate consequences for the Tribal destroyer *Mohawk*. The signal to alter course had been made on such a small lamp that she never saw it and continued blithely on towards Rhodes. She rejoined us late that day, but it cannot have been pleasant to have looked around you at dawn and found that you were alone in enemy waters!

Back in Alexandria, we were ordered to enter the huge floating dry-dock to have our bottom scraped. The warm waters of the Mediterranean greatly increased the marine life clinging to our ship's bottom with a consequent reduction in speed. The flagship was having this operation carried out, and as soon as she was clean, we would take her place.

It was fortunate perhaps that the enemy did not choose these few days to make a sortie. A ship in dry-dock is quite obviously powerless to do anything. A ship about to go into dry-dock has to divest herself of all ammunition so as to lighten her. Two huge British battleships would therefore be rendered impotent. How lucky it was not yet time for Matapan. Shells and cordite were brought up from the magazines and shell rooms, and loaded into lighters alongside. I was in charge of the 4.5" ammunition coming up. The sailors got too slap-happy, brought the 'cage' containing the ammunition up too sharply, and two cases fell down the hatch, hitting one rating on the shoulder who had been foolish enough to be inquisitive and was peering upwards. He nipped back only just in time.

Once in the huge floating dock, pumping continued and gradually the vast bulk of our ship was wholly above water. A series of long ladders led down into the dock itself, and I was able to walk about under the ship. It was an eerie experience looking up at our underside and I remember hoping that I would never see *Valiant's* bottom upside down before she sank beneath the waves. The enormous anti-torpedo bulges protruded on either side; I hoped they would be sufficient protection should a torpedo hit us. The quadruple propellers and massive twin rudders hung above me.

One factor that I had not considered when in dry-dock was the loo, our 'heads'. These were closed when pumping out began; the reason was obvious, it would have been unpleasant to say the least, for someone working below the ship. Lavatories were constructed in the dock itself which were none too clean and very hot. We had to use these, and it made a journey in the night watches both a chore and somewhat dangerous. No lights in the Alexandria blackout, you could quite easily fall to the floor of the dock and bash your brains out.

Forty-eight hours' leave was given to all midshipmen whilst we were in dry dock. I applied to spend my leave in Cairo, but was given a curt refusal. No one was to leave the city of Alexandria. I could not believe it, our ship was not even afloat, what possible reason could there be for keeping us so near at hand? All-night leave was extremely rare, and I wanted to make the most of it, but it was not to be. I now have the unenviable distinction of having spent eighteen months in Egypt, and never having seen the Pyramids!

John Cardew and I took a room at the Cecil Hotel, a beautiful and well appointed establishment facing the sea. There, we lived in considerable luxury and revelled in our civilian status away from the crowded ship.

Bad weather delayed our undocking, and we had to wait an extra day before once more becoming water-borne. The next day I reported sick, and was told I had the dreaded 'gyppy tummy', doubtless as a result of staying on shore. Numbers of the ship's company went down with it. The question was, 'Where was I to go?' I was told I had to go to bed for 24 hours, but where? Midshipmen had no proper place to sleep, they literally 'dossed down' in a convenient place. All the other officers could be ill in their cabins; such luxury was denied to us. Neither could we be ill in the Sick Bay bunks, they were reserved for ratings, and officers and ratings could not be ill together.

The problem was solved by my graciously being allowed to use the Admiral's Steward's cabin. As we were not a flagship that was occupied by the Ward Room messman. I felt too sick and ill to care where he had gone, he was a fat bladder of lard and it would do him no harm to rough it for a night or two. I said to myself, 'Really, this is a bit bloody much. Here I am, an officer, albeit a very junior one, and the only place where I can be ill is some damned steward's cabin. He shouldn't have one in the first place!'

It was 5 March 1941. Stocked again with our means of waging war, we were, in the time-honoured phrase, 'in all respects ready for sea'. And to sea again we were to go. We embarked six torpedoes and their warheads, some tractors and some 'dollies', the latter not being the film industry sort, but those used for wheeling big bombs from place to place. As none of them could be used by us, we were obviously becoming a temporary storeship. This became more evident when we embarked two Army Gunner Lieutenants, and some Fleet Air Arm ratings and stewards. I wondered maliciously whether any of the latter were going to be given cabins.

We were told we were to be based at Suda Bay in Crete, and might be there for up to six weeks. Leaving harbour the next morning was of the 'Carry on Sailoring' variety. The port anchor was weighed, and then the starboard. Unfortunately the stoker in charge of the capstan threw the lever to veer (to let out) instead of to brake. The result was that the starboard anchor promptly obeyed the law of gravity, and with a rattle and a roar we were firmly attached once more to Egyptian soil. That was nothing compared to the rattle and the roars of rage let out by the Captain and Commander. 'Number One, what the bloody hell do you think you're doing on the foc'sle?' The First Lieutenant, exposed to the wrathful gaze of his seniors on the bridge, looked suitably chastened and naturally took it out on the unfortunate stoker.

The aged battleship *Barham* was in company flying the Admiral's flag, together with six destroyers. My journal recorded wistfully: 'We have no aircraft carrier with us, so we shall have to fend for ourselves if the Junkers choose to attack.'

Twenty-four hours later Crete was in sight, its mountains snow capped. My journal, which was pompous at times, to say the least, said: 'The whole island made a very good sight.' Had I written 'a very fair sight', I might have been echoing Drake on first seeing the Cape of Good Hope! Just the same, I was writing for others to see and assess, so perhaps a spot of pretension was not out of place.

The Mediterranean gets warm early, and March was no exception. Hands were piped to bathe over the side – most welcome. Our mission in Crete was to provide protection for convoys en route to Greece. The presence of large capital ships was to discourage any warlike action on the part of the Italian Navy. We succeeded.

Our stay in Suda Bay was short-lived. Twenty-four hours and three air raid alarms (fortunately without incident) later, we proceeded to sea. We made a rendezvous with a convoy of eight ships, but having done so, we immediately turned around and headed back for Crete! Why, I never knew, perhaps for the reason given above, but whatever it was, two days later found us sheltering once more in the folds of the Cretan mountains.

Continuous naval activity in the magnificent harbour was taking place, with cruisers and destroyers steaming in proudly, oiling and making for the open sea once more. We were all very conscious that we were sitting ducks whilst anchored in the bay. There were hardly any fighter aircraft based on the island, and if there were, they were of the Brewster Buffalo type, no match for modern enemy machines. The surrounding hills should have been bristling with AA guns, but they were not; Crete was never properly fortified, and it was only after the fall of Greece that the place was defended to a certain degree.

A very accurate parallel as regards terrain can be drawn between Crete and the Falkland Islands. In both cases British ships were at their most vulnerable when in landlocked waters. It was indeed fortunate for us that the German air forces based in nearby Rhodes did not possess Exocet missiles. As it was, our anti-aircraft defences were manned constantly whilst we were in this dangerous 'haven'. The enemy could easily approach the island, skimming close to the sea surface, and then zoom up over the mountains which would block the radar. A swift descent with his bombs on the hapless ships below – it could all be over in seconds. Suda Bay and San Carlos Water had much in common.

Another complication was that the Greeks were using German-built Dornier seaplanes. When you are understandably trigger-happy, it is difficult, if not nigh impossible, to hold your fire until you can identify friendly markings. It is the enemy silhouette at which you have learned to shoot.

On 13 March we sailed once more, this time into the teeth of a gale. Let no one give you the impression that the Mediterranean is a calm sea. It can be, but the fact that it is an inland sea does not prevent it being extremely rough at times. The huge ship shook and the anemometer in my action station deep in the bowels of *Valiant* registered 100 feet per second. The turrets' crews came off badly and asked permission to train their guns fore and aft as water was pouring in. What it must have been like in the destroyers did not bear thinking of. To make matters worse, water entered the lower Power Room. This cut the fans, and after we had spent a night in those conditions, I recorded that the atmosphere was one 'that was distinctly foetid'. At times our speed was reduced to three knots – we were lucky no submarines were about.

Back to Suda Bay, there for six hours and out again. This time though, we were attacked. Aircraft alarms occurred frequently. It was bad enough having these to disturb you, it was infuriating when you learned that the radar operator had alarmed the fleet by picking up the land on a reciprocal bearing! As dusk was closing in, I was on the Flag Deck taking a sight. The fiendish bugle call of 'Repel Aircraft' blared through the loudspeakers. Rushing bodies, feet clanging on steel ladders, we dashed to our appointed stations. It seemed like chaos, but it was orderly chaos. Machinery hummed, lights flashed, orders were given. 'Open fire', from the Director Tower. Oh God, here we go again. Please not a re-run of the January air attack, for this time I am under thick armour. No fear of being machine-gunned, but real fear of being trapped down below. However, we learned fast. Bombing does not take place at dusk, this is the time for the torpedo bomber to attack. He comes in very low, his belly almost wet from the wave-tops, and difficult to see in the gathering darkness. No wonder fingers itch on triggers at dusk and dawn; since the days of primeval man, these have been the danger periods.

The AA barrage put up by the fleet may have scared our attackers, or their aim may have been bad. Two aircraft had appeared, the first hovering around astern of us. Some naïve onlookers thought it was friendly. When it dropped a torpedo aimed at us they revised their opinions. Others thought they saw bombs drop near *Barham*, whilst some held that they were unexploded shells. The second plane also attacked from astern, but fortunately its torpedo, aimed at our port quarter, missed its mark too.

Both planes then flew away. The gunnery department opined that it was our intense barrage of fire which forced them to leave. Others, more cynical, thought that it was because aircraft carry only one torpedo! Nationality? No one could tell. As a sop to the gunners we agreed they were probably German. It would. My journal records, 'it would be a brave Italian who would fly through our fire'. Floreat Whale Island (the naval gunnery school, Portsmouth).

To illustrate how twitchy we had become, an incident next day will assist. 1400 Director Tower: 'Turrets' crews close up, prepare to open fire at low-flying aircraft.' 1405 Director Tower: 'All right, it's only a flock of birds. I don't think we'd better open fire!'

Back in Alexandria, David Peck left us to join *Wryneck* for his destroyer training. The reader will remember he greeted us on joining *Valiant*. We never saw him again. On 27 April, during the evacuation of Greece, *Wryneck* stopped to pick up survivors from the *Slamat*, an unarmed transport. She and the destroyer *Diamond* between them rescued 700 men. Their survival was short lived. Both rescuing ships were bombed and sunk off Monemvasia. From all three ships only 1 officer, 41 ratings and 8 soldiers survived. Poor David Peck, he was not the officer who survived. He was eighteen years old, clever, quiet, efficient and extremely nice. We mourned his loss.

Some readers will be devotees of Peter Simple's column in the *Daily Telegraph*. One of his delightful characters is General 'Tiger' Nidgett of the Army Tailoring Corps, at one time stationed well away from the front line in Port Said. The 'Tiger's' sayings, probably based on some of Monty's, contained such phrases as: 'And crackin' good hunting to you, whoever you may be.'

Illustrious was about to depart for a refit in the United States. She sent us a farewell signal which might have been written by 'Tiger' Nidgett himself. It read: 'As one of the opening batsmen for England, we hate returning to the pavilion. Very best of luck, and may you continue to hit the bowling for six!' Dear God.

Another convoy trip to Malta occupied us. This time we had fighter cover from the new aircraft carrier *Formidable*, which had just joined the fleet. Her pilots were efficient and shot down a Heinkel bomber which had made the mistake of flying too near to the fleet. We saw it fall into the sea and everyone cheered. Well, they would, wouldn't they? It was him or us. No time for wet sentiment.

Sleep, on this trip, like so many others, was a precious commodity and in very short supply. Watches, four hours on, four hours off, were frequently interrupted by aircraft alarms, dawn and dusk action stations, and orders to other surface action stations. Meals were gobbled, you never knew when you might get the next one. Journals to be written up, sights taken and the ship's position fixed. Looking back, I wonder how we coped with it all.

We had no idea of how soon we would be involved in one of the great sea battles of the war.

9

The Battle of Matapan

The Battle of Cape Matapan, fought on 28 March 1941 has long since passed into the annals of naval history. It was fought 100 miles off the southern tip of Greece and was of great historical significance for the following reasons. Firstly, it was the first major fleet action since Jutland, a quarter of a century before. It would probably be untrue to say that Cunningham, unlike Jellicoe, could have 'lost the war in an afternoon'. Nevertheless, the victory at Matapan so affected the already poor morale of the Italian Navy that it never voluntarily offered battle again until that nation surrendered in 1943.

Secondly, it was the first time that carrier-borne aircraft had played a vital role. Thirdly, its climax was a night action, infinitely more dangerous to both sides than a similar action in daylight. The risk of collision (even with the enemy!) and of firing on one's own ships was greatly increased. Historians will argue the merits of the use by Cunningham of searchlights in such conditions. Fourthly, it was the first time that radar made a contribution of prime importance to the outcome of the battle.

When I started to write this book I had to decide how the account of naval warfare in the Mediterranean should be tackled. Was I to be an historian, observing the scene with detachment and hindsight, researching records and track charts and making Olympian comments? Or was I to set down the battles as I experienced them, a teenage midshipman's account of what happened to me and how I felt at the time? Many, more learned than myself, with access to vast amounts of material, have written naval histories of this period. *The War at Sea* by Captain S.W. Roskill is an official history, whilst *Matapan* by Captain S.W.C. Pack, is a whole book devoted to the battle. I decided on the second course. What follows therefore will be an eye-witness account of this great night action and British victory, added to which there must inevitably be explanatory passages for those unfamiliar with action at sea and its background.

The famous poem by Tennyson, *The Revenge*, begins: 'At Flores in the Azores Sir Richard Grenville lay, and a pinnace like a flutter'd bird came flying from far away. Spanish ships of war at sea, we have sighted 53!' May I paraphrase this: 'At Alexandria in Egypt, Sir Andrew Cunningham lay, and Ultra, like a wondrous bird, made call to him and say, 'Italian ships of war at sea, I have sighted 23!'

As more and more formerly Top Secret information is released by the Public Record Office, so the pieces in the martial jigsaw begin to fit together. The facts of Ultra are now common knowledge, but few in Alexandria knew on 27 March 1941 what priceless intelligence had been transmitted to British Naval headquarters. Suffice it to say that the cryptologists at Bletchley were able to read the most secret enemy ciphers with incalculable advantages to the Allied side.

By its very nature, the Ultra information had in the main to be kept for the eyes of Commanders-in-Chief only. This hampered General Freyberg in Crete, but Cunningham was determined it should not restrain him. It was vital that the sailing of the battlefleet from Alexandria should be concealed from the enemy for as long as possible. When, therefore, Cunningham received the Ultra information that the Italian battlefleet was about to put to sea, he gave his orders accordingly.

On Wednesday 26 March 1941, the British battlefleet was moored in Alexandria harbour. In *Valiant* we embarked stores which we understood were destined for Suda Bay, Crete; another 'milk run' we thought. A large convoy left harbour accompanied by destroyers, and we believed we would follow them, but no, all night leave was piped, cancelled for an hour and then restored. With half the ship's company ashore, the chances of sailing before the next day were 100 to 1.

27 March dawned, and in the early afternoon we received orders (a) there was to be no leave, and (b) we were to be at one hour's notice for steam after 1800. At that time, the aircraft carrier *Formidable* left harbour. We followed an hour later, together with our flagship *Warspite* and *Barham*.

What we did not know then was the C-in-C's deception plan. Having received the Top Secret intelligence from Ultra, Cunningham told his staff to issue the necessary orders for the departure of the fleet under cover of darkness. The C-in-C knew that the Japanese Consul in Alexandria was passing on every scrap of information that he could to his Axis partners. Britain was not then at war with Japan, and her Consul therefore had diplomatic immunity and considerable freedom of movement. The departure of the fleet must at all costs be kept from his prying eyes.

Drake is said to have played bowls whilst the Armada approached. Cunningham decided on golf. Accordingly, shortly after lunch, the spare figure of the Commander-in-Chief was to be seen descending *Warspite's* gangway, followed ostentatiously by a sailor with a bag of golf clubs slung over his shoulder. A large overnight bag was in his hand. Bosun's calls whistled, hands were raised in salute, the plain disc of a full Admiral was in place in the picket boat's midships. Cunningham took the clubs, raised his cap briefly in salute and the party left for the shore. Awnings were kept spread and the Admiral invited people to dinner. After dark the awnings were furled and the dinner cancelled. Once ashore, they took good care to be seen, and no doubt the Japanese accredited spy was soon enciphering a message to his master. Cunningham rejoined his flagship after dark and sailed with his fleet.

I have always marvelled at ships 'buzzes' or rumours, and have touched on this in an earlier chapter. The eve of Matapan produced a very accurate 'buzz'. My journal records: 'The general rumour going round the ship is that the Italian fleet has at last come out of harbour and that this is the reason for our crash departure.'

Sea routine and 2000 found me climbing up the ladder to keep the first watch on the Compass Platform. The bridge was crowded, the Captain appeared occasionally, Commander Reid made a bird-like appearance and cracked jokes, the Navigator sucked at his dead pipe and spoke little. The Gunnery Officer paced up and down with Pooley, his No. 2, and the Principal Control Officer talked to the Officer of the Watch. Good station-keeping was vital as we steamed northwest at nineteen knots. I kept a low profile, checked on the zigzag (number Ten – what else?), and made cups of rather revolting cocoa.

It may not have been Ealing Studios' idea of impending action, but there was undoubtedly an air of suppressed tension, a very tangible feeling that something was going to happen. As they would say later of the drugs scene 'we were on a 'high''', and voices were pitched that little bit higher as a result.

The huge bulks of our sister ships and *Formidable* loomed in the darkness. In company, but unseen, were nine destroyers, *Jervis, Janus, Nubian, Mohawk, Stuart, Greyhound, Griffin, Hotspur* and *Havock*.

Dawn Action found us bleary-eyed, but going through the routine of testing guns and equipment with more zest than usual. Who knew what the day might bring? Would we be using them against a surface enemy? The loudspeakers clicked, then a pause, 'This is the Commander speaking. A signal has been received from Vice Admiral Light Forces that three enemy cruisers have been reported south of Crete. He is keeping an eye on them to see which way they are going.'

So this was it, there were enemy surface vessels about, at least these were smaller than we were! At 0915 Cunningham ordered us to join VALF 'at utmost speed' in his position south of Crete. The Vice Admiral's flagship *Orion* had sighted the enemy force but it was out of range we were told. Our engineers opened all the valves they could to give us more steam, and we increased speed to 23 knots. The thrumming of the propellers made sleep in the Admiral's flat almost impossible, whilst the foam of our wake came right up to the quarterdeck. It was only to *Valiant* that this order had been given. We were more modernised than our sister ships and so were being given the privilege of assisting our cruisers to crush the enemy.

The speed of the rest of the fleet had been reduced to 20 knots in any case, because on leaving harbour *Warspite* passed too near a mud bank. This fouled her condensers and reduced her speed. What ABC said to her Captain is not on record; this fact was to have important consequences.

An hour later, our orders were countermanded – we were told to rejoin the battlefleet. What we did not know at the time was that Vice Admiral PridhamWippell (VALF) was actually under fire from the Italian 8" cruisers, a monstrous piece of impertinence.

Warspite's fleet engineer officer had by now increased her speed and she was coming up astern of us. The Italian cruisers meanwhile broke off the action, and since fuel conservancy was vital, the battlefleet reduced speed to 22 knots. This enabled the geriatric *Barham* to keep up.

Back on board *Valiant* we went to action stations at 0945. I went down to my CP where my attention was drawn to the needle of the Pitometer Log (the ship's speedometer). It was right over on 23 knots. Our usual cruising speed was fifteen or sixteen knots.

At 1130 we were sent to dinner, and at that time we were told that an enemy force composed of one *Littorio* class battleship together with attendant cruisers and destroyers, had been reported steaming south towards us. We were further told to expect action during the afternoon.

Now, my journal records: 'We went back to action stations after dinner, and waited rather excitedly for the enemy to appear.' Yes, well, perhaps, maybe the words 'waited rather excitedly' were written for perusal by our snotties' nurse and the Captain. There are two pages of synonyms of excitement in Roget's *Thesaurus*, among them 'wrought up' and on the 'qui vive', and for excitability, 'trepidation' and 'perturbation' seem apposite. I think most people were conscious of all these sensations. Certainly I was, except perhaps for wrought up.

One was excited yes, but coupled with that there was an undeniable fear of the unknown awaiting us over the horizon. All manner of thoughts went through my mind as we waited, by no means all of them heroic. Billy Bunter was at times triumphant over Walter Mitty, and had one been able to voice one's real thoughts at the time, there might have been cries of 'all right you chaps, I've had enough!'

It was all very well to pour our 15" broadsides into Valona and Bardia, but what would one 15" shell from a *Littorio*, weighing over a ton, do to us?

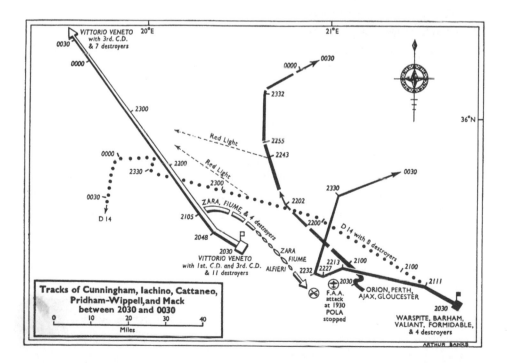

Tracks of Cunningham, Iachino, Cattaneo, Pridham-Wippell, and Mack between 2030 and 0030

I decided, ostrich-like, to try and forget about it, and since there was nothing I could do about the situation anyway, I turned to my work for comfort. The trouble was, there was as yet no work to be done. We knew what to do when action came, but even then, my action station was only concerned with the 4.5" secondary armament. This, in the normal course of events, would never fire at all, the range being too great. A few hours later I was to be proved very wrong. The afternoon wore on and it began to get dark. The 'buzz' went round (there are many telephone headsets in a big ship, in case the reader is sceptical as to how this happened at action stations) that we might have to fight at night. The enemy had not appeared by day, so what had happened?

Let us now look at events from the enemy side. The *Littorio* class battleship was the *Vittorio Veneto* of 35,000 tons and nine 15" guns – we had only eight!

She flew the flag of Admiral Angelo Iachino, the Commander-in-Chief. The forces he commanded comprised six 10,000-ton cruisers, two 8000-ton cruisers and eleven destroyers.

Iachino's flagship was reputedly very fast. She was said to be capable of 30 knots, which meant a six knot advantage over the British battlefleet. She could therefore overtake and outrange any of us whenever she wanted, a most unpleasant thought.

At 1215 on the 27th, the cruiser *Trieste* signalled that she had been sighted by a Sunderland aircraft. This was important for both sides but particularly for the British. Whenever Ultra information was to be acted upon, it was of the very greatest importance that a visual sighting of the enemy should be made, for how else would we have obtained the intelligence? The enemy had to be deceived into thinking that they had been discovered as a result of a routine sweep search, no matter that our aircraft seemed to be extraordinarily efficient!

Later that afternoon Iachino received a message to say that a reconnaissance aircraft had seen, in Alexandria harbour, 'three battleships, two aircraft carriers and some cruisers' at 1400. Cunningham's 'golfing expedition' was paying off.

Meanwhile the British cruisers under Pridham-Wippell were soon to be in a very dangerous situation, that of being sandwiched between the Italian 8" gun cruisers and Iachino's 15" guns. They saw the risk of very well being blown out of the water.

The morning of the 28th found the British cruisers being fired on by the Italian battleship whose gunnery was uncomfortably accurate. Pridham-Wippell tried to wriggle his way out of the trap and was only saved by a torpedo bomber strike by *Formidable's* aircraft. Although hits were reported at this time, none in fact had taken place, and the raid was put down to experience.

It did however, have an effect, as Iachino turned away to the north westward and, with his (then) superior speed, increased the distance between his flagship and ourselves. 'Home Angelo, whilst the going's good!' Yes, but not everybody made it.

Formidable rejoined us at 1400 having flown aircraft on a strike at the Italian fleet. We did not know it at the time but she was subjected to a torpedo-bombing attack by Italian aircraft before she came up with us. Fortunately, quick helm action by her Captain 'combed the tracks' and no hits were registered.

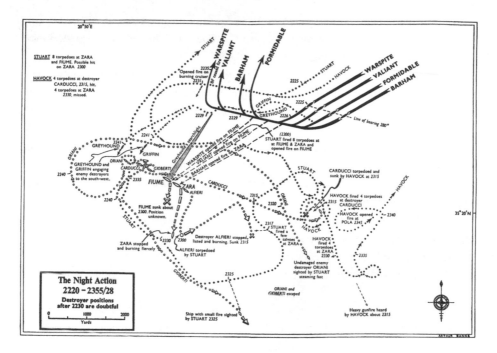

The Night Action
2220 – 2355/28

Destroyer positions
after 2230 are doubtful

During the whole of the sea chase, many sighting signals were received. The problem for Cunningham's staff, and for Iachino's, was whether to believe them or not. Aircraft Observers' positions were not by any means as accurate as they should have been, and this could prove very costly when endeavouring to catch up with a fleeing enemy.

According to Iachino, he feared air attacks more than surface attacks. His much superior speed and greater firepower should, he reasoned, allow him to outgun the British, but torpedoes and aerial bombs could cripple him and delay his race for home. The believed presence therefore, of an armoured fleet carrier was a potent factor in deciding him to turn for home.

Formidable flew off another strike of five torpedo bombers at 1500. They claimed three hits on the Italian battleship, 'reducing her speed to eight knots'. This was too optimistic a report; there was actually only one hit and the enemy's speed was reduced to 29 knots. More nightmares for the staff trying to work out Iachino's position.

Strikes against the Italian ships were also being flown by the RAF based in Crete, and as will be seen from the accompanying track chart, they had little success. On reflection, how wonderful it would have been for all of us who had to operate in the Mediterranean at that time, if Crete could have been held, like Malta. The air cover it could have given from strengthened airfields would have been of incalculable value.

By 1930 *Warspite's* aircraft had sent a very accurate description of how the enemy force was deployed. The observer reported, 'Enemy are concentrating. Total sighted consists of one battleship, six cruisers, eleven destroyers.'

The enemy's speed was estimated at 12–15 knots on a course of 300°. Such a concentration was obviously designed to protect the 'Queen Bee' battleship and made attack by any lesser foe a formidable task.

Once more, using the traditional time of dusk for a torpedo bomber attack, our carrier-based aircraft sought out the enemy. The intensive concentration now employed by the Italians also concentrated their firepower, and our pilots had to fly through a murderous hail of bullets and shells.

A contemporary record is at times untrustworthy, and my journal records that 'six torpedoes were put into *Vittorio Veneto*'. Sadly, this was not so, but one torpedo did strike the heavy cruiser *Pola* amidships and brought her to a standstill. It would not be untrue to say that this one torpedo hit was the direct cause of the Battle of Matapan.

At 2030 Iachino ordered back the return of the heavy cruisers *Zara* and *Fiume*, together with a division of destroyers to assist the damaged ship. It was perhaps just as well that he did not know he was sending them to their deaths. Pack, in his book The Battle of Matapan records the comments made at this time by Barnard, the fleet gunnery officer:

> The well-known steely blue look was in ABC's eye, and the staff had no doubt that there was going to be a party. Nevertheless, on paper the compact mass of the enemy fleet looked to the staff a pretty formidable proposition for any form of night attack. I think that ABC had probably made up his mind by about 2000 to send the light forces into attack and to follow up in person with the battlefleet, but he nevertheless, on this occasion, went through the formality of asking the opinion of certain Staff Officers. Neither the Staff Officer Operations nor the Master of the Fleet liked the idea much, and said so in their very different ways. The fleet gunnery officer said he was keen to let the guns off, but the battleships hadn't had a night practice for months and there might well be a pot mess with star-shells and search-lights if we go into confused night action. ABC took one look at his supposed helpers and said, 'You're a pack of yellow-livered skunks. I'll go and have my supper now and see after supper if my morale isn't higher than yours.

Cunningham was now determined on night action. He could do little else before the enemy's superior speed put him within range of his land-based aircraft support.

The darkened shapes of the two enemy fleets were on a closing course. Unknown to us at that time, the cruiser *Pola* was stopped, awaiting the succour of *Fiume* and *Zara*. Why Iachino detached two heavy cruisers to give assistance to a third illustrates the difference between British and Italian naval thinking. It would be most unlikely for this to happen in the Royal Navy; that was destroyers' work. They could have sunk *Pola*, if it had been thought necessary, without endangering much larger ships. Iachino believed that a senior officer 'should assess the damage and decide what should be done' – as was soon to be proved, a costly and tragic error of judgement.

Soon after 2100 Admiral Pridham-Wippell reported passing close to an unknown ship which was stopped. The C-in-C decided to investigate. On board *Valiant*, we had been closed up (or cooped up, according to where you were) at action stations for many hours.

At 1800 we were allowed to resume a lower degree of readiness, a welcome order allowing breaths of fresh air and attendance to the calls of nature. No one quite knew what was going to happen – what has been related about the enemy's movements was at that time known only to a very few in the flagship, and that, only imperfectly.

Officers and men scurried to and fro, anxious to make the most of their comparative freedom. I made my way to the quarter-deck where the guard-rails were once more upright. In action they were laid flat, with nothing to prevent one falling overboard. I had no illusions that anyone would be detached at this juncture to pick me up, even if my absence had been noticed!

The water boiled under our stern. The bulks of *Warspite*, *Barham* and *Formidable* could be seen in the darkness. The weather was fair, visibility about four miles, no stars could be seen.

In the Gunroom, midshipmen and sub-lieutenants were chattering excitedly. Conjecture ran wild, and 'buzzes' were exchanged. Probably some of the paymaster midshipmen who were on cipher duties knew considerably more than we did, but if so, they kept a discreet silence.

'Popeye' in the Gunroom pantry would insert his bald head through the serving hatch at intervals to be greeted with shouts of 'Well, Petty Officer, what do you think?' to which he would vouchsafe the latest lower deck rumour. I never remember 'Popeye' actually entering the Gunroom – he always seemed to be a half-torsoed presence on the other side.

Much discussion centred on the order that if action came, we were to switch our searchlights on instead of firing starshell. (The latter, when fired into the air, released a flare which descended on a parachute.)

With hindsight, this may well have been an unnecessary and possibly downright dangerous decision. It presupposes first that the director layer had to see the target. True, but why was no reliance placed on *Valiant's* excellent and up-to-date radar set? It was our radar which detected the enemy later on, giving the range and bearing. If the gunnery department has the information, what need is there to actually see the target? How much better therefore to have kept the searchlight masked – they could in the event add little to the radar reports, and their beams became like lighthouses pointing a path directly to us. The enemy took advantage of this, as will be seen.

After supper, the Gunroom seemed to empty and I lay back in an armchair in front of the fire. A pair of legs were outstretched opposite mine, their owner like me, trying to relax before what was likely to be an exciting as well as perhaps dangerous night. The legs belonged to Philip, Prince of Greece and Denmark. He was Searchlight Control Officer that night, a position I had once held for a short time.

I do not remember that we spoke, we both just lay there sprawled out, thinking our own thoughts.

Events were moving fast, but we did not know then that we were soon to be in battle. The PA system clicked, and we tensed, wondering what was coming next. The bugle sounded

'Action Stations' and we all ran to our allotted posts. I rushed to my High Angle Control Position down in the bowels of the ship. I felt as a submarine captain must feel as I pulled the heavy armour-plated hatch down on top of me and secured it.

So what now? It was dark outside, and the enemy was thought to be very near. Of what would his fire comprise? A battleship that might inflict terrible damage on us, cruisers which would certainly inflict damage and injure those on the upper deck, and/or destroyers whose gunfire we could ignore, but what about their torpedoes?

All these thoughts, and others besides, ran through my mind and I longed for one of my contemporaries with whom to discuss them. Leading Seaman Beechey's conversation was not on the highest plane, whilst the rest of the CP's crew muttered in low tones among themselves.

I was not entirely alone though, for I was as always at action stations, wearing my headphones. These connected me directly to Jocelyn Parker, the Sub-Lieutenant RNVR who was the port fore High Angle Control Officer. Perched in his eyrie high above the bridge, it was he who would give us the orders to open fire, and it was his director instruments, transmitted via our banks of dials, which the guns would follow. We had a good rapport, Parker and I, and he would always provide me with a running commentary of what he could see 'topside'. This I would pass on to my crew.

We waited, hoping secretly that whatever might be lurking in the darkness, we would see it first. In the event, we did, but not with eyes straining in the Mediterranean night, but with the aid of a ground glass screen on which flickered green shapes like grass, rising and falling as might a cardiograph. A higher pinnacle of 'grass' would show the trained radar operator that a surface vessel was in the vicinity. The Italian ships were not fitted with radar – we were to be thankful that some of our forces, including *Valiant*, had this wonderful aid at our disposal.

The click of the Tannoy as it was switched on alerted us all. The chilling words 'Alarm, Alarm, Alarm' electrified us. This was it, we had found the enemy, or he had found us. Whose would be the first shot? We had no time to wait or think. I glanced at the bulkhead clock – 2220. Sunset had been three and a half hours ago.

Jocelyn Parker's voice came down the Director 'phones high pitched with excitement: 'Enemy in sight, salvoes, salvoes, salvoes.' Then, before we had fired a shot, the order came: 'Check, check, check.' The imperative gunnery order to stop firing but not to cease firing – a subtle difference!

No sooner had this order been obeyed than we were ordered to open fire again and this we did. Suddenly I thought 'My God, we've been hit.' I had thoughts of the *Vittorio Veneto's* 15" guns firing at us in the dark, causing havoc above our heads. Fortunately I was quite wrong. So great is the concussion from guns of such huge calibre as ours that my mistake was a legitimate one – it was our own guns which were shaking the ship as though some giant hand had hold of us. Some measure of this may be gauged from the fact that two of the lights went out in our CP. I suppose someone had a torch. I hoped they had, as I had omitted to take this elementary precaution.

All this time it must be remembered that we were in complete ignorance of who or what was opposing us across the dark Mediterranean water. It could have been a battleship or just a destroyer. I remember rejecting the latter, since to use us in this way would have been like the old adage of the sledgehammer and the nut. All we knew was that the enemy was very close, (a) because the director tower could see him and (b) by reading the range indicator just before me. This read 5000 yards or visibility range – more of this later!

For what seemed like an age but in reality was only six minutes, the firing continued, and I began quite frankly to get anxious. If we were firing, then doubtless our gun flashes could be seen, for unlike the Italians we did not use flashless cordite. Ergo, if we could be seen, what was to prevent fire being returned or torpedoes being launched? We were doubtless handing it out, but when would it come our way?

The order came, 'Check, check, check' and the guns were silenced. We were alive, the odds were that a great many of the enemy were dead or dying, and Cunningham turned us away from the carnage. We could feel the ship shudder as she heeled in a tight turn, the compass repeater indicating a north-easterly course.

Now Jocelyn Parker's excited voice was charged with elation – 'Wonderful, wonderful, you should have seen it,' he cried. 'We blew them right out of the water, and now they're just burning hulks.' A cheer went up from my crew as I relayed the news to them. Parker went on, 'I could see brilliant orange flashes under their bridges and other bursts along their whole lengths – we've sunk two big 8" gun cruisers – a marvellous night.'

The unfortunate ships which we had destroyed were the Italian cruisers *Fiume* and *Zara*. Both were of 10,000 tons, with a speed of 32 knots. *Zara* was the flagship of Vice Admiral Cattaneo. In addition, the destroyer *Alfieri* had been destroyed by two broadsides from *Barham*. What had happened briefly was this. The *Pola*, a sister ship of *Zara* and *Fiume*, had been damaged by a successful torpedo attack by Fleet Air Arm aircraft at 1930. Explosions occurred between the engine and boiler rooms, causing complete loss of power. Helpless, she lay stopped. On hearing of *Pola's* plight the Italian Commander-in-Chief ordered *Fiume* and *Zara* together with four *Alfieri* class destroyers, to go to *Pola's* aid. History will judge whether or not it was a wise decision to detach two fine modern 8" gun cruisers for this task when the destroyers were more expendable and could easily have carried out what was necessary.

Iachino's excuse was that the presence of a flag officer was necessary 'to make the correct decisions'. This does not say much for the initiative of his junior officers nor for his trust in the Captain of *Pola*.

Whatever historians decide, Iachino's orders to *Fiume* and *Zara* sent them to the bottom of the Mediterranean.

The two rescuing cruisers had practically reached the stricken *Pola* when we fell upon them. Fortunately for us, our radar picked up *Pola* first, and had it not been for Charles Morgan's quick action we might have fired upon her. This would have alerted *Fiume* and *Zara* and the 'bag' would have been one cruiser instead of three plus two destroyers. Morgan told us after the battle that he would not give the Gunnery Officer permission to open fire as he was sure 'something bigger was to come'. How right he was.

Pola was soon to share the fate of her sister ships, but not from our huge guns. She was found by the destroyers two miles to the east. They shone a searchlight on her to find her guns still trained fore and aft, her ensign still flying.

Her upper deck presented a sorry spectacle; half drunken sailors staggered about and her quarter-deck was littered with bottles and clothing.

From interrogation of her crew when taken prisoner, there came the extraordinary story of why she never fired a shot. When this question was put to him, one officer replied, 'We didn't fire at you, because we thought that if we did, you would fire back!' Nelson would have relished that delicious morsel.

The destroyer *Jervis* went alongside *Pola*. Some of *Jervis'* sailors, armed with old-fashioned, pirate-style cutlasses, boarded the stricken ship. They found only 257 of the ship's company out of a total of 1000 still on board. They filed peacefully over the brow on to *Jervis*, thankful that, apart from what might be a bombed journey to captivity, their war was over.

The destroyer *Nubian* then fired a torpedo at *Pola*. This appeared to have little effect, so another was fired and she sank. Earlier on, the destroyer *Havock* had sunk the destroyer *Carducci* with torpedoes and gunfire.

The Battle of Matapan thus ended in a glorious victory for British arms. Three heavy cruisers and two destroyers had been sunk, with no loss to ourselves. Cunningham summed it up in his despatch to Admiralty: 'In spite of the almost unbelievable incompetence of the Italians in night fighting, there are solid grounds for satisfaction in the results of this action.'

My journal records that after all this excitement, life in the ship had to go on as usual, and I left my action station down below to act as Midshipman of the Watch on the bridge. The Middle Watch (midnight to 0400) found us making away to the north-east. I could not help thinking that splicing the mainbrace with champagne would have been more appropriate than the hot cocoa I was busily brewing, but naturally no such order was given.

You would have imagined that a buzz of excited chatter would have filled the compass platform, everyone exchanging his experiences and views of the battle, but on reflection one can see that this could not be. Keyed up we all were, but the bridge is the place from where the ship is conned and fought. It was now the middle of the night, the enemy might be out there still, and the great battlefleet had to keep good station. It was not a time for distracting talk.

Daylight came, and with it a turn to the westward, taking us back over the exact spot where the battle had been fought. We were now to see the aftermath of our night encounter. There were many small boats, Carley rafts and pieces of wreckage in the water, some of them with occupants. It was a pathetic sight, the remains of proud units of the Italian fleet now reduced to so much flotsam in Mussolini's so-called 'Mare Nostrum'. Although still in our teens, we had become hardened and could look upon the vanquished with detachment.

They would have inflicted the same terrible fate on us had they been better sailors; in war it is the survival of the fittest and best trained. Crete was to prove a different story.

We in the battleships did not of course stop to pick up the survivors. This was left to the destroyers, the maids of-all-work of the fleet. Cynically, they were more expendable than we were in the event of enemy attack. They were also more manoeuvrable, and picked up many survivors.

Besides those who were alive, there were many corpses floating in a sea covered with a film of oil. A variant on the Dantesque pictures of hell.

Our destroyers picked up 900 survivors, but rescue work halted abruptly with the arrival of a German aircraft. The fact that the fleet was engaged in rescuing what remained of their allies would not have deterred a Nazi attack, nor did it.

Our own aircraft reconnaissance had produced no sign of *Vittorio Veneto* and accordingly we set course for Alexandria. The C-in-C flew off an aircraft which, when it was a safe distance from the fleet, made a signal to the Italian naval command giving the position of the survivors. An Italian hospital ship picked them up. There can be humanity even in war.

The German reconnaissance plane had done its work only too well, and at 1500 our radar reported a group of unidentified aircraft closing from astern.

The chilling bugle call of 'Repel Aircraft' echoed over the loudspeakers and the ship's passages were full of men running to their action stations. This was to be a particularly vicious and accurate attack in which we were nearly hit.

Records vary as to the number of aircraft which attacked us; my journal says six, (incorrect). Pack says twelve (correct). As on my eighteenth birthday, their tactics were the same; go for the aircraft carrier and make her your main target, whilst others attack the battleships.

Poor *Formidable*, she was therefore selected, having just managed to fly off three fighters to intercept. Fighter Direction was then in its infancy, and had the carrier's fighter directors possessed the experience learned later, they would not have sent two fighters already in the air on a chase which later proved to be a feint. Later, when I qualified as a Fighter Direction Officer I saw to it that my CAP (Combat Air Patrol) was never so denuded that it was incapable of its main purpose; the defence of the fleet.

The fighters, catapulted so tardily, were at first unable to gain sufficient height to be effective, and the German JU88s arrived overhead unmolested.

The entry in my journal reads: 'Their bombing was extremely accurate, one bomb landing close to the starboard bow, and one falling on the port quarter. This latter bomb was an extremely near miss, and many people thought we had been hit. Down in the CP the deck heaved in a most ominous manner and I am told that the Sick Bay ratings in the starboard dip were so convinced that we had been hit that they rang up forward to enquire if there were any casualties.'

Formidable received four very near misses but no damage. The last few enemy aircraft were forced to jettison their bomb loads when finally engaged by her fighters. Two bombers were shot down, and guns' crews cheered as one disintegrated in mid-air, the other hitting the sea. Like all bombing attacks, this one, although only probably lasting a minute, seemed as though it was going on for ever.

Our return to our home port was still not without incident. On the morning of our arrival an Italian S79 reconnaissance aircraft was shot down by our fleet fighters. As if that was not enough, a submarine was reported in the swept channel of Alexandria's Great Pass. Because there was no room for manoeuvre in the narrow channel, Cunningham ordered the destroyers ahead to clear the way for the battleships with depth charges. The wording of his despatch on this incident was laconic: 'This operation had no result apart from creating a marked impression on the Italian survivors!' The latter had had enough action to last them a lifetime and many were clearly horrified at the prospect of more. Some though, cheered, but whether this was in admiration at the Royal Navy's fighting capabilities or the fact that they were nearing the shore is in some doubt. I have a personal preference for the latter.

Aftermath and Reflections

Five Italian warships had been sent to the bottom with no loss to ourselves which was an undoubted cause for great satisfaction. Nevertheless, despatches reveal that the launching of an air attack on the Italian battleship too early had the effect which Cunningham feared; the enemy turned for home with a lead that could not be closed in daylight.

The Battle of Matapan had such an effect on Italian morale that their naval forces never again sailed in strength against us.

Our reception in Alexandria was a noisy one, with every ship at anchor there, down to the humblest tug, letting off resounding blasts on their sirens and steam whistles. What the Japanese Consul had to say at his failure to note our departure is not recorded.

It was only now that we heard about our battle from the BBC, and this reporting was the cause of much resentment.

The flagship *Warspite* was mentioned by the BBC three times whilst no other ship was mentioned at all. Our ship's company, and that of *Barham*, were greatly incensed. They lined the guard-rails and shouts of 'Three cheers for *Warspite*' together with less polite lower deck suggestions as to where *Warspite's* sailors should put their ammunition, echoed across the harbour.

Charles Morgan was furious, and after a thanksgiving service had been held on the quarter-deck, he cleared lower deck and delivered a scathing admonition concerning this behaviour. He was quite right of course, but nevertheless the broadcast had been particularly inept PR. It had infuriated us all, though we as officers had naturally kept our own counsel. The BBC later gave mention to the previously unnamed ships and honour was satisfied.

A somewhat inglorious action of mine may have accounted for the fact that I was not mentioned in despatches. The morning after our return to harbour I was sent for by Mr Scrutton, the Commissioned Gunner. A gunnery rating promoted from the lower deck, he was efficiency itself, and all the Gunroom was in awe of him. Scrutton was in charge of the Transmitting Station (or TS) at Action Stations. This compartment, crammed with instruments and dials, was where all the calculations for the main armament were carried out, the resultant ranges and bearings being passed to the heavy gun turrets. Its operations today are carried out by computers; the TS was their cumbersome forerunner.

Although he was only a one-striper in rank, I had some qualms as to the reason for my summons. I was not long left in doubt. 'Holloway', he said, 'why did you not tune the 4.5"s to the main armament range when you saw my straddle lamp flashing?'

Scrutton's technical question requires an explanation. The straddle lamp referred to was a small bulb set in the overhead bulkhead of my CP. In the unlikely event of the range at which the mighty 15" guns were hitting being within the range of the 4.5" guns, its flashing would indicate that I must signal this range to the guns under my control. This of course was precisely what had happened at Matapan. The range at which we sank the enemy was between 3225 and 4000 yards. Records show that the port side 4.5"s opened fire at visibility range of 5000 yards.

I was now in somewhat of a quandary. What Mr Scrutton did not know was that there was no bulb in the straddle lamp socket. Why was there no bulb in the socket? Because I had ordered its removal. Why had I ordered its removal? Ah, yes, well ... we were allowed to doze off during our watch below in the CP. Rest was at a premium and the TS would flash the straddle lamp every watch to test it. This annoyed me, its winking woke me up, so I took it out and when the TS 'phoned through, saying, 'Testing straddle lamp', a rating would whisper back, 'Straddle lamp correct.' Naughty perhaps, but there you are. We were undoubtedly hitting the upperworks of the Italian cruisers with the 4.5"s at some stage, so our contribution did not materially affect the result.

'Mr Scrutton,' I said, 'we were so intent on our other duties in the CP that we just never saw the lamp.' Naturally we didn't!

Scrutton gave a snort and dismissed me. I doubled off smartly and gave orders for a new bulb to be put in the straddle lamp socket – the last one had shattered in our 15" broadsides...?

Rest was evidently a problem for the Italians too as interrogation of our prisoners revealed. In their navy it was apparently customary for ships' companies to remain closed up at action stations from the time of leaving harbour until their return! Food was brought to them and they were allowed to sleep, but on the fateful night of 28 March, they said they were suffering from weariness and lack of food.

It is interesting, with the benefit of records which were naturally Top Secret at that time, to have confirmation of the part that Ultra played in Matapan. It was not some valet like Cicero operation from an Axis embassy whose information led to our meeting with the enemy.

Cunningham's signal to the Admiralty reads as follows:

1.   Press communique designed to conceal fact that information on which fleet put to sea came from 'Y' (Ultra) sources.
2.   For security reasons, no press correspondents sailed with the Fleet.

How wise; whilst no doubt some newsmen would have been souls of discretion, others would doubtless have failed to keep their pens from scratching, resulting in the gravest possible breaches of security. It would have been instructive to know what the senior British officers in the Falklands campaign would have thought of Cunningham's action.

The Italians in their communique must have felt the need for a boost to morale, albeit somewhat illusory. (Rear-Admiral Commanding First Battle Squadron) sent the following signal to his Commander-in-Chief:

Intercepted Italian communique – reads as follows:
   One British cruiser sunk, German aircraft severely damaged British aircraft carrier – three hits and sank destroyer.

Cunningham replied dryly, 'I regret these heavy losses to our fleet.'

Tragically, the Italian communique, had it been written at the time of the Battle of Crete six weeks later, would have been economical, not with the truth, but with our losses.

The Italians very naturally did not refer in any communique to the fact that in the dark melee of Matapan, they fought among themselves after the battlefleet action.

Destroyer reports speak of gun flashes where none of our forces were known to be. The British use of night-fighting lights to identify friend from foe seems to have been unknown to the Italians. It seems also to have been unknown or at least forgotten, by the destroyer *Havock*, who, having failed to switch on her fighting lights was straddled by a 6" salvo from *Warspite*. She emerged unscathed, but it doubtless taught her captain a lesson he was unlikely to forget.

So ended a great naval battle, in which the training and high morale of the British was to be victorious over the inefficiency and low morale of the Italians. A night battle is fraught with danger. It took a brave and dogged fighter like Cunningham to seek it out and carry it through with such a brilliant result.

The Italian Navy received a blow from which it never fully recovered. Two years later, its ships were to lie surrendered under the guns of Fortress Malta.

10

The Battlefleet
Bombards Tripoli

From the sublime to the ridiculous, from violent action one minute, to almost peacetime peevishness. My journal entry for Thursday 3 April runs as follows:

I went ashore [in Alexandria] in the afternoon, prepared to bathe, and was very annoyed to find that the swimming bath [sic] at the Sporting Club did not open until 15th April. The situation in the Balkans is unchanged and may flare into war at any minute.

A transatlantic comment might well have been: 'Buddy, you can say that again!'

Relaxing, and almost bored after our excitement, we midshipmen continued our routine of instruction, interspersed with 'runs ashore'. Baulked at the Sporting Club, I bathed at Stanley Bay, a very pleasant stretch of sand in the suburbs of Alexandria. My first swim in the Mediterranean, and I remember thinking that the water was much saltier than at home.

The beaches were deserted as few of Alexandria's European civilian population remained. We swam, and on occasion surfed. Deck chairs and drinks were brought to us by attendants clad in their white robes with red sashes. No aircraft screamed overhead and the sun shone in a cloudless sky. Compared to what we had been through, and to what was to come, it was idyllic. Once again I was glad that my service was in a warm climate instead of the swirling mists of Iceland, or counting endless sheep in the Orkneys.

Eden was only temporary, however, and the stark reality that we were only very transient visitors to the Garden was brought home to us in no uncertain manner by Eighth Army Communiques.

Journal: Friday, 4 April 1941.

It was announced this morning that Italo-German forces occupied Benghazi late last night. The reason given in the Cairo communique is that the enemy force was well-equipped with tanks and that as Benghazi was not used by us as a port (though I feel this is stretching the truth somewhat) and the city is indefensible, we decided to withdraw to the now well known 'strong posts in the rear' and not risk jeopardizing our already long lines of communication.

From the phrase I used 70 years ago it would seem that I had almost anticipated word for word Sir Robert Armstrong's famous utterance in the 'Spycatcher' hearing.

Our instruction continued unabated. Engineering was now to be our study, and I found it of far more interest than the boring workshops at Dartmouth.

Down into 'B' Boiler Room we went, a Dante's Inferno of noise and stifling heat. Our instructor, finding that we could not hear a word of what he was saying, moved us to 'Y' Boiler Room. Here, a boiler was being cleaned, and as its twin was also cold, we were told to get inside! Feeling like escapees from Colditz, we crawled in through one of the holes usually reserved for the sprayers. I felt again the claustrophobic 'Alice syndrome' which I had felt when climbing up the barbette of 'B' turret. What if I got stuck? Would the engineers stuff a ram up my rear and push me inside, or would they pull me out ignominiously? Fortune smiled on me, I was very thin (Nanny: 'The child lives on a rasher of wind!') and I arrived inside the boiler without any need of assistance.

Ian Fleming had yet to create James Bond, but looking back, what better place for Bond to be imprisoned? We were told that the engineers had great difficulty with cracking of the boiler walls due to the intense heat. Imagine James inside the boiler as he waits impotently for the sprayers to be turned on and the boiler 'flashed up'. A ghastly death, but one which would doubtless have been averted by the last minute intervention of a beautiful girl, her boiler suit open to her navel, and of course, with an exact knowledge of how the complicated machinery worked. Mr Broccoli could do with me as a scriptwriter.

The boiler rooms were followed by the engine rooms. Here, with pipes and dials everywhere, we were able to grasp what a difficult world it was for these men and what little chance they had of escape in an emergency. Drowned, or killed by the escape of scalding steam, the proverbial cat in hell would have been more fortunate.

We crawled through the propeller shaft passages and hoped no one would test propellers as we did so. The function of plummer-blocks was explained to us (they support the propeller shaft) and we became, temporarily at least, minor experts on the Ring Main system. I even drew a diagram of the latter, so I suppose I knew something about it at the time! When next the engine room asked permission of the bridge to 'blow soot' we would have some idea of their problems.

'A midshipman, Mr Byam' Captain Bligh is reputed to have said, 'is the lowest form of animal life in the British navy.' He could have been right. Under instruction one minute, under enemy fire or bombs the next, always changing our cruising or action stations, we certainly had a varied life and only lacked for sleep, peace and quiet. 'Popeye' continued to provide us with quantities of passable food, and although it was not up to Ward Room standards, our mess bills were lower. The Warrant Officers' Mess always had the best fare; the fact that the Warrant messman was a member of the mess may have had something to do with it.

Low species that we were, we were naturally not privy to the Top Secret signals which were flashing to and fro between the Admiralty and our Commander-in-Chief. Briefly, according to Roskill what was happening was this. The War Cabinet was deeply concerned at the high rate of flow of reinforcements and supplies which were reaching General Erwin Rommel through the port of Tripoli. The prognosis reached by them was that unless some immediate and drastic action was taken, the Afrika Korps would soon be in possession of Egypt.

The Admiralty set out two blunt alternatives to Cunningham. He was either to bombard Tripoli or to block the port. Having set out the alternatives, the Admiralty went on to choose the latter. They ordered that the venerable battleship *Barham*, together with the old 'C' class cruiser *Caledon* should be used as blockships. Poor *Barham*, was her long career to end like this, a temporary wall against the enemy's supply ships? She had just poured 15" shells into two enemy cruisers at Matapan, was this now to be her fate; and her ship's company, what of them? Killed or at best prisoners in a desperate enterprise. No one was to know she had only seven months to survive before German torpedoes were to send her to the bottom. But more of that later.

Cunningham was horrified at the prospective loss of one third of his battlefleet and was strong enough to say so. He therefore withdrew his previous aversion to bombardment which he considered the lesser of two evils.

It was a terrible decision for him to take, and on the face of it he could have sentenced all of us in the battlefleet to a watery grave instead of sacrificing one battleship and one cruiser. The old principle of 'the buck stops here' applied to C-in-C Med, and he accepted it.

We midshipmen, of course, and indeed everyone on board *Valiant* with the exception of the Captain and Navigator, were in blissful ignorance of our next destination. No doubt it was just as well, for our mission would take us through extremely dangerous waters.

At 0600 on Friday 18 April, the Mediterranean Fleet weighed and proceeded to sea. Our destination at first was Suda Bay, Crete, (where else?) for the destroyers to fuel. That night, as always at sea, the Night Intentions were signalled by lamp before it got dark. These consisted of alterations of course and speed which would be carried out by the fleet during the night without further signal.

My journal records that at 0400 we were ordered 'to observe attentively the Admiral's motions'. Those less acquainted with the Senior Service might legitimately assume that this was an unusual command for a close inspection of our Commander-in-Chiefs faeces to take place – a sort of seagoing anal investigation. This fortunately was not the case, and if the Admiral did have, or effect, any unusual motions at that early hour, they were invisible.

'Alas poor Yorrick' is the cry in Hamlet. 'Alas, poor *York*' was the cry as we entered Suda Bay. There, beached, and surrounded by a cluster of small ships and boats, was this once proud heavy cruiser. She had been attacked on 26 March by an Italian 'one man torpedo boat' and had suffered great damage. With the totally inadequate repair facilities at Suda, little could be done, and she was eventually to fall into German hands after the surrender of the island.

Little did we think at the time that we in *Valiant* were later to suffer the same fate. Roskill comments: 'This was the price to be paid for an inadequately defended harbour.' Perhaps, but when it came to our turn, that could never have been said of Alexandria.

Our departure from Suda was considerably delayed due to our picket boat being away on a long trip. Despite the hoist of its recall, and two 20" signalling projectors burning on them, the crew took their time. I was glad I was not midshipman of the boat; perhaps like me, his Morse was abysmal! As a result, instead of leading the fleet to sea as ordered, we left last, an ignominious exit. As soon as we were at sea, the Commander made his broadcast. 'We are to bombard Tripoli on Monday morning,' he said, 'with the co-operation of the RAF.'

Astonishment coupled with apprehension was most people's reaction. It was as if the Italian Navy proposed to bombard Alexandria. What were we being let in for?

On our way, shooting conditions were good, and our fighters from *Formidable* shot down one enemy aircraft and then four JU52 troop carriers, presumably on their way to Tripoli. Doubtless before they died they might have wondered where their opponents had come from, that far west.

At dusk, our friendly aircraft carrier left us taking a destroyer screen with her. We, that is, *Warspite*, ourselves, the former blockship-designate *Barham* and the 6" gun cruiser *Gloucester*, proceeded towards Tripoli. Talk about Drake singeing the King of Spain's beard!

Midnight on the fateful Monday 21st, and I was on watch on the bridge. 'White light on the starboard bow,' shouted an alert lookout. 'Alarm Action' was sounded off, bells rang, buzzers buzzed, rattlers rattled and everyone ran. It was the enemy, true, but for once not an enemy we could touch. An Italian hospital ship was steaming north-eastwards, doubtless crowded with wounded. She was well lighted, as required by the Geneva Convention. It was extraordinary to see a ship lighted up as though it was peacetime. We were so used to peering through the darkness at darkened ships that we gazed at this unusual sight in wonderment. We thought that it was unlikely we had been seen, and continued to steer stealthily on towards our objective. The Geneva Convention should have precluded the Italian ship from reporting our presence, but it would have been unwise to rely on it.

I made cocoa, checked the zigzag and tried to keep out of the way at the back of the bridge. The latter was beginning to fill up now; officers drifted in and out, some were there quite legitimately like the two gunnery officers, Unwin and Pooley. Others, very wrongly, were quite obviously there to 'have a look at the show', but they were lieutenant-commanders at least, and who was I to chase them away?

At 0230 our radar began reporting large formations of aircraft. How nice, their IFF showed them to be ours, obviously the RAF bombers on their way to 'soften up' our target.

Twenty minutes later heavy anti-aircraft fire could be seen on the port bow, indicating that our friends were at work. The trouble was that (a) they were early, and (b) they did their work too well. As a result, huge clouds of smoke and dust were raised 100 feet above the port. Our own aircraft which was flying overhead to spot our fall of shot, found its mission rendered practically useless. Its crew could see nothing and was reduced to impotence over a prime enemy target just when it was most wanted.

Coloured tracer was shooting up from the ground, and Larry Allen, our American Press Correspondent, was unoriginal enough to exclaim that it was 'just like the Fourth of July'. Having other things on our minds, the irony of his 'end of British rule' description was, at that time, lost upon us.

Naval bombardment of a shore target necessitates the bombarding ships proceeding in line ahead for the duration of the bombardment run. With no zigzag in operation they are thus sitting ducks for any enemy submarine. It follows also that if the shore batteries are alert, it would not take any great gunnery expertise to hit the bombarding ships, whose projected course and speed could be easily calculated.

We, as the bombarding ships, also needed a marker point on which to align. In the case of Tripoli we could of course make out the general direction of the city from the aerial bombing and the enemy's counter-fire. We needed to be much more accurate than that if we were to achieve our purpose; namely that of denying the enemy his use of harbour facilities for some time to come.

The naval staff in Alexandria however, had done their homework. Sitting on station four miles offshore was His Majesty's submarine *Truant*. She calmly flashed a light seawards to mark the spot where we should turn for the bombardment run, almost like an usherette at a cinema!

'Action Stations' was at 0300. I ran to my CP and waited for the order to fire. Readers will remember that at Matapan, I had had what Harold Macmillan called 'a little local difficulty' with a certain straddle lamp. I had seen to it that it worked this time, but typically it never burned, although the 15" guns were hitting their target! Such is fate.

The whole ship shuddered as the main armament commenced firing, and the secondary followed suit three minutes later. Seen from shore it must have been an awesome sight, huge orange flashes lighting up the sides of the three battleships only six miles away. The terrible roar overhead of the 15" shells, each weighing one ton, must have been enough to strike terror into the bravest. They had only seconds to wait before the devastating crump of the shell landing and exploding. Our own 4.5" guns were loaded with semi-armour piercing shells whilst the 15" used bombardment shells.

Our target was the mole and administrative buildings, *Warspite* bombarded the Spanish Quay with HE whilst *Barham* shot at the power station and marshalling yards.

Warspite, going on the principle that any shells falling short would fall into the sea, commenced her bombardment at a range which was 3000 yards over. From this she 'laddered down' through the town to her objective. The swathe she must have cut through the streets would have been quite impressive. In retrospect it seems a pity that the parents of a certain Colonel Gaddafi were not in the path of the shells.

Books written many years later say that 'the enemy was taken completely by surprise'. Perhaps, but that did not stop them having the impertinence to fire back at us, although they did no damage. Doubtless thinking that we were standing far out to sea and thus firing at extreme range, they did the same and their shells all went over. Their firing was sporadic only. *Gloucester* claimed to have silenced one of the batteries.

Their firing did lead to a cry of 'Alarm Port', everyone thinking it was an E-Boat, but it was only enemy shells falling over as before.

Our bombardment of Rommel' s main supply port continued for 20 minutes on the port side, then, as in some warlike gavotte, we turned round and gave the starboard side their chance.

Our 15" guns fired off 205 rounds, by which time the C-in-C called off his dogs of war and turned us to 030° at 21 knots to get as far away as possible from retaliatory dive-bombers. *Formidable* rejoined us at 0730 and now came proof of the value of having a modern fleet carrier with us together with good fighter direction technique.

Several attempts were made by enemy aircraft to attack us, the largest group coming from the direction of Derna. None came within sight of the fleet and our fighters shot down three German JU88s.

In retrospect, no action against the enemy in which I have taken part has impressed on me more how exceptionally lucky we were off Tripoli. Granted, we achieved complete surprise, it was dark, so no bombers could attack us, and the shore batteries were but a pinprick. But, what about a menace hidden beneath the waves, one which never slept, and was of the gravest danger to us by day or night? I speak of course, of mines. How on earth was it that we did not, six miles off the enemy's chief supply port, run slap into a minefield, with devastating consequent effect upon the balance of sea power in the Mediterranean? We had no mine sweepers with us, so we were just incredibly lucky. How fortunate we were was brought home to me in the most forcible manner possible in mid December of that fateful year.

At Dartmouth there had been another cadet of the same surname in my term. Dick Holloway came from Bristol, a solicitor's son. We were no relation, but became good friends. No doubt the 'twinned' surname had something to do with it.

Dick Holloway and a friend, David Houston, were appointed to the cruiser *Neptune*, a beautiful 6" gun ship commanded by Captain Rory O'Conor. The latter was greatly liked and took a special interest in midshipmen. He wrote a much-read tome for use before their seamanship examinations.

Dick Holloway dined with me on board HMAS *Nizam* in July 1941. It was nice to see him again, and we had so much to discuss that one of the Australian lieutenants rudely observed, 'You both talk too much.'

Within five months Holloway was dead, killed along with almost every other member of *Neptune's* ship's company, off Tripoli.

Briefly what happened was this: *Neptune*, together with the cruisers *Aurora* and *Penelope*, and attendant destroyers comprised Force 'K'. This small fleet operated from Malta, and was used in harrying enemy convoys carrying war material to Tripoli. On the night of 18/19 December 1941 this force was, as a result of Ultra intelligence, ordered to seek out an enemy convoy. Twenty miles off Tripoli (remember, we were only six miles offshore on our bombardment run) *Neptune* struck a mine. The time was 0100. She and the other cruisers had entered a hitherto unknown minefield, the ultimate horror of sailors.

Minutes later *Neptune* struck two more mines. Without power and unable to steam, she drifted helplessly towards her inevitable doom. The log of visual signals tells the whole tragic story in one graphic page (see Appendix I).

The feelings of those on board *Neptune* during those ghastly last hours do not bear thinking about. With their only illumination a torch or two (and these shaded on the upper deck) they must have waited in utter despair for the waves to take them to their deaths. Friends were so near and yet so far; both *Penelope* and *Aurora* were mined, and could not help. This applied also to the destroyer *Kandahar* who otherwise might have assisted in a rescue operation.

For others in company it was *sauve qui peut*. Terrible as the decision was to abandon *Neptune* to her fate, it was obviously the correct one. Further penetration of the minefield in a gallant rescue attempt would have been the sheerest folly, putting the rescuing ships at great risk of harm to themselves and thus no possibility of succour for *Neptune*.

At 0400 the inevitable happened. *Neptune* struck a fourth mine, a brilliant flash was seen below her bridge – she blew up, capsized and sank within minutes.

There was only one survivor; 600 officers and men including my friend Dick Holloway died instantly. Like all of us, he was only eighteen. His death, and the manner in which he died, affected me profoundly.

It could so easily have been us five months before. It may well have been that our incredibly lucky passage through those most dangerous waters in April contributed to *Neptune's* loss. No doubt the enemy decided that never again should Tripoli be bombarded from the sea. Three Italian cruisers and four destroyers laid a most extensive minefield off Tripoli in May and June 1941. Most of the mines were Italian but the long ones on cables were German. Beside the tragedy of the loss of our ships in Force K referred to earlier, two of our submarines were lost in the newly laid minefields.

That Cunningham so endangered his battle fleet as to take it within six miles of Tripoli is evidence of the extreme pressure being brought to bear upon him by London. In a signal to the Admiralty after the bombardment he made his protest, saying: 'We have got away with it once, and only because the German Air Force was engaged elsewhere.' Quite rightly, he considered the job should have been done by heavy bomber squadrons from Egypt.

Back in Alexandria, tangible signs began to appear that the gallant Greeks were being overwhelmed by the Germans.

The ancient cruiser *Averoff* accompanied by three antiquated Greek destroyers sailed into sanctuary. A Yugoslav submarine and an MTB also arrived. What subsequent use was made of them I never found out.

Commander Reid made this comment in his Daily Orders:

> *Valiant* fired many more rounds of main and secondary armament at Tripoli than either of the other two battleships. We were the first to complete ammunitioning and we have surveyed the two bower cables in twelve hours for which a week is normally allowed in peacetime.

And then a pompous but nonetheless heartening footnote: 'This is up to *Valiant* standard.'

It was disheartening to anyone on the Allied side in the Middle East at that time to witness the to-ing and fro-ing of the Eighth Army. At one moment it was marching into Benghazi, the next moment it was thrown back on its heels and as now, the enemy was across the Egyptian frontier at Sollum.

I began to wonder idly what would happen to us if events took an even further turn for the worse. Would we steam at full speed for the Suez Canal and escape down the Red Sea? What if enemy paratroops sabotaged the Canal? We would be bottled up in the eastern Mediterranean like rats cornered by terriers in a barn. There would be no escape, there would be nowhere to go. It was unthinkable that British naval units should scuttle themselves, but better that than allow three 15" battleships to fall into enemy hands. Turkey perhaps, a neutral country, but then, like the *Graf Spee* in Montevideo, we could not seek indefinite sanctuary. I find it helpful in a crisis to emulate the ostrich. I did so on this occasion and felt considerably better.

Again I reflected how lucky we were to have Alexandria in which to relax after our sorties against the enemy. Rommel might be knocking at Egypt's back door, but in the meantime the ostriches could bury their heads in the sands of Sidi Bishr and Stanley Bay, play tennis at the Sporting Club, and if in funds, have dinner at Pastroudi' s.

'Stands still the Liebfraumilch at eight o'clock?!' 'Eat drink and be merry for tomorrow we die' is, and was, a hackneyed phrase, but it had more than a ring of truth in it for us.

The next month was going to prove to be one of the worst in our lives. It was fortunate we did not know what was in store for us.

What was about to occur was the inevitable outcome of a vastly superior and magnificently equipped army pitted against brave forces, but tiny in comparison and ill-equipped. The German thrust into the Balkans was gathering momentum all the time. A brave but weaker man can resist a determined attacker for a while but soon brute force will overcome, and so it was with the Wehrmacht and the gallant Greeks who were fighting for their country and their honour. Sadly, soon the unequal struggle would be over. My journal entry for 28 April 1941 reads: 'It is reported today that the evacuation from Greece has begun, and the first operations are reported to be going well.'

Yes, well they would say that wouldn't they. It is instructive, and at times very galling to be in the thick of fighting, to know very well that matters are not proceeding according to plan, and then to hear the bland, cultured (in those days) voice of the BBC announcer telling the world that matters are proceeding like clockwork. Sadly, it is very often being 'economical with the truth'.

The next day, 29 April, the battlefleet, plus our carrier *Formidable*, sailed from Alexandria. We were told we were to cover the army's evacuation from Greece, take a convoy some of the way back to Egypt, then turn westwards and cover some more evacuated troops.

Formidable flew on all her aircraft at 1700, and we proceeded north-westwards at seventeen knots.

The warships spread out over the sea looked magnificent. We had left our flagship *Warspite* in harbour, but the sight presented still looked powerful and menacing. In the rear, *Barham*, wearing the flag of RAI (Rear-Admiral First Battle-squadron), in place astern *Valiant* steamed on, better equipped than her flagship, but mounting the same huge 15" guns which had wrought so much destruction at Matapan. Astern again was our carrier, her flight deck dipping gracefully in the swell. We prayed that she would not be so damaged as to be unable to give us the air cover we so desperately needed in these waters.

The cruiser *Phoebe* steamed on the port quarter, whilst the anti-submarine screen of eight destroyers proceeded in an inverted 'V' formation ahead of us all. British sea power was being paraded – in the face of such force it was unlikely that the response from the Italians would be anything more than token. I stood on *Valiant's* quarter-deck and gazed at our display of power. We seemed invincible; how stupid, we were nothing of the kind, but it gave me heart to think of it.

To those who are unfamiliar with life at sea in a warship, there may be some unexpected departures from the pictures conjured up by novelists and film directors. Sea routine was always more relaxed than in harbour. Those senior were not saluted by those junior to them unless the latter had a report to make, or on first meeting them in the morning. In colder weather, roll neck sweaters beneath reefer jackets replaced collar and tie, whilst in warm weather and particularly at night if no one could see, flip-flop sandals took the place of long white stockings and shoes.

No officer drank at sea, although the bars of the various messes were open if required. Sleep was taken as and when possible, and, since we were not entitled to the luxury of a cabin, midshipmen would often be found lying prone on the banquette seats of the Gunroom.

In a rough sea, deadlights would be fixed in the scuttles, allowing air to come in but keeping water and light out. At night, the ship would be battened down for darkening, and obviously in a warm climate, fresh, cool air was at a premium. Meals were served at the usual times but they had to overlap the times of watches. We did not suffer from indigestion but we ought to have done!

The Gunroom had its own bathroom with baths, showers and wash-basins. A matter of some concern when at sea in wartime was how much or how little clothing should be discarded. If a bomb hit the ship, or you were torpedoed, would it be best, having just had a shower, to try and escape naked, thus unencumbered when in water? This was debatable. Naturally it depended how far out we were from land. At best, it would be preferable to have shoes on terra firma, but these would be a hindrance in the water. Most survivors to whom I talked after their ordeals favoured tropical rig – shirt and shorts, but no shoes. Fortunately I never had to put this to the test, but often wondered how long I would have survived had I been unlucky.

Unless we were closed up at Action Stations the ship's routine was carried out as if it was peacetime. Commander's Defaulters and Requestmen were seen between decks. The Captain, who never left the bridge at sea, performed a similar duty outside his sea cabin.

The whole sea-going ant-hill was alive with purpose. Divisions cleaned their parts of ship, divisional officers saw their ratings, sick parades were held, and the Captain's Secretary, overloaded with work, looked permanently harassed.

I was attached to the Torpedo Division which, since we had no torpedoes, was rather an Irish description. It did however, contain all the electrical ratings, clever chaps who knew their amps from their watts and how to use a megger. I was handed all their S264s, or personal records, in order to keep them up-to-date. It was a job I loathed and found intensely boring. How anyone could have stood Pompey Naval Barracks where all the paper work received much more attention, I could never comprehend. I enjoyed the technical side of the

Navy, but the keeping of records and seeing the ship was clean was tedious to the nth degree and induced instant ennui in me. Later, when I became a Fighter Direction Officer I would use the scornful Fleet Air Arm expression 'Leave that to the deck scrubbers!'

On Wednesday, 30 April, our convoy came into sight at 0700. Comprising six ships, including the Royal Fleet Auxiliary *Brambleleaf*, it steamed at only ten knots. This was too slow and dangerous for the battlefleet, and occasionally we altered course so as to circle round our charges; rather reminiscent of sheep dog trials, I thought.

About 2000 there was a submarine scare. A Swordfish aircraft dropped depth charges and destroyers raced to the spot. The latter dropped 'patterns' of depth charges but a tragic mishap ensued. The destroyer *Juno* dropped her charges, but one exploded before it hit the water, killing two officers and eight ratings beside injuring others.

The result of our attack was unknown but my journal records: 'It is thought it was sunk.' Wishful thinking perhaps.

The ever-present menace of enemy aircraft persisted, and at 1000 we opened fire. This was one of the Fred Karno sides of war – vide my journal: 'The target was somewhat obscure, as although *Barham* opened fire as well, the control officer in the director tower admits he could not see what he was meant to be firing at!'

Actually, there were four Italian CR42 fighters lurking, protecting five German JU88s. Our carrier based fighters saw them off; oh, the sheer luxury of friendly fighter cover! It wasn't to last for long.

Our convoy duty completed, we looked forward to a spell in harbour, but it was not to be. Enemy bombers had once more mined the Great Pass, the entrance to Alexandria harbour. There was nothing for it but to spend the night steaming up and down whilst the destroyers ran dangerously short of fuel.

After 24 hours, all was pronounced clear and it was then that we received an extraordinary signal from RA1 our Admiral. This read: 'Ships are to proceed into harbour one at a time.'

Morgan snorted and remarked, 'We don't usually enter harbour in line abreast!'

11

Crete – The Battle is Joined

My life was now about to change dramatically. Every midshipman, as part of his training, was required to serve three months' 'destroyer time'. This made sense of course; destroyers are the maids-of-all-work of the fleet. They are constantly at sea and are sent to places to which no battleship or cruiser would dare venture. This was to be more than amply demonstrated during the coming months.

As related earlier, 'destroyer time' had proved fatal for poor David Peck, bombed and sunk in the destroyer *Wryneck* during the evacuation of Greece. German bombers were once more to try and eliminate me, fortunately without success.

On Monday, 4 May 1941 I was given four hours to get ready to join HMAS *Nizam*. What was she, of what was she capable; she sounded almost Indian. The latter comment was not far off the mark. The fabulously rich *Nizam* of Hyderabad had made a grand gesture and donated enough money to build this brand new destroyer.

An 'N' class destroyer displacing 1760 tons, *Nizam* had a top speed of 36 knots. Her armament consisted of 6 x 4.7" guns, 1 x 4" gun, 4 Oerlikons, 1 x 2-pdr gun and a set of 21" torpedo tubes. Built by John Brown of Clydebank, she was commissioned by the Royal Australian Navy on 19 December 1940.

I had very mixed feelings about joining her. There are those naval officers who love the small ship life, the informality, the absence of big ship ceremonial. I was not one of them. I would be leaving my Gunroom friends and going to an alien environment, not even an English one at that! What would the Australians be like? I had no experience of them whatsoever and feared a culture shock.

I had got used to life in *Valiant* and was very fond of the ship. Furthermore, I had private doubts as to whether my seamanship would prove adequate in a small ship. I had always disliked the subject right from Dartmouth days and likened it to the boring deck scrubbing. How would I measure up? Doubtless all would soon be revealed.

I packed hurriedly. Although *Nizam* had not yet even entered Alexandria (she had made the long journey from the UK via the Cape, and was now en route from Port Said), there was need for haste. In wartime there is no knowing how soon one will receive orders to sail. *Valiant* might have to put to sea, and if I did not make haste I would still be on board thus missing my new appointment. Black marks all round.

Napier, the flotilla leader and *Nizam* entered harbour at 1400 looking very smart. In the event, I did not leave *Valiant* until 1830 and after doing the rounds of practically all the destroyers in the harbour, eventually found my future home, moored alongside Mahmoudiyeh Quay.

I was welcomed by Richardson, the Australian midshipman whom I was to relieve. He was my idea of the typical Australian, tall, well built, bronzed and healthy, he might have been a lifeguard on Manley Beach – not Bondi – too common! Charming though he was, he also seemed frightfully efficient, and I hoped that *Nizam* would not regret the exchange.

The Aussie accents jarred, and I detected at once an informality between officers and ratings which jangled on my Dartmouth training. The lower deck did not actually call you 'cobber' but you had the feeling that it was only awaiting an excuse to pop out!

Among the new experiences for me on joining *Nizam* there were two that stood out. First and foremost I had a cabin, all to myself! I could not believe my luck. I was never to have such luxury again throughout my sea-going time as a midshipman, and revelled in it. Later, a lieutenant joined for a while and then it was the Ward Room cushions for me, but while it lasted I made the most of it. Secondly, for the first time in my life I became a Ward Room officer. There are no Gunrooms for the 'young gentlemen' in destroyers, and so I messed with two and a half and two-stripers.

The Gunner (T) and I were the only Englishmen on board, and at times it became irksome. You can take badinage and remarks about 'the Poms' for a while but there comes a time when you feel you have to hit back. After a particularly provoking session, I fear I retorted 'Well, your bloody country is only five cities and a desert' which may not have endeared me to some.

The Captain, Lieutenant-Commander M.S. Clark, RAN was a charming and courteous man. Coming from Melbourne, he had no trace of an Aussie accent. Not renowned for his ability at ship handling when manoeuvring at close quarters, he nevertheless saved our lives when we were being bombed in the open sea off Crete. Like many another captain he would assess the direction the bomb would take on its release and then give the order to turn out of its path. A destroyer answers to her helm at once, and a number of bombs landed exactly where we would have been had he not taken violent avoiding action.

The navigator, Lieutenant 'Dusty' Miller, RAN was tall and resembled the film actor Fred MacMurray. His friend, Sub-Lieutenant 'Nigger' Black, RAN was dark, short and curly-haired. I must confess to amusement when writing his soliloquy. What a fuss the race relations industry would make of it today. Nobody gave it a second thought in 1941 –it was no more a term of disparagement than Nigger Brown was for gloves.

Lieutenant-Commander Carter, RAN was in charge of me. I did not like him and I fancy the feeling was mutual. He was porcine, spoke only in monosyllables and took little or no interest in my welfare.

The rest of the Ward Room was made up with the doctor, a quiet, charming man and the 'Chief' a two and a half striper RAN engineer officer, also a pleasure to mess with. Life was unusual for me in that very naturally conversation, when not of the war, concentrated on places in Australia, a country I had yet to visit. The equivalent of the *Tatler* carried photographs of Speech Day at Geelong Grammar School and so on.

Gradually I grew a second skin but tended to like the ratings more than the officers. They were not for ever going on about the Poms, or if they did, it was obviously not meant to hurt but was part of an inbred feeling of nationalism.

I went to sleep in my cabin, but not before an air raid which lasted from 2100 till 2230. Sleep was always at a premium! All the ships and shore batteries opened fire and the noise was terrific.

Two days after I had joined her, *Nizam* put to sea, preceded by the battlefleet and our carrier *Formidable*. It was then that I discovered one of the differences between a 30,000-ton battleship and a 1760-ton destroyer. She pitched and rolled and I was horribly seasick. This awful malady, now much less in evidence because of modern-day medicine, was the one thing I had in common with Admiral Lord Nelson. It is highly unpleasant having to go on watch when you are feeling wretched. Further, it is bound to impair your efficiency.

Having got over it, after 24 to 36 hours it does not recur, but the whole unpleasant cycle starts again on leaving harbour. A convoy to Malta was our objective, together with the 'passing through' the Strait of Pantellaria of the battleship *Queen Elizabeth* and the cruiser *Fiji*.

The reader will remember the Stuka dive-bomber attacks on us off Pantellaria in January. It was therefore a courageous or foolhardy decision to send two such valuable warships through Bomb Alley. As it turned out it was a courageous and correct decision, for both ships emerged from Hell's Mouth unscathed.

And where was the Luftwaffe? Luckily, not in evidence. We oiled at sea, and this brought forth a comment in my journal. 'It is obvious,' I wrote, 'that Suda Bay in Crete can no longer be considered safe for oiling the fleet, as on previous occasions. The Germans are already in the islands of Lemnos and Milo, six minutes' flying time from the Bay.' Things were hotting up. They were soon to get much hotter.

There were many air raid alarms but our faithful Fulmar fighters chased away all the would-be raiders, except on one occasion. No fault of the Fulmars, the raid took place at night and sticks of bombs were dropped, one falling between the fast minelayer *Abdiel* and our sister ship *Napier*. Near misses were reported on the battleships. 'All clear' at 2230 and then keeping the Middle Watch from midnight to 0400; it was lucky I was so young.

After many further reports of enemy aircraft closing the fleet, none of which came within sight, we reached Alexandria without further incident.

I was sent to get a secret message from the destroyer *Voyager*. Her officers told me she had just returned from Suda Bay. 'Great efforts,' they said, 'are being made to defend the place, and 6" guns are being mounted everywhere.' I hoped the preparations would prove effective – at that time in the war we were so used to retreats and defeats that we became cynical as to the possibilities of success.

Rumours of a German attack on Crete abounded. It was now firmly fixed in everyone's mind that an attack could not long be delayed, for even those most ignorant of strategy could see that the island was the obvious next target for Axis attention.

Twenty-four hours in harbour was all the respite we had, and on 13 May we put to sea after dark. Escorts to the battlefleet, we steamed north-west, the purpose of our sailing and our destination unknown.

The next day my journal entry reads: 'Today we learned that although we had been sent out at first to cover a convoy, it was heard later that Axis forces were going to try and invade Crete and we were to stop it. The invasion would most probably be from the air, and we are to stop the supplies which will inevitably come by sea.'

My words 'heard later' are verbatim as written at the time, but with hindsight this information was undoubtedly the result of an Ultra decrypt.

So there we were; the balloon was about to go up, the starting gun had gone off, battle was about to be joined, or whatever cliché you like to use, and we were going to be in the thick of it. I must admit, I felt somewhat smug. Aged only eighteen and five months, a fairly junior midshipman, I had already seen far more action against the enemy than anyone else on board! *Nizam* had only been engaged on convoy escort duty after leaving her builder's yard in the UK. Her ship's company had arrived fresh from Australia to commission her and had seen no action at home; the Japanese were yet to erupt in the Pacific. Meanwhile I had taken part in three bombardments, been dive-bombed off Pantellaria and had been present at the Battle of Matapan. In spite of all this vast war experience, no one asked my advice. They were probably right. If I had had more experience of war than my shipmates, it did little to instil confidence in me of my chances of survival. I had seen what enemy dive-bombing could do to ships completely exposed in the open sea. The Aussies were in utter and blissful ignorance of what was, literally, to fall upon them.

As a curtain-raiser to the Battle of Crete, I quote from David Thomas' book *Crete 1941*. He wrote: 'The battles which will be related were almost exclusively between warships of the Royal Navy and aircraft of the German Luftwaffe.

They proved to be a series of sustained aerial bombardments the like of which no navy in the world had experienced before. Not until the Kamikaze suicide missions of the Japanese pilots at Okinawa four years later, was the severity of the Mediterranean ordeal to be surpassed.'

As had happened on numerous occasions already, and was to happen later, we were to suffer for the criminal refusal of politicians to listen to Winston Churchill's pre-war warnings of the necessity to rearm. This, coupled with a highly pacifist Socialist opposition which did its best to ensure the deaths of numerous servicemen by its pathetic bleatings that all would be settled amicably by the League of Nations. No one learns – Michael Foot was to blather on about appeals to the United Nations whilst Argentina reinforced the Falkland Islands. *Si vis pacem para bellum.*

Meanwhile at sea in *Nizam*, we had warnings of large groups of enemy aircraft closing, and with no aircraft carrier to protect us, we waited in some trepidation. I would rather have prior warning of an attack than hear a sudden 'swoosh' and explosion, but the anticipatory waiting is, to say the least, stomach-churning. Miraculously, the aircraft detected by radar never materialised. What they were doing south of Crete we never knew . We were only thankful they left us alone.

On 17 May we intercepted a cypher message from C-in-C Med to NOIC Suda (Naval Officer in Charge, Suda Bay) asking him what the situation was there, and telling him that the whole operational plan of the Mediterranean fleet at this time would be based on his reply.

The reply from Suda said that seventeen enemy aircraft had made a dive-bombing attack on the Bay during which HMS *Salvia* had been hit with two killed and twelve wounded.

The cruisers *Gloucester*, *Fiji* and *Perth*, having made a more northerly sweep than ourselves, joined us during the morning, but all was uneventful and later we received orders to return to Alexandria and refuel. The calm before the storm.

Back in harbour at 0700 we received orders to sail again at 1300 and at 1400 were steaming northwards at 25 knots. As soon as we left harbour, I heard of our destination. We were to bombard Scarpanto, a small island 50 miles east of Crete. Here, the Germans had established a dive-bomber base and we were to endeavour to shell the planes on the ground and destroy the runways.

My father made a speciality of 'taking' wasps' nests as he used to call it. Armed only with a rag dipped in potassium cyanide on the end of a long poker, and with no protective netting, he would insert the poker into the rockery. Wasps inside would die, those returning, with luck, would also fall foul of the poisonous fumes. It struck me somewhat forcibly that we were about to emulate my father, and without the protective netting. Moreover, he was on terra firma. Should his attempt at destruction fail and the wasps, angry, flew around, stings at the ready, he would not sink. We had hundreds of fathoms of ocean beneath us in like case.

In company were the destroyers *Ilex*, *Jarvis* and *Havock*. The four ships made a brave sight in the warm Mediterranean sunshine, our bows cleaving the water, boiling waters indicating our high speed. Everyone was tense, anti-flash gear was checked (very hot to wear in that climate) ammunition stacked and ready, the gunlayers going through their drill. This was to be a night bombardment; they would need to know how to do their jobs blindfold.

At midnight we went to Action Stations. From now on people talked in whispers on the upper deck, as though 'careless talk costs lives!' I didn't think the enemy could hear, but perhaps those who whispered, although secretly anxious and not a little afraid, may have had a point.

'Bloody hell, look at that,' said Leading Signalman Peters, a huge fair-haired young man from Sydney. Similar exclamations came – the time was 0230 and My journal reads: 'We very nearly stayed at Scarpanto, a broken wreck.'

A torpedo had passed right under the ship – its track had been spotted on the port side and everyone held their breath awaiting what seemed to them the inevitable explosion, and then miraculously the track emerged on the starboard side and what might have sent us to the bottom continued on its deadly way. Seconds later we heard a loud explosion.

The torpedo had exploded against the land. Whoever fired the torpedo had set its depth too low. We had been saved from drowning or being taken prisoner by what Wimbledon commentator Dan Maskell would have called 'an unforced error'!

Who fired it? Controversy raged that night and for long afterwards, but the general consensus of opinion was that it was an E-Boat. My journal records that 'it made off under cover of a smokescreen'. Well, a submarine would not have needed that kind of protection, would it? This near-fatal incident sent the adrenalin coursing through everyone's veins, and had almost made us forget the object of the exercise – our bombardment!

Swinging into line ahead, we commenced firing at 0245, with an initial range of 9000 yards. I reckoned five miles was quite near enough to get to the enemy; we were to be much nearer than that later on.

Our flotilla leader kept signalling us 'Give me your range' but true to the routine communications cock-ups when in action, he kept on signalling his instead, so we were unable to reply.

The gun flashes in the darkness did nothing to allay my fears (and I dare say those of others too) that we were prime illuminated targets for another, and more accurate torpedo, but nothing happened.

Firing ceased and we hoped we had done some damage to the wasps' nest – we would know when it became light.

We illuminated a bay further north with starshell. Accuracy was excellent, Brock's Benefit could not have done better. How nice it would have been if the bay had been full of Greek caiques, crammed with German troops and stores. What havoc we could have caused. But the bay was empty, and disappointed, we turned away watching the last of our starshell float down on its parachute, guttering out in the sea. It was now 0341. Daylight would break at 0530. Anti-aircraft stations were manned at 0500 and we waited tensely as we pounded back towards Egypt at 25 knots.

Daylight streaked the sky and soon we were a target for everyone to see, especially those with swept-back wings.

We scanned the sky anxiously, but the pure blue was unscarred by black crosses. A miracle, or had we 'taken' the wasps' nest? For us there was respite that day for which we were thankful, but Roskill in his *History of the War at Sea* says 'a further attack by naval bombers on the enemy's main air base at Scarpanto took place on 25 May, but although it achieved surprise, the bombers were too few to have much permanent effect on the enemy's air effort'.

So there you are – a task force of two battleships, one aircraft carrier and nine destroyers together with our preceding effort with four destroyers had not succeeded in checking the enemy. What a dreadful waste of time, precious fuel and the endangering of five ships, and all for nothing. Good job we didn't know it at the time.

Unscathed, we arrived back in Alexandria at 2100 but the gruelling pace was not to slacken for another week. We had fired 56 rounds into Scarpanto these we replaced, oiled and were ready for sea once more.

Three hours was all we were allowed in harbour and this was no rest period with everyone making the ship ready for sea. We slipped and proceeded at midnight, our orders to patrol around the Heraklion area.

In order to understand the complexities and dangers of the battle for Crete, it is well to study the map. From this, it will be seen that the best harbours, such as Heraklion and Suda Bay, are to the north of the island whilst to the south there is virtually nothing except Sphakia. The latter was useless except as a sandy beach for the subsequent evacuation.

Cunningham wrote later, 'it would have been best if the island had been turned upside down', and how right he was.

There were only two 'entrances' to the north of the island, the Antikithera Channel to the west, and the Kaso Strait to the east. Both were to become the most sinister of 'Bomb Alleys'.

We were due to enter the Kaso Strait at 0900 and as we got nearer and nearer, so did our apprehensions of the immediate future become uppermost in our minds. Our orders as before, were to intercept any attempts by the Germans to reinforce their airborne landings by sea transport from Greece. The Italian Navy presented few problems; it was the Luftwaffe we feared, and with good reason. Throughout the whole of our passage to Crete, we intercepted signal after signal which, as recorded in my journal 'showed that the fleet to the west of us was having an appalling time from dive-bombers. First, *Gloucester*, which I had seen launched at Plymouth in 1937 (and was my home county cruiser) was reported sunk; the signal said there were men in the water showing lights. It also instructed the cruiser *Fiji* to pick up survivors, but

The sinking of HMS *Gloucester* taken from a German aircraft.

then a later signal told us that *Fiji* had herself been sunk, and then the destroyer *Juno*. Hits were also made on the cruisers *Perth* and *Carlisle*.'

As officer in charge of the plot at Action Stations I read all these signals and endeavoured to present some sort of coherent situation report to the Captain. As any intelligence officer will know (and I had had no training in this) it is extremely difficult to sift the wheat from the chaff. Signalled reports are sent at the height of action, they may be inaccurate and may well conflict with other reports purporting to be of the same incident. From 1700 onwards we kept the most vigilant anti-aircraft lookout. Our radar was nowhere near as efficient and reliable as the big sets installed in *Valiant* and *Formidable*. Consequently, the human eye was all-important. Those who have not experienced it can have no idea how utterly naked and defenceless one can feel in a ship at sea awaiting a bomber attack. A large bird appearing from nowhere can cause gun barrels to train instantly on to its bearing. Men very naturally become trigger happy and on one occasion the order 'Open Fire' was given there were sheepish faces when it was discovered that it was merely the evening star, Venus, rising!

On land there is usually some cover from aircraft – a tree, a house, a trench, but at sea there is nothing, absolutely nothing to hide you, and in the beautiful Mediterranean weather, conditions were perfect for an Axis kill.

As we steamed on and on northwards, more reports came in of fearful enemy air activity; surely we were not going to be spared? We were even closer to the enemy air-bases than our luckless companions to the west. We shall never know what happened. Perhaps we were spotted without our knowledge and deemed too small a fry, at that time, to warrant attention. I doubt it, anything that moved on the sea was being bombed, and if it was a survivor in the water, he was machine-gunned. The machine-gunning of survivors in the water was a dreadful, dreadful thing but it had been considered by the Germans and coolly translated into orders to their forces in action. For the Jews, the final solution. For those who were struggling for their lives in cold seas and oil fuel, there was to be '*Schrecklichkeit*'. Translated literally, this means 'terribleness' or 'frightfulness', and the logic was thought through with Teutonic thoroughness.

Why, went German thinking, sink the ship and let the sailors who survived her sinking escape to fight another day? After all, they reasoned, a ship can be replaced in a matter of perhaps nine months to a year. But, the trained men who sail in her cannot be replaced for at least seventeen to eighteen years and these would be only the rawest of juniors.

How much more cost-effective therefore to kill the men who were in the water and thus literally to drive yet another nail into the enemy's coffin? I leave the reader to decide on the morality of this decision. In fairness, it has to be said that some German U-boat commanders would not implement this policy, but most, certainly in the Mediterranean, carried out their orders with relish.

The reason for the ferocious attacks by German aircraft on the cruisers *Fiji* and *Gloucester* was revealed after the war. An order issued to his pilots by the Luftwaffe commander in Crete said:

Fly to the west of the island. There you will see two battleships [sic]. These are the ships which so callously killed our troops with their propellors on their way in their caiques to the island. Give them hell.

Plane after plane swooped down on the helpless cruisers. Eventually, having fired all their anti-aircraft ammunition they were reduced to firing starshell. The end, when it came, was inevitable. Both ships were sunk with great loss of life. I lost two midshipmen friends who had been cadets in the same house house as me at Dartmouth, together with our former Captain of Royal Marines, Dick Formby.

That is not the end of the story. The few survivors who were picked up by the Italian Navy were initially treated quite well. It was later when the Germans found out that they were from the two cruisers that they were very nearly shot. It was only the intervention of a German doctor who mentioned the Geneva Convention that they were spared. Their journey through Italy to Germany, packed tightly into a railway truck in stifling heat was a foretaste of what our soldiers were to endure at the hands of the Japanese after the fall of Singapore. They spent the next four years in POW camps in Greece, Austria and Poland. Towards the end of the war they were marched westwards in the depths of a terrible winter to prevent their release by the advancing Red Army. Frostbite took its toll and one man had to have his toes amputated without anaesthetic.

I have always been of the opinion that we on the *Nizam* were spared when we steamed towards Suda Bay on 26 May because the German pilots were too busy with their attacks to the west. John Cardew and I could easily have chosen to go to sea in the *Gloucester*; he came from Cheltenham, I was Gloucestershire born and bred. The county affiliation and the fact that we had seen her launched might well have influenced us. How lucky we had been.

Suffice it to say that miraculously we entered the Kaso Strait on time and the blessed cloak of darkness enveloped us. Phew, what a relief, but, I had to remind myself, don't get too euphoric, you have to face the return journey.

Down in the plot I kept track of the ship's position by dead reckoning. Occasionally it was possible to get bearings of the islands of Ovo and Standia which, together with their distances measured by our surface radar, gave us an accurate idea of where we were. Those islands are so small that they do not appear on the map showing our losses in the Cretan campaign printed in Roskill's History. However, their small size assisted us in more accurate pilotage. Even I could do it!

We were now, in pitch darkness, to the north of Crete, steaming right past Heraklion and practically to Suda Bay.

It must be remembered that although I had a good picture of the ghastly bombing to which our less fortunate ships were being subjected, I had, at least until now, no idea of how we were faring on land. No army signals came our way, we shared no common wavelength, and therefore apart from BBC communiques which were mere verbiage, we were completely in the dark as to events which were happening only a few miles away from us! As records came to be published after the war it transpired that due to communications failures, the various units of the British Army ashore in Crete were in like case. However, that was their misfortune, and something over which naturally we had no control.

For our part, we hoped to meet and destroy the enemy. In this area, only 24 hours before, a force of our cruisers and destroyers had wreaked havoc amongst a convoy of light craft crowded with German troops and escorted by Italian MTBs. 'Buzzes' went round the fleet later of bodies in the water being churned up by ships' screws. This may have happened but it cannot have been anything but unintentional. Cruisers cannot, in the melee of a night action, turn on searchlights so that they can side-step survivors. Liberals like Ludovic Kennedy might protest as he did over the shooting by 'Crap' Miers of Germans who had allegedly surrendered. You cannot be too pussyfooting in war, and if some Axis troops died in this way, well, as they said in the navy: 'You shouldn't have joined, mate!' Our own Schrecklichkeit?

At 0300, having found nothing, we turned east for our return journey. No wonder we had an empty sea before us; a decision had just been taken by the German High Command, again unknown to us until after the war, that their paratroops must first subdue the British defences and only then might sea-borne reinforcements sail for the island. What a pity Ultra had not picked this up!

Just after turning east we received a signal from C-in-C saying 'all forces proceed Alexandria at best possible speed'. Now what was afoot? Ours not to reason why, and we were glad of the order, which because of its emphasis on speed would allow us to clear the Kaso Strait that much earlier.

'Oh no you don't,' said the Luftwaffe commander, 'oh no you bloody don't.' It was 0545 and the sky was just beginning to lighten when we spotted them. Two high-level bombers hung in the heavens, harbingers of death doubtless setting their bomb sights for the targets below them.

All hell broke loose as the horrible crack of the 4.7" guns assailed our ears. Nowadays, and quite rightly, everyone is issued with ear-plugs and/or ear muffs. In those days it was considered cissy even to put your hands to your ears during gun fire.

Our open bridge now came into its own. Exposed to the elements, as were those keeping watch on any destroyer's bridge, when it comes to fighting the ship and especially during aircraft attack, it has no rival.

The bridge was full, Captain, Navigator, Officer of the Watch, lookouts and two signalmen made it a crowded place. The signal was hoisted 'take individual avoiding action', but we needed no order. Lieutenant-Commander Clark zigzagged the ship violently in anticipation of what was to come and, as a car at speed pulls itself round a bend, so we at our best speed twisted and turned to save the ship and our lives. The bombs fell all around us, great spouts of water erupting from their impact. 'They seemed to have an inexhaustible supply of bombs,' I wrote in my journal. Sometimes I put my head up on to the bridge but I mostly kept to my Action Station, the plot just below the bridge. The ship would heel right over, the Leading Seaman and I would know this meant that another 'stick' was on its way down. We would then hear the bomb's scream as it made its deadly descent and then he and I would be 'sheltering' under the extremely dubious protection of the plot table. This was a purely animal and ostrich-like dash for cover, but I suppose that in the event of splinters we might only receive them in our buttocks and not in our heads. The attack ceased, everyone was all right. We breathed again.

Through the Kaso Strait, but this was no magic exit. The bombers came for us again at 0700. We twisted and turned as before, and either the enemy's aim was poor (not so, if you looked at how close the bursts were) or our Captain's shiphandling was becoming better. We survived.

Breakfast was gobbled, everyone on tenterhooks as to whether we would make it or suffer the fate of our friends further west.

It was 0830 and 'Alarm Aircraft' was sounded. Six dive-bombers were after us this time and our group did not escape unscathed. A cry went up, '*Havock* is hit.' Indeed she was, two boilers being put out of action, and she sustained casualties of five killed and ten wounded.

My journal takes up the story: 'However, to make up for this (*Havock's* damage), our gunners in *Nizam* shot the tail off one bomber, and another disappeared over the horizon, flying very low and with smoke pouring from it. No hits were scored on us. By this time the ammunition situation was getting serious – none of the guns had much left.

At 1000 just as everyone thought the bombing was over, without warning there was a horrible whistling noise and a large bomb fell in the water very close to us. A long-range high-level bomber had managed to get right over-head without being seen, and we were only saved by the inaccuracy of his aim.' That we shot the tail off one bomber and may have mortally wounded another was very creditable indeed. From what I had seen previously of close-range weapons I did not think much of them except as a deterrent to a dive-bomber. I felt now that my opinion should be revised, and joined in the cheers which greeted the gunners' success.

The Aussies were being 'blooded' in no uncertain fashion.

We arrived at Alexandria at 2000, fuelled and ammunitioned, and were on our buoy by 2300. Then, guess what, to help us sleep? Yes, you are right, an air raid! We were too tired to care. If they hit us we could do nothing about it. Kismet.

The morning of 24 May dawned, and with it orders to raise steam for full speed by 0800. We then proceeded to No. 13 quay in company with the destroyers *Decoy*, *Hero* and *Isis*. As we drew alongside we saw hundreds of troops waiting. We were told (in confidence) that these were something called 'commandos' (we had never heard the term before!) They looked a piratical lot (my journal: 'a mixed and rather motley crowd') festooned with weapons of every description, wearing balaclavas beneath which were blackened faces. Our confidential informant whispered: 'Some are even deserters from the French Foreign Legion!' We were suitably impressed and like the Duke of Wellington, thought: 'I don't know what they do to the enemy, but by God Sir, they frighten me!' The men of Layforce were to be our passengers. We embarked 108. There is little room in a destroyer for this sort of thing. The officers of course, slept on the deck in the Ward Room. I, as junior boy, gave up my cabin.

The other ranks either crammed the mess decks or littered the iron deck topside. They did not remain in the latter position for very long.

Off we went at 1030 at 28 knots, increasing to 30 knots an hour later. The object of the exercise was to put the troops ashore at Sphakia on the south coast of Crete. Little did we know that this self-same little fishing port was to be the scene of a Cretan Dunkirk within the space of only a few days.

What on earth 400 troops could do to redress the balance of power on the island I thought was debatable at the time. The fighting never was in the south. Our commandos would have had an arduous climb up the cliffs after landing, and would then have had to march. They would have had to cross an 11,000-foot high mountain range, and having marched for 50 miles might then have just reached the battle zone. Tough they might have been, but in what condition to fight, one wonders! If they had doubts, the weather came to their rescue. During the First Watch (2000 to midnight) it came on to blow very hard and we were shipping water badly. Let no one believe the blandishments of travel agents when they tell you that the Mediterranean is 'calm as a millpond, especially in summer'. It can be a bitch in winter and not much better on occasions in the summer months. What we had encountered was a real gale, force nine, and it was highly unpleasant. The troops had long since abandoned the iron deck and were packed in on the mess decks where vomit mixed with seawater.

Huge waves broke over the foc'sle, and to venture on to the iron deck without a line around you was foolhardy to say the least. This highlights one of the handicaps of a destroyer. I had been used to the luxury of being able to walk the whole length of *Valiant* below decks even though at times I had to unclip a great number of watertight doors. This cannot be done in a destroyer. To have added watertight doors would increase the ship's weight, and so whilst many bulkheads ran transversely throughout the ship, there were no openings in them. The only method therefore of getting from, say, the Ward Room (aft) to the bridge (forward) was by way of the iron deck. Lovely, and safe on a balmy June night. Sheer hell and very dangerous in conditions such as we were now to experience.

We had taken on board four additional whalers in Alexandria for the purpose of ferrying the troops ashore. Mighty waves now smashed these to smithereens and they disappeared over the side. My journal reads: 'Trying to make 30 knots in this gale was no joke. The ship shivered and shuddered a great deal.' As a result, at 2300 our destination was changed to Port Mudros, since Sphakia's open beach would have turned an attempted landing into a suicide attempt.

It was at this time that those listening to the BBC World Service heard the almost unbelievable news that HMS *Hood* had been hit by a salvo from *Bismarck* and that she had blown up. It was incredible, and a body blow to morale. All of us knew of her as a most powerful warship – to me, who had actually been on board in pre-war days, a dreadful feeling of loss was created. I thought *Hood* the most beautiful ship I had ever seen. She combined perfect symmetry of line with sleek latent power. I would have considered it an honour to have served in her. Now I was glad I had not.

Later in the war I met the only officer survivor, a midshipman named Dundas who had been with me at Dartmouth. 'I was on the bridge,' he said. 'The next thing I knew I was in the water.' Poor Dundas, he was a Jonah. Another ship he was in was bombed. Later he was killed in a car accident.

The wind screamed, the sea heaved, we were tossed hither and thither like a cork. Watch-keeping on the bridge or indeed anywhere else on the upper deck was sheer hell. Although down in the plot I was protected to a certain extent from the ferocity of the storm, it was nevertheless uncomfortable. The deck of the plot was swimming with water which swooshed in through the wheel-house door and even down the voicepipes! Station keeping was almost impossible, and finally much to my undisguised relief, the landing was cancelled and we turned back for home. I was glad someone had had some sense.

It was said that a second attempt at landing the troops was to be made, but this too was cancelled due to lack of oil fuel. Steaming at such high speed and trying to maintain it in the teeth of the gale had proved extremely expensive in burning up our fuel supplies; no one wanted to run out of motive power with the Luftwaffe overhead!

At 1100 two unidentified aircraft suddenly appeared. All guns trained on them, but fortunately did not open fire, as they flew on and disappeared. We breathed again.

The storm abated as we neared the Egyptian coast. How nice it was to see that brown line ahead of us indicating sanctuary; if only temporary. We oiled and awaited orders.

12

Crete – Evacuation

Monday 26 May 1941 dawned as it nearly always did in Alexandria. The sun blazed down, the water in the harbour was like glass, unrippled, but crowded with shipping. The ever-present smell of oil fuel mixed with the odour of unwashed gyppo bodies drifted offshore. The wail of the muezzins calling the faithful to prayer had made dawn hideous with its cacophony.

Tourists from early times had paid handsomely to see this sight, and even if their nostrils were assailed by the smells, they doubtless put it down to 'the romance of the East'. Rich Egyptians had seaside villas in Alexandria, rich Greeks enjoyed their Egyptian mistresses in large houses along the Grande Corniche or out at Stanley Bay.

All very delightful, but now the fun had had to stop. Months ago, the rich had left Alexandria for the safety of South Africa, and many of the houses were empty. Alexandria was now very much at war, and I for one had no time to appreciate the one-time tourists' delight.

Nizam had hummed with activity throughout the night and there had been little time for rest. Ammunition and food had to be brought on board – more of the latter because the troops like the poor, were still with us, and indeed we had taken on board a few more. Poor devils, I did not envy them their task. I spoke to a number of them. They seemed cheerful enough and were eager to get into the fight, although many were rather white around the gills as the aftermath of their recent unpleasant and abortive voyage.

They were allowed to walk around on the quay side, something which had been arranged for their convenience and for ours. They were not forever literally getting under our feet. Some honed fearsome-looking knives, others oiled their submachine guns.

It must be reiterated that all this time we, at our lowly level, had little or no idea how the battle on Crete was progressing. We were only small cogs in the campaign wheel and went where we were sent, doing our duty as well as possible under conditions which at best might be described as 'adverse'.

Had we known that our army command on Crete had not much more idea than we had of what was going on, we might have been even less sanguine than we were. As we now know, communications were poor to say the least, the Germans had secured the airfield at Maleme and were reinforcing their troops as fast as they could go through a sky devoid of opposing planes.

Our troops were pinned down through ferocious and almost continuous dive-bombing whilst enemy troops crept ever and ever nearer. Short of food and water, ammunition supplies beginning to look precarious, no wonder the sour odour of defeat began to manifest itself. There was talk ashore of a move towards the beaches on the south coast, and evacuation. Such talk, even if officers and NCOs tried to stop it, was hardly conducive to our offensive spirit. Blissfully ignorant of all this, we received orders at 0700 for our next 'milk run'. With the commandos still on board, no prizes were given as to our destination; we thought it unlikely that we were to land them off Tripoli in a Keyesian attack on Rommel's HQ.

When it was given out where we were to go, I must confess to a feeling of bile in the pit of my stomach. Oh no, please not Suda Bay! This was going to be a hazardous trip with a vengeance, and one in which our chances of survival would not have had the directors of Ladbroke's rushing to open a book.

Roskill writes of the situation at this time:

On land the garrison had fared ill on the 21st and 22nd and Suda Bay had been so heavily bombed that its continual use as a base, even for small craft, or as an entry for supplies and reinforcements for the Army, was practically impossible. Destroyers and the fast minelayer *Abdiel* [capable of 40knots] were now the only ships able to get through with urgently needed stores and they made a number of hazardous

HMAS *Nizam* – carrying troops evacuated from Crete – enters Alexandria harbour, May 1941. (Author's collection)

dashes in and out of Suda Bay on successive nights. The use of merchant ships for this purpose was several times attempted but was found to be suicidal. Even the fast 'Glen' ships could not do the round trip quickly enough to escape loss.

So there it was, but the foregoing extract from the history *The War at Sea* was written and published thirteen years after the events it described. We knew nothing of these attempts to use Suda Bay, but a shrewd guess would have produced the answer that it was probably a rather unhealthy place at the present time.

'Ours not to reason why...' Yes, well, the rest was best left unsaid. In any case, we were tired and getting more and more tired by the hour. We were mostly so busy that we did not have time to think, which was probably all to the good. You snatched a bit of rest when you could, but it certainly was not sleep as such. You snatched a meal when possible and attended to the calls of nature. I remember thinking several times when enthroned in the 'heads' how inconvenient it would be if the Luftwaffe chose to arrive overhead at that inauspicious moment! It was really quite miraculous but I never heard of anyone who was caught in such a situation. I suppose it must have happened to someone!

The storm had ceased, the Mediterranean had returned to its idyllic blue colour, the sea was calm. Ideal conditions for a pleasure cruise.

The quirks of fate are like a hand at bridge, capricious and unpredictable. We had had the storm with its attendant dark overcast when we were sailing to the south of Crete. Now, we had glorious weather which would be perfect for our aerial attackers, and our destination was to the north of the island which was now almost certainly enemy-held territory or at least a good part of it.

The troops revelled in it and sprawled out on deck sunning themselves and generally getting in the way once more. The Australian sailors exchanged good-humoured banter with the soldiers. The varied accents would have kept Professor Higgins occupied for years. For the outward journey at least, we had been dealt a bridge hand on which you could have called a Grand Slam, and made it.

Lord Haw Haw, our traitorous broadcaster from 'Gairmany' during the war used to taunt 'And where is the Ark Royal?' On this journey right into the wasps' nest, we might have retorted: 'And where is the Luftwaffe?'

It was quite incredible, but we never saw or heard an enemy aircraft (we had long ago given up expecting to see ours) during our passage of the Kaso Strait and beyond. My journal:

We entered the Kaso Strait at 1800, having gone to action stations at 1700. It seemed an absolute miracle that we were not bombed out of the water, as for about three hours we were steaming in full view of Crete and in broad daylight. However, we did not even sight one enemy plane, for which we have a lot to be thankful.

From now on, at action stations and steaming westwards along the northern coast of Crete, we were keyed up, and apprehensive of what was to come. I was glad I was not in

Evacuation from Crete.
(Author's collection)

charge of the flotilla's pilotage. To enter an unknown harbour in broad daylight, which is unencumbered with wrecks, is one thing. To enter the same harbour in pitch darkness, in company with other ships, no lights or buoys to guide you, blazing and sunken wrecks all around, and the German Army battering at the gates of the port, is quite another. That was our task. The reader will perhaps now gather why I was somewhat glad to be so junior that my powers of ship handling, navigation and general guidance were not called upon. It is at times best to know one's place.

Abdiel, the fast minelayer, was our leader followed by Captain (D) in *Napier*, ourselves and *Hero*. A tiny shaded white light shone its feeble beam astern of *Abdiel*. Every other ship shone a similar light except of course the after destroyer. We entered Suda Bay at 2300 but it was not for another one and a half hours that we secured alongside the quay. The bay is long, wide and is situated in an east-west direction. In more peaceful times it made a good fleet anchorage; now it had become a maritime graveyard, and about as dangerous a place into which to sail as one could imagine.

We crept into the bay as slowly and as cautiously as we could. This required the most expert ship handling. A ship is not like a car in a traffic jam. If she steams too slowly she loses steerage way and cannot be adequately controlled. Put on too many revs and you could easily run into a partially or wholly submerged wreck, in which position the Luftwaffe or the Wehrmacht or both would find you in the morning. An unpleasant prospect. Muttered orders came from the bridge, the engine room telegraph clanged – couldn't they mute that, it seemed as though the whole German Army could hear it.

Dusty Miller and the Captain came down into the plot on occasions to look at the chart. The night vision lights now in use in Combat Information Centres had yet to be invented.

The plot lights would automatically be extinguished when the door was opened and they studied the chart by torchlight, so that on return to the pitch darkness of the bridge they would not be too 'blinded'.

Everyone spoke in undertones, even in parts of the ship where it did not matter. The hazards of our undertaking were appreciated by all, and reflected in our actions. It was like being in a submarine whose Captain has ordered 'Silent routine' to fox the enemy's hydrophones.

How *Abdiel*, our leader, found the way in, I shall never know. For us, there was no way of measuring her speed, it just had to be done by the size of the already small white sternlight. If and when she turned, that was not immediately apparent either. For those on the bridge it was a nightmare, unfortunately real and one which could end in great tragedy. The length of time it took us to come alongside the quay at Suda is a measure of the difficulties of our passage.

One sees many depictions of what Hell is supposed to be like. If I could paint, I need only portray Suda Bay on that ghastly, hideous night. Nothing would be needed to embellish it, all the Satanic ingredients were there to complete the picture. The harbour was full of sinking vessels. Some were still burning and gurgling as they settled down to a watery grave. To the north of the bay a ship burned fiercely making a beacon for enemy bombers. The darkness, apart from the fires, was intense, but you could smell dense smoke. The whole place reeked of death and defeat.

As soon as we were secured alongside, we ushered the troops of Layforce ashore. I had, as usual, very little time to think about anything but I do remember thinking, 'Dear God, how awful, quite awful, to be a soldier.' There these wretches were, being pitchforked into the, as yet, bloodiest battle of the war. As we shall see later Layforce acquitted itself admirably and lived to fight another day. It appeared to be sheer and utter chaos in Suda Bay. Those ashore said that there was no organisation at all and everything was a complete shambles. People just wandered about, you could not tell friend from foe.

Poor Layforce. That very morning, 27 May, General Freyberg, C-in-C Crete, sent a message to London. Transmitted at 0930 it pointed out that the situation in Crete had become 'most serious' and that it was unlikely that Suda Bay could be held for another 24 hours, if as long.

So, although we did not know it at the time, we were the last British ships to enter and leave the port. What a prospect, we might have entered in the pitch darkness to find the Germans in control! Far too near capture for comfort.

At that time though, we needed no telling how precarious the situation was. My journal records: 'The sound of German machine guns could be heard whilst we were in the bay, and we were told that units of their army were only four miles away.' And we were landing puny reinforcements to march straight into their arms along with all their weapons and supplies which we had transported over those hazardous waters. Dear Heaven, what a mess, what a pathetic waste.

It is not often that 'Clear lower deck' is piped in the Royal Navy. It is usually ordered for a pronouncement by the Captain, which he wishes, by his physical presence, to carry more weight than a broadcast over the loudspeakers. It is also ordered when a particularly serious situation demands that as many hands as possible are put to work, including officers. The old days of coaling ship was one case in point, our delivery of Layforce and urgent supplies was another.

I helped with everyone else, passing packing cases, guns, ammunition. Had I known that I was being an acting quartermaster for the Wehrmacht, I would not have worked with such a will. There is a story that the British quartermaster in Alexandria sent a number of packing cases containing shoe polish instead of food. What the wretched soldiers who unpacked them said does not bear thinking about. Doubtless, many German feldwebels were smartly turned out for long afterwards.

My journal goes on: 'Unloading troops and stores took only 40 minutes – a magnificent effort on the part of everyone when one realises it was done in complete darkness with not even a torch allowed. I wondered if someone, or a packing case, would fall in the 'drink' but no one did!

Having disembarked 750 troops and 150 tons of ammunition we set about embarking some wounded. These were mostly 'walking wounded', and some of their injuries appeared to be superficial. Others though had been badly mutilated by bombs.' Our doctor got busy.

Meanwhile, precious minutes were ticking by, and whenever one's mind had a moment for reflection, it zeroed in on the ghastly thought of the return journey. That we were to make the return journey at all was something, but the picture of dawn and waiting Stukas was highly unpleasant.

We left the doomed harbour of Suda at 0215. Never have I been so glad to leave a place or to feel the engines thrumming once more beneath my feet.

Our ordeal started almost as soon as we had slipped and were a little distance from Suda Harbour. An enemy plane began dropping flares just where we had been unloading. Again my journal: 'Flares were also dropped over the burning ship, and then they were dropped just astern of *Abdiel* who was coming up astern of us. The plane followed us up the bay for some distance, but we had always moved into shadow just as the water space we had so recently vacated was made light as day. Fortunately for us no bombs were dropped, but Suda was bombed just after we left.'

How lucky we had been. Had we been a little later, we would have been sitting ducks alongside and I have little doubt that to the awful gurgling of the sinking ships would have been added our own plug-hole noises. I breathed a sigh of relief as we cleared the end of the bay, turned and headed eastward at 31 knots.

We were too late. Dawn found us still to the west of the Kaso Strait, and at 0545 we were attacked by five planes. Dive-bombers these, they screamed down at us whilst we jinxed desperately this way and that to avoid their unloaded cargoes. *Hero* was damaged but managed to continue under her own steam. *Abdiel* and ourselves came through unscathed.

It was in this attack that we found our poor wounded passengers such a hindrance. Some were accommodated on the upper deck, and because we could not, as previously explained, rush through between decks, we found getting to our action stations much more difficult.

Once more we felt how utterly naked and exposed we were to whatever the enemy cared to do to us. There was no cover whatsoever, we could only twist and turn and hope for the best.

An aerial bombardment leaves you very much shaken for a while, but we had survived our ordeal and hoped we would survive others which would doubtless come our way. At 0800 we were once more under aerial attack, this time from high-level bombers. If I have to be bombed at all, and basically it is something I could do without, I would rather be bombed from on high than be dive-bombed.

The infinite menace of the swept-back wings of the Stuka, the scream of the machine itself and then of its bomb are enough to strike terror into the bravest. Add to that the ever-present possibility of being machine-gunned as it howls down, and on levelling-out, and you will see the lesser of two evils is high in the sky.

It is difficult though, to ascertain the path of a bomb dropped from a great height, and it can arrive uncomfortably close before you see it, making avoiding action almost impossible. You just hope you have a bad bomb aimer above you! Huge spouts of water rose all around us, but we bore a charmed life and survived.

Incredibly, no more attacks came our way and we arrived in Alexandria at 1900. A ghastly sight caught our eyes as we entered harbour. There was our beautiful former protectress, the aircraft carrier *Formidable*. She had a great gaping hole in her starboard side extending through from the flight deck down to her waterline.

So that was that, no more naval fighter protection for the Eastern Mediterranean Fleet until Italy surrendered. Why had *Formidable* been allowed to get so near enemy air-bases? Would the non-aviator admirals never learn that you should not so hazard your one and only precious carrier? Probably not.

We secured to our buoy at 2130 and, exhausted, slept like logs. What, no air raid? No – thankfully.

There was to be little rest for us. The situation in Crete had deteriorated speedily, with the Germans flying in reinforcements and the British completely unable, with the loss of Suda Bay, to do anything to assist the army but evacuate the troops. This was now to be our task.

Once more provisioned and ammunitioned, we left Alexandria at 0800 on 28 May after only thirteen hours in We had been lent a whaler from *Formidable* who obviously had no further use for it. It would increase the number and speed with which we could evacuate the troops. Our fellow rescuers were the destroyers *Napier* (Australian), *Kandahar* and *Kelvin*.

Once more we pounded northwards at full speed, and as before, the nearer we got to Crete, the more anxiously we scanned the sky, the more trigger-happy the gunners became.

Maybe there were people praying for us. If so, their intercessions with the Almighty were bearing fruit – miracle of miracles, no enemy aircraft appeared. Where were they? No one knew, but as long as they were not in our vicinity we did not much care.

Strangely, after we had been so nearly torpedoed and sunk off Scarpanto, nobody seemed to think of a submarine attack. We could contemplate only the bombing threat after we had been subjected to so much of it. Perhaps our high speed and zigzag made it difficult for a submarine to position itself, and so subconsciously we relaxed as far as that danger was concerned.

We were bound, we were told, for the small fishing village of Sphakia which lay on the southern coast of Crete. We all heaved a sigh of relief. At last, someone had had some sense and had realised that the north coast of Crete was untenable for the Royal Navy.

I.M.G. Stewart in his book *The Struggle for Crete* puts the situation in a nutshell:

> The island of Crete was not well-endowed with port facilities suitable for evacuating our army. Indeed, [since Suda Bay had been lost – author] Heraklion was the only place with any port facilities at all where warships could berth alongside a jetty or quay.
>
> The bulk of the evacuation from Crete had to be made from the small open beach at Sphakia. Sphakia lay at the foot of a 500-foot escarpment, access to which was gained by a near two-hour scramble down a narrow, twisting goat track in the dark. The fishing village, for that is all it was, possessed a shingle beach which it wore like an apron. About 200 yards in width, it shelved ideally for small boats to embark troops.

We arrived at Sphakia at midnight, and immediately lowered our boats. The Gunner (T) was in charge of the little flotilla consisting of our two motor boats towing whalers. Off they went in the dark, meanwhile some troops were already arriving at our gangway in their own boats. This showed initiative, but were they queue jumpers? We did not ask.

As these dirty, desperately weary men hauled themselves on board I was struck by the melodrama of the situation. Often a man would arrive at the guard-rail, flop on to the iron deck and gasp, 'Thank God for the Navy.' That it was genuine there was no doubt, but I

Sphakia,
Crete.
(Imperial War
Museum)

remember thinking in a detached way that it seemed like a script from a rather second-rate war film.

Roskill writes on this:

> In every one of the evacuation accounts left by troops in the ships that took them off appears the sustaining, almost blind faith that, if they could only reach the coast somewhere, the Navy would rescue them. One young New Zealander called it the ever-present hope of contacting the Navy, and another wrote that during all the long retreat our one hope and thought was the Navy.

It was nice to know that our sacrifices and efforts had not gone unappreciated.

Wounded came off too. I was sorry we had no better facilities for getting them on board; they just had to climb up the ladder like anyone else which must have been hell.

'The Germans are only eight miles away,' someone gasped as he collapsed on deck like a large floundering fish. We were getting blasé. Only two nights ago we had been half that distance from German machine guns – what was eight miles! They were not far from the hilltops overlooking Sphakia, so speed was of the essence. Fortunately no one bombed the little port, why, I cannot imagine, but the enemy bombed neighbouring beaches throughout the night, and as we left we could see flashes up in the hills.

The ship was crammed and could take no more. We left at 0300 and headed for base. My journal records:

> We were not attacked at dawn, and by 0900 we thought we were fairly safe. However at 0910, as I was sitting in the Ward Room, the alarm bells went and before I had time to get out of the door, a terrific explosion threw us all back. All the glasses shattered, and some of the lights as well. A high-level bomber had approached unseen and dropped a 'stick' – one of which was this extremely near miss on the port quarter. I thought the damage caused would be very great, but it amounted to one shell-hoist being put temporarily out of action and a slight leak aft.

I was wrong about the damage being only slight, as will be seen later, but the above was written only hours after the attack.

Alexandria was reached at teatime without further incident. We disembarked our troops, oiled and went on our buoy at 2130.

There had been little time to get to know any of the soldiers personally. They had flopped down on the upper or mess decks, dead tired. So were we, but we had not had to march across gruelling country in blazing heat with the enemy at our heels. Once again I thanked my lucky stars that if I had to fight a war at all, it was not as a poor bloody infantryman.

The hour of midnight passed, and with it came Friday 30 May and the inevitable air raid. We were again too tired to bother. There was no shelter to which we could go anyway (in Malta servicemen sheltered in the caves), so let the army gunners deal with the enemy. We desperately needed sleep to deal with another evacuation trip. The latter was delayed,

HMAS
Nizam lands
her troops,
evacuated
from Crete, in
Alexandria. The
author can be
seen just below
the bridge.
(Imperial War
Museum)

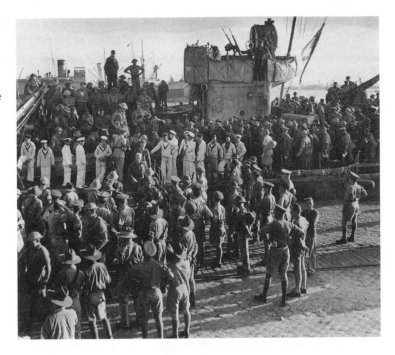

for which the air raid was to be thanked. Aircraft-laid mines were suspected, and until the passage out of harbour was pronounced clear, we could not leave.

Precious hours went by – we should have left at 0530 but did not sail until 1000. Our flotilla leader, *Napier*, was in the rear accompanied by the destroyers *Kandahar* and *Kelvin*. All the trips we had undertaken to Crete had been eventful. This one was to be more eventful than most. According to my journal:

> Just as we got outside [the harbour entrance] we stopped suddenly and white smoke poured from our funnel. The Captain sent for me. He ordered me to go and ask Commander [E] what was wrong. I found that as a result of the near miss yesterday, water had entered Nos. 7 and 8 oil fuel tanks, and of course, as we were steaming on these, water had seeped into the boilers.
>
> We got under way again in a quarter of an hour, making twenty-four knots on one boiler. We signalled to *Napier*, informing D7 that naturally Nos. 7 and 8 oil fuel tanks were useless, necessitating the discharge of 120 tons of oil fuel which we could ill afford to do. We were told to carry on.

How lucky our enforced stop had not taken place much later. Just how lucky will be seen in a moment.

At teatime we sighted a large convoy headed towards Alexandria, presumably full of evacuated soldiers. My journal entry reads: 'This convoy was being bombed, and we soon received the attentions of the bombers.'

Alarm bells had rung, everyone was at Action Stations once more (we never seemed to do anything else), the ship zigzagging and squirming at our best possible speed. The deck heeled over at an angle of about 45 degrees and then back again as Lieutenant-Commander Clark tried desperately to avoid the falling bombs.

The 4.5" guns, now in high angle, shook the whole ship, whilst the eight-barrel pom-poms added their multiple chatter to the din. Shell and cartridge cases littered the deck.

Six enemy aircraft were attacking us. It was a miracle that we were not hit, but suddenly a cry went up, '*Kandahar*'s been hit.' A moment later, '*Kelvin's* been hit.' Who was to be next? Fortunately it turned out that both destroyers had sustained near misses, not hits, but these were bad enough to make them a liability on our mission and they were ordered to return to Alexandria. Lucky them I thought. *Napier* and ourselves were left alone in the ocean to continue on towards Crete and further danger.

Our former companions signalled: 'We hate to have to leave you. God speed.' Yes, well, nice of them, but it was with leaden hearts that we watched their departure. We two ships would make a much more compact target for the Luftwaffe. We could have done with their concentrated firepower too. We longed for darkness. Blessed night enveloped us once more and we were comparatively safe, although a sharp lookout was kept for E-boats. The thought of our near sinking off Scarpanto was fresh in our memories.

The ship's clock showed midnight, the date Saturday 31 May. We, the only two destroyers left, were still pounding towards Crete. On the bridge, shadowy figures peered into shaded instruments. Muted reports were heard, disembodied, echoing from voicepipes, the recipients sometimes unnecessarily fearful, closed the cover, shutting off the voice in a strangled gurgle. The inevitable cocoa appeared (not made by me thank goodness) and was gulped as eagerly as though it was a large tot of brandy.

The Captain sat, immobile now, in his bridge chair, peering like all of us, into the darkness which surrounded us. Below the bridge, sailors checked the whalers and motor-boats which would bring succour to the beleaguered troops awaiting our arrival.

Landfall at Sphakia was made at 0025. 'Stop engines' was ordered, the anchor chain rattled through the hawse pipe. Privately I could not help wishing the order had been 'Finished with engines' given at Alexandria!

Ashore, someone had done his homework. Where they had been found, no one knew, but troops began making their way out to us in invasion barges, whilst our own boats helped swell the number. As before, they made their awkward way on board, some with weapons, others with just their lives. It was appropriate I thought, that those we were saving were nearly all Anzac troops – New Zealand Maoris, some Australians, some Greeks plus naval and RAF personnel.

The messdecks began to be crammed. We were first and foremost a fighting ship, not a troopship, and the Captain started to get worried. To alleviate his worries he sent for his most junior officer – me. I arrived breathless on the bridge. 'Snotty,' he said, 'I am concerned that we may get too many troops on board, and the ship may become unstable. Go and count them and report back to me.'

What an order I thought. I thought it even more forcibly when I arrived on the messdecks.

Soldiers were everywhere, jam-packed like sardines. Most had cups of tea in their hands and 'wads' of gorgeous white bread and ham were being wolfed down, their first food and drink for a very long time. I thought dear God, how am I going to count this lot; it was not exactly a time to enforce discipline and yet I had to try.

It was then that I had a brilliant idea. Instead of my counting the troops, why not let them count themselves? I pulled out a whistle attached to my lifebelt and blew it hard. Conversation ceased and very weary heads turned towards me.

'Listen to me,' I shouted, 'We must know how many of you are on board.' (I did not dwell on the possibilities dependent on too many having partaken of our hospitality already; it was unthinkable, I imagined, that we should disembark any surplus!)

'I want you to number as though you were on parade,' I said, 'starting from where I stand and going back away from me.' There were murmurs, and then, blessed relief, it started. 'One, two, three,' and so on. It may not have been parade ground stuff but it was music to my ears. I reported 645 to the Captain. In addition, we had 53 officers.

We learned later that *Napier*, our sister ship, had a more varied assortment of personnel on board. Their tally, beside the troops, included three women, one Greek, one Chinaman, ten merchant seamen, two children and one dog! Everyone was afraid of the bombing – I am glad I did not know of the children and the dog until we had arrived safely in Alexandria. The dog especially must have been terrified, but I am delighted it was saved. What ever had caused the Chinaman's presence on Crete? History does not relate.

At last we could take no more, and the ladder was pulled up, our boats hoisted inboard. I felt so desperately sorry for those left behind on the beach. Later, after the war, survivors of the POW camps told their stories. A number recalled that it was the most awful moment of their lives when they heard the rattle of our anchor chain, and knew that there was now no hope of rescue. They had endured a terrible, long and arduous march, over mountains and goat tracks, short of food and tortured with thirst only to find that it had all been for nothing. Some could not take it and shot themselves in nearby caves.

There had been a picket on the beach, four deep and with fixed bayonets, holding back those who were trying to rush the boats. Oh yes, there was panic among some, as there was to be at Singapore later. It was confined mostly to unformed bodies of men, stragglers from their units. They were the flotsam left to the not so tender mercies of the Germans. Only organised formations of troops were allowed off the beach.

The next morning, German officers, towels in their hands, were bathing on the beach we had so recently vacated, whilst their prisoners began their weary march back to the north and the prison camps. Only the bravest of spirits could have survived that.

We left at 0300, making best possible speed of 30 knots. There were several E-boat scares and we were challenged by a ship just as we left, but all was well. Not for long. My journal:

At 0900 we were bombed. We had, however, some fighter protection, and but for this we would probably have now ceased swimming. We were attacked by no less than 34 aircraft, all JU88 long-range bombers. A stick of bombs landed right in the track of this ship, and where we would have been if we had not been zigzagging violently. Bombs whistled very close to us, but I am glad to say none actually hit us. [All this was written only hours after the event. It sounds the understatement of the day!]

With *Napier* however, it was a very different story. She received a very near miss which cracked her port turbine and reduced her speed to 23 knots. During the afternoon, about 1500, *Napier* suddenly stopped and blew off a lot of steam. We asked if we could tow her but she replied No, she was going ahead slowly. Eventually she made twenty knots and steered a steady course, whilst we were told to zigzag ahead of her, doing an anti-submarine sweep. This we continued to do all the way back to Alexandria, where we arrived at 1830.

Just outside the boom, *Jackal* [a destroyer], was lying and she gave us three hearty cheers as we steamed past. We went alongside the quay where all the troops disembarked. It was evidently quite an event, as there were lots of officers to receive us, as well as 'newsreel cameramen and reporters'.

As for us, we were completely exhausted. I would have liked at that moment, to have slept for a week. The resilience of the human body however is very high, particularly when you are only eighteen years of age. But, just at that time I felt deathly tired and could not have lifted a finger to evacuate anyone else. A selfish view perhaps, but one just thought how lucky one was to have gone through that infernal torment of bombs, machine-gun fire and torpedoes, and come out safely the other side.

Cunningham, in his memoirs, writes of that day:

I shall never forget the sight of those ships coming up harbour, the guns of their fore turrets awry, one or two broken off and pointing forlornly skyward, their upper decks crowded with troops, and the marks of their ordeal only too plainly visible.

How did the balance sheet look then, and now, after 70 years have elapsed?

Firstly, the entry in my journal about Layforce (whom we had landed in Suda Bay) falling into the hands of the enemy was fortunately premature and pessimistic. They had apparently fought with skill, vigour and great courage, and had provided the rear-guard all the way across the mountains to Sphakia. As a reward for their efforts they were among the first to be taken off by sea. No one had the time to question any of the troops evacuated, but later I discovered that we had brought off units of Layforce including their CO, Brigadier Laycock.

It was long after the war, when I made one of my frequent trips to the Imperial War Museum, that I found out that amongst the Layforce officers we had rescued was none other than Evelyn Waugh, a fact I found in his war diary. In the diary was the entry: 'our journey back to Alexandria was without incident.' All I can conclude is that Waugh, like so many others, must have been worn out and slept through the bombing attack we

Ships lost and damaged during the campaign to evacuate the British Army from Greece and Crete, April/May 1941. (Blandford Press)

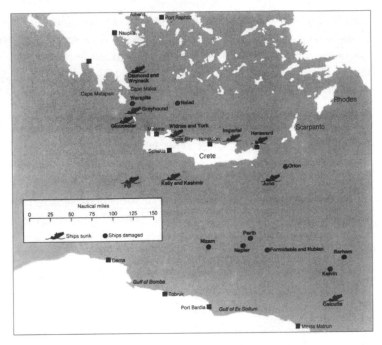

had undergone. I had done so myself in harbour when our own guns were firing during an air raid.

A semi-fictional account of Waugh's service in Crete appears in his novel *Officers and Gentlemen*. Waugh had joined the commandos at a senior age and had been posted as Intelligence Officer to Layforce.

At a dinner party years later I recounted the story and a guest inquired 'what had he got to say for himself, was he polite?' Waugh could on occasion be very rude. My dinner companion did not realise that in those conditions officers just dossed down on the deck of the Ward Room, dead tired. It was not exactly a social occasion. Still, I count my very minor part in rescuing Evelyn Waugh as a great contribution to English literature...

But back to the balance sheet. Secondly, it was more than fortunate for the course of the war that we had the Italian Navy opposing us and not the German.

The day after our return from our final trip to Crete we were put at one hour's notice for steam. The reason, we understood, was that the Italian Navy might very well make a sortie as a result of the sad depletion of the British Mediterranean fleet.

There would have been very little to stop them. Practically every one of our ships had been damaged in some way, some very seriously indeed, necessitating docking for months. That the Italians did not venture out was no doubt due in great part to the slaughter we had inflicted on them at Matapan.

Thirdly, had it all been worth it? Was our incursion into Greece and then Crete with the most fearful losses in men and ships, a creditable enterprise or a 'Charge of the Light

Brigade'. Had it been in that immortal phrase: '*C'est magnifique. Mais ce n'est pas la guerre?*'

The answer is, seen in June 1941 and from the viewpoint of a very junior officer, emphatically no. We could never have maintained our forces in Greece and Crete, in the face of overwhelming German air superiority. Malta and Tobruk were difficult enough to supply by sea, and the latter fell anyway. We could never have succoured them plus Greece and Crete.

Looked at after 70 years have elapsed however, and with the 30-year rule letting some, but not all felines out of bags, it is a very different story indeed.

The most important point and the whole purpose of the Greece and Crete operations was to gain time for Russia. Churchill, with wondrous bounty afforded to him by Ultra, knew of Operation *Barbarossa*, the German plan to invade Russia, months before it took place. Veteran strategist that he was, he saw instantly that if Russia was not to be crushed within weeks, the German onslaught must be so delayed that it would be slowed up or stopped with the onset of the terrible Russian winter.

The original date for the German invasion of Russia had been April 1941. In fact, due to the drain imposed on the German forces by our resistance in Greece and Crete, it did not take place until 21 June. The delay of two months was vital for Russia and fatal for Germany.

So certain had Hitler and his staff been of a blitzkrieg in Russia, that the Wehrmacht was not issued with winter clothing. It was assumed that the German army would have been in Moscow in six weeks, snug in warm houses and barracks. So they might have been if it had not been for the Royal Navy and the British Dominion troops.

The *Dad's Army* song speaks of 'Mr Hitler, we've stopped your little game'. Well, it was no little game, but our resistance in the Balkans may well have been Churchill's hinge of fate. Thank Heaven no Hollywood film producer has had the nerve to star Errol Flynn as a latter-day Byron.

We may also have saved Malta in this way. The Germans had plans for a paratroop landing on the island, prior to an Axis invasion. The German paratroops landed in Crete were picked off like pheasants by our troops, and thousands were killed. Hitler never unleashed them again. Further, it is now known that had not Freyberg given orders to evacuate Crete, the Germans themselves were going to have given in the next day! Such is fate.

We in the Navy had fulfilled all the tasks given to us. No seaborne landings were made by the enemy until his airborne forces had conquered the island. About 18,000 out of the 32,000 men that made up the garrison were evacuated. But at what price? Two battleships and one aircraft carrier had been damaged, the *Warspite* and *Formidable* so severely, they were sent to the US for extensive repairs. Dear *Valiant*, she stayed on station in spite of bomb damage. Three cruisers and six destroyers were sunk, and six cruisers and seven destroyers damaged. All this had been accomplished by air power alone. The old men who, pre-war, sat in the Admiralty and pooh-poohed the idea of air attack overwhelming naval vessels had a great deal to answer for. Air Marshal Tedder: 'Sea power could not henceforth be exercised independently of air power.'

13

Syria

'I am one of the few Englishmen since Waterloo who has actually fought the French'
– Author

After the trials and tribulations, not to say extreme weariness of the Battle of Crete, we all thought, perhaps not unjustifiably, that we were entitled to some respite. Yes, well, of sorts, but not for long. This was war, and like firemen, whenever there was a call, we had to answer it. It was soon to come.

What remained of the fleet lay in Alexandria harbour licking its wounds. The lovely cruiser *Orion* was moored near us. My journal records: 'She looks extremely battered, the covering being off 'B' turret altogether.' What I wrote then was an understatement. *Orion* had been attacked by eleven Stuka dive-bombers. Her captain had been killed by an explosive bullet. A bomb had pierced her bridge, exploding on the stokers' mess-deck. Crowded with evacuated troops, she had 260 killed and 280 wounded. For some hours she had limped out of control and on fire. Had we received such a hit, being a much smaller ship we would undoubtedly have sunk within minutes.

Crete however, was behind us, the island had surrendered to the Germans and the poor devils we had to leave there were consigned to the camps. After the war I was to hear the following from a neighbour who gave himself up to some German officers in the north of the island. The latter were cleaning their weapons. One, who spoke English, said to him, 'We are rather busy today, could you come back tomorrow?' Sadly, my friend reflected that he had little better to do. The daily routine of a ship must, like good housekeeping, go on, and we were no exception. Parts of ship and weapons had to be cleaned, stores and ammunition taken on board, charts brought up to date. I was ordered to collect some of the latter from the Chart Depot, and to correct them, using the information in Notices to Mariners. Poor *Orion*, it was some of her charts that I was given. I considered she was unlikely to require them for many months to come. I was ordered to give priority to the charts of Cyprus. Rumour had it that this would be the Germans' next objective, with a view to taking Syria and driving on to the Suez Canal. Oh God, I thought, please, not another Crete! That would really be too much.

We bathed over the side and relaxed as much as we could. It was a relief not to have the engines throbbing and thrumming under our feet. The latter, and their attendant staff, came in for much praise from the Captain when he addressed the assembled ship's company after prayers on Sunday. He said that from 4 May to 4 June (all the time I had been aboard, and the ship on the Mediterranean station) she had steamed 10,700 miles, which if worked out, is equivalent to steaming at well over fifteen knots for every minute of the time she had been out here. No wonder we were tired!

On 4 June there was the inevitable air raid. We opened fire but I was so exhausted that I never woke up even whilst our own guns were belching forth their defiance! This may have accounted for the fact that my journal records: 'Some bombs were dropped, and one landed on a quay about 100 yards from the ship, but it did not do much damage.' My entry for the next day corrects this: 'Apparently the air raid last night was on a much bigger scale than I thought. (It certainly was!) High explosive and incendiary bombs were dropped, 150 people killed and 200 injured. Many of the bombs dropped in the native quarter and I do not think any naval ships were hit.' As far as I know, they never were.

The near miss which we had received on 29 May had caused more damage than we thought. Our 'A' bracket was rattling badly, causing wear on the propeller shaft. (The 'A' bracket is a support for the propeller shaft.) Docking us was the only answer and we duly entered the small Gabbari dock on 11 June. I had not realised before what a dreadful plague flies can be. Like mosquitoes they do not like salt water, and so, attached to our buoy as we usually were, they were no problem. Here in Gabbari dock we were literally ashore. It was awful, intense heat, flies everywhere and you could not close scuttles (portholes) as then you could hardly breathe. Once again I thought of soldiers enduring not only the enemy but flies as well. Rather them than me!

Two days previously, British and Free French troops had marched into Syria.

Put very briefly, Raschid Ali had attacked the British air base of Habbaniyah in Iraq on 2 May 1941. He employed 9000 Iraqi troops and 50 field guns. He then appealed for help to Germany on 4 May. Germany demanded the immediate use of Syrian airfields for German squadrons on their way to Iraq. Vichy France, to which Syria was bound, agreed to comply with the German demands.

Britain had no other course but to invade Syria in order to put a stop to what was potentially an extremely serious threat to her eastern flank in the Middle East. My journal entry of 9 June 1941 is a masterpiece of understatement coupled with no little naïveté: 'Nothing much happened today except that Great Britain and Free France marched into Syria to prevent further German infiltration. This was done only this morning.'

In my own defence, I must point out that a midshipman's journal was meant to contain firstly, an account of the doings of the ship in which he was serving, and secondly any events of international importance. That the happenings in Syria were very soon to involve *Nizam* and hence myself was crystal ball stuff and would have been rightly stamped upon by any 'snotties' nurse' worthy of his salt – or gin.

We spent four days in dock, our docking and undocking being delayed due to the absence of Egyptian labour. The fellaheen had panicked after the last two air raids and were conspicuous by their absence. We provided the docking parties; much sucking of teeth on the part of the lower deck.

As we were now literally ashore, the ship's company emulated the practice as in Malta and evacuated the ship by night except for security parties. Those lucky enough to be on watch ashore were billeted at Sidi Bishr, a pre-war bathing beach for the wealthy and out of reach of enemy bombs unless they were very inaccurate. I had yet to see a bomb strike any of HM ships, and elected to stay on board revelling in the luxury of my cabin – in spite of the flies!

We undocked at 1900 on 16 June and hoped for a further night in harbour. Did I say I was naive? I must have been, we had our operational orders (fetched by me from the office of C-in-C, feeling most important), and at 2230 we sailed alone for Haifa.

Making 30 knots, we arrived off Haifa at 1115 the following day. The signal station was situated on top of Mount Carmel which dominates the town. We called it up and received no reply. Only much later, when we were abeam, did they wake up and ask us who we were!

The sight of three cruisers and six destroyers met our eyes. One destroyer, *Isis*, was damaged as the result of a bomb. Whose bomb? German? Italian? No, French. It really beat the band, gall rose into my mouth. Here we were, we who had held the line absolutely alone against Germany and Italy for fourteen months, and now we were confronted with this destruction caused by none other than our former ally!

I fully realise that this is too simplistic an approach to take. High politics, so-called national honour, coupled with pig-headedness were to blame. General Dentz, the French C-in-C Syria, clung to the 'legality' of the Franco-German armistice. General de Gaulle thought that Syria, once it knew of Free French involvement, would fall into our arms.

Both were wrong. Dentz was sentenced to death in 1945 for his adherence to Vichy. De Gaulle continued to trade on national pride for many a year. The fact remains that Dentz's opposition to us cost 6500 French casualties and 4600 Allied. What a tragedy, and how Hitler must have roared with laughter, if he was capable of such a thing.

The cold, stark fact remains that we were now based in Haifa to fight the French, and it was thus that I became one of the few Englishmen since Waterloo to do so. It is not one of my opening conversational gambits when I am in that country.

Oiling was easy. The 600-mile long pipeline ended in Haifa. All you had to do was berth alongside the oil quay and connect up, rather like a filling station!

No peace for the wicked, and although some ships were giving leave that night, we were to spend it at sea. Off at 1900 in company with one cruiser and three destroyers, our orders were to bombard Tripoli (no, not Libya, Syria), and then 'have a look in' at Beirut (my journal) on the way back. All a false alarm, and we could have given leave or got our heads down. At 2330 we received the signal 'Bombardment cancelled', and we made for home without 'looking in' at Beirut. I was grateful. I could not help feeling that a Government Health Warning might have been added to the orders to 'look in' on that city.

On our return to Haifa I went ashore for the first time to look around. My first impression was what a pleasant change it made from Alexandria. Green hills could be seen instead of a dingy brown everywhere. The town was clean and did not smell. It had an air of modernity about it, and, apart from French air raids(!), safety. You were unlikely to be mugged or set upon going back to the docks. That was to follow after the war with the murderous activities of Irgun Zwai Leumi and the Stern Gang.

The prime purpose of our presence in Haifa was to assist the army's advance northwards along the coast road by bombardment and, should we come across any French naval forces in so doing, to engage them and sink them if possible. Memories of history lessons at Dartmouth flooded back. Nelson at the Battle of the Nile, Aboukir. What an extraordinary and tragic 'grand bouleversement' to find ourselves once more pitted against our traditional enemy. David Price-Jones in his *Paris in the Third Reich*, describes how Admiral Darlan as prime minister, consented that German supplies should flow through Vichy-controlled Syria. What is worse is that Rudolf Rahn, the German embassy troubleshooter, was dispatched to Syria where he quickly arranged for French armaments to be released for use against the British and for air-bases to become available. In Rahn's memoirs, he described the goodwill he found among the French in Syria. So much for our allies. We found a distinct absence of goodwill among them. Their goodwill to us consisted of bombs, torpedoes and shelling. Who was perfidious in Syria in June 1941? John Bull or Marianne?

The next day we sailed in the evening and swept up the coast. Morning came and with its light we bombarded the coast road. Nobody really seemed to mind this, and with some feeling that we had been gallant for nothing, we turned around and headed for Haifa. Our sweep had taken us up past Beirut however, and it was odd to see the city brilliantly lighted against the Stygian blackness of the rest of the coast. The French had declared it an open city, so of course we were not supposed to poop off at it. There were those who were unkind enough to say that this was merely a ruse of the wily French to bring reinforcements into the port more easily. I am sure that these unworthy thoughts were swiftly suppressed in their minds. I had not seen a lighted city since we left Durban in October 1940. Whatever the reason for the illumination, it was a wonderful sight to those used to dreary blackouts for so long.

Back in Haifa at 0800, out again at 2000 that evening. When did we sleep? I never seem to remember. My family laugh at me and say, 'Daddy spent most of the war asleep.' Very wise too, but they were thinking of the incidents of the bulkhead light at Matapan, and later the 'human torpedo' attack in Alexandria. The reverse is probably nearer the truth, at least in this particular stage of the war!

We were a big force this time. The cruisers *Naiad* and *Leander*, the former flying the flag of the Admiral Commanding the Fifteenth Cruiser Squadron (CS15), plus eight destroyers.

This powerful array of ships was being sent out to look for and destroy the French 36-knot destroyer *Cassard*, which had been reported coming down the Syrian coast under cover of darkness. Could it be she had sailed from the open port of Beirut? Oh, surely not, what base and unworthy thoughts enter one's head.

CS15 ordered us to spread out in two search bodies, ourselves and four other destroyers being the searching force, while the two cruisers and three destroyers made up the striking force. I wondered idly which was the most dangerous, search or strike? And if we chanced upon the *Cassard*, how long before the cavalry came to our rescue? There should be a good old melee in that event!

As things turned out, an opportunity was missed, a foretaste of the next day's happenings. Let my journal describe the scene: 'Just as we went to Action Stations at midnight, a submarine report came through from *Jervis* (one of our search party). We expected to hear that she had sunk it, but no report came through, and it was only later we heard what had happened. *Jervis* came unexpectedly upon a submarine which was on the surface. She did not locate her by Asdic. The submarine was as surprised as *Jervis* and immediately crash-dived. Her conning-tower was just awash as the destroyer rushed past. All the hands being at Action Stations, there was no one on the depth charges, they were at the (torpedo) tubes!' So there was a wasted opportunity. Captain (D) would not wait, said enough time had been wasted already, and called off the hounds. But how damned silly; surely one destroyer could have been told to search for the sub by Asdic? That would still have left two cruisers and seven destroyers to deal with one enemy (sic) destroyer. Sledgehammers and nuts would appear to come into the picture somewhere.

The rest of the night was uneventful, and we never saw the *Cassard*. One unusual event did occur however, soon after dawn. An air alarm alert was flashed to us all, and we thought, 'Oh God, not a re-run of Crete after all the bombing we have undergone.' Well no, it was a wonderful, marvellous surprise. There up in the sky a few minutes later were our own fighters, our very own special fighter cover! We could not believe it, being so used in recent weeks to being utterly at the not so tender mercies of the Luftwaffe. Indeed, so badly did the fleet feel about lack of air cover in Greece and Crete that after the island had fallen, RAF personnel did not dare appear on the streets of Alexandria for fear of being beaten up by sailors suffering from prolonged enemy air attacks.

Quite unjustified of course – the RAF could not operate because the enemy had either bombed their airfields to pieces or overrun them and were using them instead. Try telling this to 'chocker' sailors though, you would receive a lusty response!

In that respect, Syria was a marvellous contrast to our previous aerial nakedness. The RAF gave us excellent fighter cover throughout the campaign, one of the pilots being Roald Dahl, the story writer, who has written his own account of his operations. Make the most of it boys, the future will not afford you such luxury again!

Back in harbour my journal records: 'N.O.L.C.'s. [Naval officer in charge] office is the only camouflaged building in Haifa, and therefore the most conspicuous!'

We had the night in harbour with no air raids. If we did not sleep the sleep of the just, we certainly slept the sleep of the exhausted.

Sunday 22 June 1941. 'Today, Germany declared war on Russia,' says my journal. Looking back, I do not think a declaration of war was the expression to have used. Attacked would probably have been nearer the mark. I have always loathed Communists, but I thought then, 'Well, if they are going to help us win the war, all well and good.'

Off we went again at nightfall, a large search and strike force as before. My journal:

We were to sweep up to Beirut and have a look right in to the harbour. [As I wrote it then, it sounds as though some huge naval doctor was going to say 'open wide please and say ALLAH!' before we administered some unpleasant medicine.] We were told to expect the shore batteries to open fire on us and 'to be ready to lay a smoke screen.'

Er, well, yes, quite – it sounded as though the 'throat inspection' was not going to be without its unpleasantness. Should I ask the MO for some binding medicine?   ·

The alarm buzzers sounded their terrible stomach-churning noise at midnight and we all rushed to our action stations. I busied myself keeping our DR position on the plot and wondered what was afoot. We were soon to know. My journal, written up the next day, gives a graphic account of events: 'All was peaceful until 0150 when an enemy report came from *Naiad* [cruiser] of a ship bearing 150°. Almost immediately after the enemy report came the sound of gun fire.

We had stumbled upon two Vichy French destroyers, one undoubtedly of the *Cassard* class. At 0155 we opened fire, and ceased fire at 0159 having fired 62 rounds in that time.

I went up to have a look at the action and found the whole scene lit up by starshell whilst tracer was all over the place. The range was only 055x and we ought to have blown them out of the water. However, although we saw at least a dozen hits on the *Cassard*, she and the other destroyer got away to the safety of the minefields.

Unlike Matapan, the enemy replied to our fire, and one shell from her 5.4" guns splashed into the sea not ten yards from our stern! *Naiad* fired three torpedoes, *Leander* two, and *Jaguar* two, whilst the French destroyer fired two at us, although without scoring any hits.

Altogether, it cannot be called a very successful action, since two cruisers and eight destroyers failed to sink the enemy at a range of less than a mile! All the time the action was in progress, the shore batteries in Beirut were firing at us, although luckily their fire was not very accurate.'

Well there we are, that was my contemporary account of our brush with the French navy. Looking back, I think I was either brave, naive or foolish to have made the acid comment with which I ended my entry. Whoever was later to inspect my journal might have thought it reflected on him, and certainly the Captain would have to see it before I left the ship! However, I felt the comment was right then and I feel it was right now. Cunningham probably still turns in his grave when he reflects on how we allowed them to get away. Nobody had deferred to Midshipman Holloway, that veteran of night fighting, fresh from Matapan and victory over three cruisers. Perhaps just as well, but a little more night encounter exercises would have stood our strike force in good stead. Few of our ships had been at Matapan; as a 'force de frappe' we had not 'frapped' so well!

The action did have its amusing side. A bearded officer on the bridge sported a green beard for a fortnight. The shell which had so nearly hit us showered the bridge with spray, the latter full of the chemical dye used by the French to spot their fall of shot!

I was furious that the enemy had had the temerity to actually fire back! I expected them to be like the Italians who seldom did such an ungentlemanly thing. It was really most off-putting and set me against the thought of French cuisine for a long time.

Should anyone ask me, if I had to undergo one or the other, which would I choose – to be bombed or shelled, I think I would choose the latter. To be bombed from the air at sea is a highly unpleasant experience because it is more prolonged. The aircraft wheels in the sky, a predatory bird eyeing its prey. We, the prey, await anxiously the unleashing of its deadly cargo, a cargo that can kill us outright, maim us horribly, or sink the ship, when we shall struggle for our lives in the water choking on oil fuel. We watch the aircraft as it circles, positions itself, and then commences its terrible screaming dive, a dive which will only end with the release of the bomb or stick of bombs and possible machine-gun bullets as well.

To be shelled is different. You are opposite your enemy, but suddenly a ripple of fire lights up his side; if he is using flashless cordite you do not even see this. You wait, rather like a rabbit fascinated by a snake, and then there is a whoosh and you are either hit or the shells splash into the sea and you hope fervently that his range-finder has been rendered U/S by the blast (unlikely), or that he has a stupid gunnery officer (perhaps), or that for whatever reason, the next salvo won't fall so close!

Modern science had by then made the rabbit and snake analogy horribly real, for I used to watch the radar screen, peer into it fixedly with fascination as the green trace showed the enemy shell leave its gun muzzle and make a lazy arc towards us. Oh, Sir Robert Watson-Watt (the British inventor of RD/F (radar), you had a lot to answer for on those occasions!

Back to Haifa at 0700 on 23 June, and on board arrived an Australian Naval Reserve midshipman. He and I were thrown together because of our rank, age and the close quarters in which we were forced to live. He came from a rather seedy part of 'Sydneye', with an accent to match. The reader will by now have guessed that we were not on the closest of terms. One day he said to me: 'Aouw, 'Olloway, are you going ashore on a beer run or a neyture run?' I think the fellow was referring to the 'Hotel Excelsior', a house of ill-repute in Haifa. Somehow I do not fancy that in later life he was to become an aficionado of the new Sydney Opera House.

As Pepys would have written: 'To sea at eight of the evening o'clock.' This was becoming a nightly 'milk run' but it had a deadly purpose. Up the Syrian Coast we went, one cruiser and three destroyers. Beirut abeam at midnight, we cruised up and down outside as we had time to waste. Minefields? To be honest, I never thought of them, although they must have been talked about when *Cassard* and her sister ship made good their escape into them.

The whole town was lit up as usual, but my journal records: 'There was a heavy gun shelling it.' Brilliant flashes of flame could be seen coming from the coast, and the scene was reminiscent of Bardia just before we had bombarded it in January.

Why, if Beirut was an open town was a heavy gun shelling it? Don't ask me, ask General, later Field Marshal, Sir Henry Maitland Wilson, British Army C-in-C!

Soon, hundreds of flares were dropped, lighting up the coastal area like day, and then we saw bombs dropping, all this presumably from our own aircraft. How nice it was to watch our own side dishing it out for a change. At dawn we bombarded the town of Saida, during which time the French shore batteries fired back at us. Their ranging was poor and it was more interesting than frightening.

Return to Haifa and a step back in time, for at noon a party of 50 of us accompanied by the sin bosun (padre) from *Jaguar* were ready for a mini-tour of the Holy Land. We set off in buses for Nazareth and the Sea of Galilee. Nazareth was a dusty Arab town. There were about five different religions or sects, each claiming its particular cavern in the rocks to be the authentic Biblical carpenter's shop. This did not help to instil religious fervour in those whose faith required a boost. I took a photograph of a laden donkey being led past a petrol pump, giving myself a metaphorical pat on the back for having thus brilliantly recorded the meeting of old and new.

Tiberias was different. Here, you could imagine yourself back in the time of the New Testament. Think of a huge Scottish loch, but substitute brown hills for the blue of the heather, and a dry, very hot day for a mist, then you have a fair idea of the place. I never saw Jerusalem, but then I was never allowed to visit Cairo to see the Pyramids either.

On arrival back in Haifa we learned that our dawn bombardment had been a successful one. We had apparently destroyed some machine-gun nests which were holding up our troops. As a result our gallant pongoes were now only ten miles from Beirut.

Bombardments in support of the army are dull in one respect because you seldom know the target at which you are requested to fire. You are given a map reference and told to poop off. I like to see a few houses demolished or a water tower or two. Of course it is not dull when the enemy returns your fire – that is a different story!

That night an air raid on Haifa took place, setting some oil tanks on fire. One bomb landed between the cruiser *Leander* and the destroyer *Ilex*. Some planes made a determined attack on Acre of Crusader fame, and just across the bay. My journal records: 'I hope they (the French pilots) received a reprimand at their debriefing – Acre has no military importance and the oil pipe-line is a mile and a half away.'

Another 'night excursion' to Beirut followed and then a dawn bombardment of Damour where enemy emplacements were holding up our advance.

On 28 June, the powers that be had evidently decided that, given adequate fighter cover we could operate in daylight with impunity, and so it proved. A large force, comprising two cruisers and six destroyers, including ourselves, left Haifa just after noon, our destination once more Damour. At 1330 we heard the noise of aircraft. Still very 'twitchy' after Crete, everyone grew anxious and guns were trained skywards. We waited, and then someone who was better at aircraft recognition than I (which wouldn't be difficult) shouted 'friendlies' and cheers went up. There in the blue sky were six beautiful Hurricanes waggling their wings. What a contrast to our merciless bombings of only three weeks ago. Morale went sky-high, we were going to be all right.

Firing at Damour took place after we had had lunch and time to digest it 1520. This was right and proper, and the correct way to fight a war. Napoleon, who was mindful of his troops' stomachs, would have approved. Whether his descendants on shore did so is in doubt.

The main targets were a WT station near Beirut and a wide wadi. The former had a very tall mast, and my hopes previously expressed, of seeing it topple to the ground, were raised. Sadly, such a target is necessarily extremely narrow and good as our gunnery was, gravity did not assert itself.

Up and down three times we went, slinging in shells on to the coastline. Shore batteries fired at us but ineffectually. Captain Hornblower could not hold a candle to us. We felt we had the French on the run; which was indeed the case. Teatime, we ceased firing and turned for home. It might have been a good shoot over Norfolk farmland.

Everyone got excited at the thought of a 'run ashore' in Haifa. Poor bloody fools; never anticipate good things in wartime. We received orders to escort a damaged destroyer to Port Said in tow. So, instead of either a 'beer run' or even a 'neyture run' we spent the night at sea. Served us right for being so cocky.

We were never still for long. We did not even enter Port Said but said goodbye to our charge and were ordered to Alexandria. En route we received an 'emergency air attack' message from the destroyer Waterhen, asking for help in a position just east of Sollum. We thought we might be told to assist her, but were not. Two days later we heard that the unfortunate ship had been sunk but her survivors were brought in to Alexandria. No one can say the Mediterranean at that time was ever dull.

On 2 July, at one hour's notice for steam we were a captive audience and Rear Admiral (Destroyers) Rear Admiral Glennie, took the opportunity to inspect the ship. Later, as was customary, he addressed the ship's company. Some admirals are good at speeches, some are mediocre. Glennie's speech was somewhat platitudinous. 'The destroyers,' he said, 'have been called upon to perform tasks which were really not theirs but they have performed them cheerfully and well.' What else could have performed the tasks we were set, except perhaps J.C.? I don't know what else could have evacuated hundreds of troops or entered the hell-hole of Suda Bay when the Germans were only three miles away. Really. Glennie went on: 'Our work had been especially appreciated by our two sister (sic) services.' Even at the tender age of eighteen my journal recorded the caustic comment: '1 imagine the army is, or should be, the most appreciative!'

3 July came and off we went to Lebanon, once more, in company with a large force. My journal: 'There was a report of three French destroyers trying to effect a landing near Tyre but they later turned out to be our own ships.' Bloody marvellous intelligence; a combination of Peter Sellers and Dad's Army. I wondered what bright spark at HQ had originated this report!

A night in harbour, then off to bombard the town of Damour again. I felt our shells ought to have written on them, 'Doomy was here!' We had our fighter umbrella so we were protected, but once again the shore batteries had what a friend of mine used to call 'the impertinance' to fire at us. I went down to 'X' gun to watch proceedings and got splashed by French near misses (fortunately uncoloured!). Fire from the shore was horribly accurate. A bombarding ship is on a predictable course and thus an easy target. We were often straddled, and as we had the inside berth and were therefore the ship closest to the land, ours was an unenviable position.

One sees so many photographs nowadays of men at action stations wearing quite properly – anti-flash gear. We never did in those fiercely hot summer months. We would have been roasted and preferred to man the guns in shorts alone, whilst risking the possible danger to our skins. The sun fortunately did more damage than cordite.

A night in harbour and blessed sleep. That was one benefit which Haifa offered – everyone was so goddamned tired that there were no parties of drunken Australian (and British) sailors beating up the town. It was a case of heads down hoping we might have some much needed rest.

On 5 July, and after breakfast (the whole thing was becoming much more gentlemanly), we sailed in company with the cruisers *Perth* and *Ajax*, plus other destroyers. Damour was once again our target, and after luncheon had been consumed we commenced bombarding it. Coastal batteries had evidently been sparing with their dejeuner as their salvoes screamed in close with a stomach-churning noise. No one could say that lunch aboard *Nizam* was even a succulent feast but one did not want to bring up the fare so recently consumed. Sleep was denied us once again, for on our return to Haifa we were told we should not enter harbour but anchor outside as we were 'required' that night. It was the phantom Vichy destroyer force once more, so we swept up towards Cyprus all night but saw nothing.

6 July, and at 0500 we were joined by *Ajax* and the rest of the Haifa force, our task as usual to bombard the coast. This lasted all day, and was what you might call 'shoot on request'. We made signals to the army asking them what targets they wanted blasted, and then we obliged. Friendly fighters patrolled overhead, and as always the contrast between this conflict and our recent terrifying experiences off Crete was uppermost in our minds. The fact that the French were still firing at us was, in comparison, a minor factor. We had air cover, and if we were sunk, as we were within sight of land, we were sure anyway that someone would pick us up. Strangely, we never gave a thought to enemy (French) submarines. In spite of the earlier submarine encounter, we never credited the French with many in Syria. It was not until after the war that we learned they had five stationed there. We did a 'shoot' every hour, but then like good trade unionists, we had 'a tea break at 4 o'clock' and we ceased firing, turning for home. The French are not tea conscious. A few despairing salvoes were fired at us and then as we drew out of range they stopped. Doubtless the army, after its own 'brew-up' was pressing them.

Two more days of bombardments followed, and then the charming news that the French had so effectively mined Haifa harbour from the air that no one could get in or out! As we were 'out' we remained 'out' and had to cruise up and down impotently waiting for clearance.

11 July came, and with it news that General Dentz, Vichy French C-in-C, had asked for an armistice. The following day a cipher signal came through from naval HQ: 'Our troops are standing fast in Syria as from 0000.' My bland journal entry reads: 'Needless to say we were very pleased, as I for one was rather sick of the fighting in Syria, but perhaps not so much of Haifa itself.' So there it was – I did not think of it then, but I had taken part in an event unique in British history. For the first time since hostilities commenced we had won a complete victory. This was not the to and fro of the desert war or the defeats in France, Greece and Crete. We were the masters of Syria, but against whom had our victory been won? Against the French, our enemies for centuries. The French, with whom we went to war against Germany in 1939 as a result of a guarantee to a country which in September of that year we did nothing to help in its hour of agony and dire need.

'*Un grand bouleversement*' would be the French phrase for what had occurred. To have to fight one's former ally was indeed a terrible thing to do. It is however not the job of this book to look into the machinations and grovelling collaboration with Germany that had penetrated the Vichy ministers like a plague bacillus. General Dentz paid, both for his treatment of our prisoners of war and for his defence of Syria.

It became known to British Army HQ in Syria that those of our forces who had been taken prisoner during the campaign had been transported to Vichy France. Undoubtedly had they remained there they would eventually have been taken to POW camps in Germany, there to languish in cold and hunger until the Allied victory. Maitland Wilson acted swiftly. General Dentz and his staff were placed under close arrest and informed in no uncertain terms that they would remain close prisoners until the wrong perpetrated against our captives had been righted. Dentz, as Girard was later to prove in Algeria, was a prima donna and acted like one. He was furious at the affront to a French general and was loud in his protestations. The balloon was soon pricked however, and the British prisoners, much to their joy, were released. Not until the last one had been returned was General Dentz and his staff allowed to leave their cells.

Immediately after the war Dentz was arraigned by the Free French government and sentenced to death, commuted to life imprisonment. He served a year and then died. He had paid the price for the 11,000 French and Allied (note the separation!) casualties sustained during the Syrian conflict.

For us to have fought in Syria was absolutely right. By our swift intervention we had prevented a German thrust and right hook which could easily have seen the forces of the Reich march from Russia, joining hands with their comrades from the Western Desert on the banks of the Suez Canal. What a tragedy that what had formerly been a common cause should have been resolved in bitterness and bloodshed between the 'Allies' of 1939.

14

Temporary Respite

Our war in Syria having been brought to a satisfactory conclusion, we received orders to return to Alexandria. As we left, we learned of one of the conditions of the armistice which pleased us greatly. The French were to be responsible for clearing all the mines laid by them. Excellent, why should our chaps run the risk of being blown up!

I left Haifa with some regret. Although no one could label it 'Sin city of the Middle East' (Beirut might have qualified) it was nevertheless a quiet and restful place when our former allies were not bombing it. It was pleasant to walk in, clean and well kept, and in the few brief hours I managed occasionally ashore there, I found it an agreeable change from Alexandria.

18 July 1941 saw us off Alexandria at noon. A sighting of other vessels at sea is always exciting. First the lookout will spot masts on the horizon, or as in our case, the surface radar may make a report. Then, if you are expecting friendly ships, you are pleased that someone has got his navigation right. If you do not know who it is, you hope it is not the director tower of a ship bigger than you, which will blow you out of the water before you have a chance to close the range. The tragic sinking of *Hood* by *Bismarck* is a classic case in point.

We were all right – the masts grew taller, familiar superstructures appeared, and we welcomed the sight of a force of our cruisers including *Abdiel*, *Latona*, *Phoebe* and *Naiad*. Ten minutes later two huge shapes began to grow on the horizon and we recognised *Valiant* and *Queen Elizabeth*. We were home again among the Mediterranean Fleet.

Twenty-four hours of exercises followed, one of them being a night encounter. The battleships fired starshell, and once *Queen Elizabeth's* searchlight swept round and locked on to us for three minutes. The effect was dazzling not to say frightening, and we now knew what it must have been like for the hapless Italians caught in a similar situation at Matapan. Rabbits and headlights came to mind.

The aerial mining of Alexandria harbour was always a potent menace in those days, far more so than any bombing. So it proved that morning, a mine having been dropped in or near *Valiant's* berth. This necessitated a slow processional return to harbour, minesweepers in the van, and ourselves in the rear. *Valiant* secured elsewhere and the search for the mines continued for ten days. On I August there was a huge explosion together with an enormous water spout right in the battleship's usual berth. An hour later another exploded. My much-loved first ship had until then borne a charmed life from underwater menace. Her time of charm was beginning to run out – those two mines were a forerunner.

A power boat from one of the interned French cruisers was not so lucky as *Valiant*. Entering an area of the harbour designated as dangerous, it exploded an acoustic mine. The boat, with its occupants, was sucked down in the resultant whirlpool of water. Its crew were rescued afterwards, their spot of involuntary minesweeping being probably their only contribution to the fight against the Axis since June 1940. My journal records that this explosion was the subject of a caustic signal from the Rear Admiral Commanding Alexandria, warning ships' boats of the danger from mines in the harbour.

I rather nastily hoped that the signal had not been repeated to the French ships – *'Continuez le minesweeping, s'il vous plait!'*

Back to *Nizam*, and as soon as we entered harbour on 19 July I was told that my destroyer time was over, and I was to return to *Valiant*. My time had been cut short; there were too many midshipmen awaiting their turn. My journal could not record it but I was overjoyed at the prospect of leaving *Nizam*. I had never felt that I had fitted into its Ward Room and I got the feeling that this was mutual. There had been no one else of my tender age (eighteen) and rank (except the disenchanting Australian midshipman referred to earlier), and my life on board had perforce been a lonely one interspersed with conversations with the English Gunner (T). Being the only two representatives of the United Kingdom in an Australian ship, we were drawn together by a common bond of country. We came however, from different backgrounds of class and evolution (he had to his great credit risen from the lower deck) and so close contact did not really occur.

However, I said good-bye to certain ratings with regret. We had shared many watches together during which they had told me stories of life Down Under. We had tried to take what cover we could together during the terrible time of the battle for Crete, and altogether I left them with more repining than some members of the Ward Room. An exception was the Captain, Lieutenant-Commander M.J. Clark. I had received nothing but courtesy from him and we parted with, I hope and think, respect on his side as well as on mine. No one could say I had not seen action whilst on board *Nizam*. However, to return to the noisy camaraderie of *Valiant's* Gunroom would be a pleasure to which I looked forward eagerly. I might even get some sleep, although not in a cabin any more!

My relief was well known to me. He was Dudley Cunliffe-Owen, son of Sir Hugo Cunliffe-Owen, chairman of British American Tobacco and a very rich man indeed. He owned not one steam yacht before the war, but two. Sir Hugo, not a man to mince words, had written to the formidable E.W. Kempson, Headmaster of Dartmouth, when Dudley and I were in our sixth term there. 'My son,' he thundered, 'writes like a housemaid. Please see that his writing improves!'

Nowadays of course, hardly anyone employs a housemaid, let alone knows what they write like. But Sir Hugo was quite right. Most housemaids then had the common denominator of a similar script culled from their council schools. Neat it may have been, but there was no character in it and precious little style if any. It is good that Sir Hugo did not live till today when the misspelt atrocities perpetrated by the pupils of left-wing teachers fresh from their political 'training colleges' would put the pre-war housemaids top of the class.

Dudley Cunliffe-Owen had been a member of my term at Dartmouth, and in the same house. We had travelled to Egypt together round the Cape and then joined *Valiant* instead of the torpedoed *Kent*. At Dartmouth I had disliked him, but in *Valiant* we had become good friends, and it was with pleasure that I greeted him on the quayside. I had only two hours in which to show him round and introduce him before *Valiant'* s smart black picket boat with its distinctive white lines came to fetch me. I waved good-bye to Dudley – I came near to waving my cap around my head as in the traditional three cheers but thought it might be unkind to him. I silently wished him luck and turned my back on *Nizam*.

The picket boat, doing only eight knots instead of its usual powerful 25 due to the suspected presence of acoustic mines, drew alongside the port after gangway of *Valiant*. I ran up the steps, stopped at the top, saluted the quarterdeck and stepped on board. I was back home. 'Ah, Holloway,' said the Midshipman of the Watch, 'been away long? You are keeping the last watch this evening.' I was indeed home again but very happy to be back.

July to October 1941 was a period of relative quiet for the Eastern Mediterranean Fleet if you compare it with the recent events of Matapan, Greece, Crete and Syria. I emphasize most strongly the word relative, since the happenings which unfolded were by no means unexciting. Sudden death was always lurking round the corner if not actually staring one in the face. At times the Gunroom assumed an almost peacetime air. Watches of course were kept, but often midshipmen and Sub-Lieutenants would be reading quietly, or playing the gramophone. (Judy Garland and darling Deanna Durbin – what would we have done without your records?) Others would be seated at the long meal table which ran the length of the mess, writing up their journals, drawing track charts (see illustration) or writing home. The hot African sunshine streamed in through the open scuttles, whilst outside the harsh Arabic words of the felucca boatmen could be heard as they plied for hire.

At other times, lectures would be given in the mess on all manner of subjects varying from ship construction to navigation or the advancement prospects of gunnery ratings. As can be imagined, this latter was hardly the most fascinating of subjects, and in the heat and boredom I could hardly keep my eyelids from drooping. Years later, sitting as Chairman of my Bench of magistrates I have been in like case on a hot, airless afternoon. Trying valiantly to listen to some boring advocate or a particularly inarticulate witness, I have only been prevented from nodding off by the thought of the headline: 'Chairman of Bench asleep in court, appeal sought!'

It is said that one old colonel sitting on the Bench did indeed doze off. This was in the days when unacceptable language given in evidence was written down, not related as now in monotonous tones by a policeman. The offending word was duly passed along the magisterial line until it reached a lady magistrate. She read it with composure and then nudged the dormant colonel in the ribs whilst passing him the piece of paper. The colonel jerked awake, and looked at the word **** held before his eyes. He turned to his lady colleague, his face went purple and in a stage whisper exclaimed, 'Good God, madam, what, now?' But I digress.

The ever-present possibility of being sunk at sea naturally receded when in harbour. Whilst we knew we were not out of danger by any manner of means, the thought that if we survived a bomb or mine we would be certain to be picked up helped morale considerably. Once again it was tennis and tea at the Sporting Club, bathing at Stanley Bay or Sidi Bishr, a film, or dinner at Pastroudi's. What a contrast to the previous few months! I present no excuses though; we thoroughly deserved a period of relaxation, and since I only had two nights' all-night leave in the seventeen months I spent in the Mediterranean, it was a minor recompense.

On 23 July the fleet put to sea for the purpose of creating a diversion for Force 'H' in the Western Mediterranean. We had the luxury of six fighters protecting us all day – someone had at last learned that HM ships are no match for aircraft attack. Fighter Direction was poor however, and the current CAP (Combat Air Patrol) was often sent to intercept their reliefs! IFF, where were you? Our sortie was uneventful and we returned to Alexandria.

The next day I was granted a wish which I had entertained for a long time. I became an intrepid birdman, or in other words, went aloft in an aeroplane for the first time. My aerial chariot was to be our Swordfish, that wonderful biplane built by Fairey which distinguished itself so well during the war. Although only capable of 120 knots in a following wind, it was indeed a maid of all work, and because of its unbelievable slowness, made an excellent torpedo bomber.

The pilot (from *Queen Elizabeth*) greeted me with the somewhat disquieting news that he had not flown one of these aircraft for nine months. I did not dare ask him how good a memory he had, but put on my helmet and Mae West. I wondered which I resembled more closely, Wilbur Wright or Baron Manfred von Richthofen. The ghost of Walter Mitty had joined me again.

Being a floatplane, our 'runway' was the harbour. Always crowded, I hoped we would not hit anything. It was lucky, I reflected, that we were not fighter interceptors – it took us half an hour to attain 6000 feet. Perhaps my pilot was familiarizing himself with the controls. I began to wish he had done more preflight checks.

We circled round the harbour for a while and then in company with *Valiant's* other Swordfish and *Queen Elizabeth's* Walrus (the 'steam chicken') flew out to sea in arrow-head formation. Whether Reichsmarshal Hermann Goering, Feldmarshall Milch and General Galland were quaking in their shoes that day, history does not relate. Doubtless had they seen this powerful aerial armada with Midshipman Holloway in the open observer's cockpit, they would have tried to persuade the Führer to sue for peace at once. As it was, I heard on landing that the exercise for which we had gone aloft had been completely disorganised due to our landing too early and our Gunnery Officer had given it up in despair.

Never mind, I enjoyed it and the Japanese Consul was no doubt feverishly telling Tokyo of this formidable display of Allied air power.

The next day found me attending a court martial – not, fortunately, my own. A sailor from the Australian destroyer *Stuart* had been foc'sle sentry on 11th June. As such, he was armed with a Webley .45 pistol and ammunition. It was night time and his best friend came up to chat to him thus relieving the boredom. The boredom was relieved all right. The friend jokingly asked the sentry to shoot him. The sentry obligingly complied and was put under close arrest. Found guilty, he was sentenced to four months' imprisonment for manslaughter. I was fascinated by the solemn procedure. I have been intrigued by court proceedings ever since.

That night, a very severe air raid took place. The radar recorded 25 enemy aircraft, identified as German JU88s. They were unsporting enough to bomb the harbour instead of the town thus making things highly unpleasant. We were dive-bombed, whilst mines and flares were dropped. One bomb dropped very near us and a stick dropped exactly where *Valiant* would have been if she had been moored in her old berth.

It was a salutary reminder that we were vulnerable in harbour as well as at sea. Not for us the sixteen-foot thick concrete pens in which U-boats sheltered at Brest, Lorient and la Pallice. Their crews must have put two fingers in the air whenever the RAF came over. We had no such umbrella.

Destroyers continued to come and go from the Tobruk 'Milk Run', disembarking wounded as we had from Crete. I was glad I was no longer in destroyers.

Following an attack on Malta by the Italians on 27 July it was thought wise to take precautions in Alexandria. The attack on Malta had been made by seventeen E-boats, supported by torpedo bombers. This must have been Italy's Dieppe as the whole force was destroyed. Nevertheless a dummy attack on Alexandria harbour was mounted on 9 August, and the pyrotechnics were impressive. Green Very lights shot up over the breakwater, and artificial fog was used. This meant that when the searchlights were turned on we could not see anything in the direction of Dekheila aerodrome. I suppose this meant something to the army who were there to defend us. It had no message for me.

The next day three cruisers and two destroyers, one of the latter being *Nizam*, returned to harbour from 'Fortress Tobruk'. This force had been the victim of a severe dive-bombing attack on the journey home and was only saved from disaster by the arrival of friendly Tomahawk fighters. *Nizam*'s radar aerial was hanging drunkenly over the side. Her engines had been strained by a near miss. Poor Dudley Cunliffe-Owen I thought, he was getting a taste of what I had suffered off Crete.

The authorities, naval and military, had become further concerned that an enemy midget submarine attack might be mounted against Alexandria harbour. Their prescience was admirable – at least they were trying to prevent an occurrence which had already taken place in Gibraltar and Suda Bay.

Accordingly, a conference was convened on 26 August 1941 at Ras-el-Tin, the naval HQ. I was ordered to attend, together with other midshipmen. Why was it that I, a lowly midshipman, should be summoned to a conference on the security of Alexandria harbour? All will be revealed, but as I sped in *Valiant*'s picket boat across the calm waters of the harbour, I felt immensely proud that at my tender age I was already involved with security matters. Thoughts of Sherlock Holmes, *The 39 Steps* and Bulldog Drummond flitted through my brain here at last was my metier, they might even ask me to join MI5 or MI6.

Arriving at Ras-el-Tin I nearly forfeited my high-level security rating by tripping on getting out of the boat. It would have been invidious for a future member of the security forces to have fallen flat on his face at the start of the conference, I mused. Picking myself up I marched smartly into the large room set aside for the meeting. An impressive sight met my eyes. High-ranking gold braid shone everywhere on tropical epaulettes, and to my surprise, there were many Egyptian officials present, their khaki uniforms and red tarbooshes contrasting with the British white shirts and shorts.

Air conditioning was in its infancy then and the room was hot. No women Wrens did not appear in Alexandria until the Italian surrender, and it seemed 'local talent' was at a premium. I found a chair and sat down.

Then an interesting and amusing thing happened. A slip of paper was passed round all the English officers. This said: 'Owing to the mixed nature (sic) of the audience, certain information is being withheld, and would officers please refrain from asking pointed questions at the end.' My thoughts of asking a barbed question which would in one sentence pin-point with unerring accuracy the chief weakness of Alexandria's defences were dashed. The post of head of MI5 seemed to recede into the distance. I contented myself with wondering what would happen if the slip of paper now going the rounds was to fall into Egyptian hands? This had partly been foreseen as the latter were all 'corralled' in one section of the room. Doubtless some diplomatic reason for this had been given to the gyppos – 'It will make consultation among your colleagues easier Effendi.'

The lecture (for the slip of paper had altered it to that) was to be given by Captain Binney, commanding officer of 'Nile', the naval shore establishment in Alexandria. He started with a short summary of the Italian attacks on Gibraltar, Suda Bay (where the cruiser *York* was severely damaged and had to be left to the Germans) and the recent E-boat attack on Malta. 'The latter,' he remarked with smug satisfaction, 'had been repulsed with heavy losses owing to the alertness of the defences.' He did not need to add that he hoped our defences would be equally as alert if and when tested. (In the event, they were not.)

Binney then continued, and it became plain very soon what the 'certain information' was that he was withholding from our reluctant host country. When he reached the point where he had to detail the type of craft which the Italians used, he repeated time and again that we 'had no knowledge of the mechanism of these craft or even what they looked like'.

I might not have been privy to the secrets of Ultra at that time, but it was common knowledge in the Mediterranean Fleet that the craft which attacked Suda Bay had been captured intact and brought to Alexandria for examination. If it was such common knowledge, then it was highly possible that the gyppos knew it also? Maybe, maybe not. Anyway, quite rightly, Binney was taking no chances, but he did, however, say: 'We thought they looked like the 'human torpedo' which was used in the abortive raid on Gibraltar, and that a sort of motor-boat-cum-raft had been used at Suda Bay.' By saying that, he had virtually told everyone present what the craft did look like, but no matter. He was a nice chap.

Binney ended his lecture with a short summary of Alexandria's defences and then said that greater emphasis should be placed on and vigilance exercised in the Boom Gate Patrol. All was now revealed, and it was plain as to why we midshipmen had been ordered to attend the lecture.

Every harbour in wartime, if it is to be reasonably secure against E-boat or submarine attack, has to have its entrance(s) protected by an underwater boom. This is virtually a steel/wire mesh gate which is opened only to allow ships to enter or leave.

The requirements for each harbour obviously vary, and this was made tragically clear in the winter of 1939 at Scapa Flow. The battleship *Royal Oak* was torpedoed and sunk with terrible loss of life because she was in a part of the Flow as then unprotected by a boom or blockship. Ironically the latter arrived at her appointed station the day after the battleship was sunk!

Alexandria harbour has only one entrance (see the author's sketch taken from his journal) and therefore should in theory have been much easier to defend than Scapa Flow. Enter the Boom Gate Patrol.

Queen Elizabeth and *Valiant* were both required to provide a fast picket boat which would patrol just outside the boom at night. I was frequently in charge of one boat, and at first it was really quite fun. The trouble was that, like today's security operations against the IRA, you patrol and patrol, you get bored when nothing happens and unconsciously you relax.

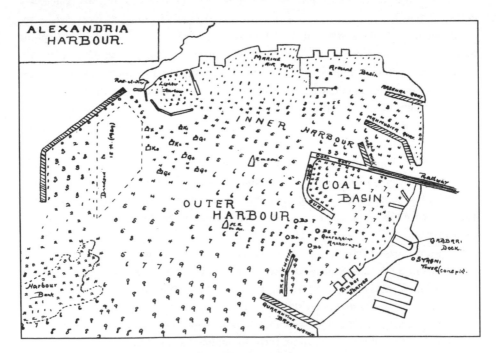

Sketch of Alexandria harbour from the author's journal.

What would happen was this. At dusk we would set off in our picket boat with its powerful Ford V8 engine growling as though straining at the leash, the exhaust water gurgling astern. I would be in the cockpit handling the wheel, occasionally manipulating the Bendix cable throttle controls, not unlike those of an aircraft. The usual crew would be on board, bowman, stoker and sternsheetman, the coxswain beside me. An extra crew member would be carried, a torpedoman who had charge of the small bombs. Throttles a quarter astern, we drifted clear of the gangway. Wheel over, throttles half ahead and then full as we raced towards the harbour mouth. Our draught being virtually negligible, it was with ease that we travelled over the closed boom having first made our recognition signals to Ras-el-Tin. I had no desire to be shot at by my own side!

We slowed down just outside the harbour mouth and then drifted in the slight swell whilst the torpedoman busied himself in the stern. Then he would shout 'Ready', I would shout 'Drop', and at the same time shove the throttle forward. The engine would respond eagerly, we would suddenly surge forward, leaving astern a small 2–3lb bomb or minor depth charge, to descend to its appointed depth.

There would be a thump and a spout of water, the explosion having taken place just near the boom. If any enemy was trying to use wire-cutters on the boom he would have had a nasty shock. So would we, I often reflected, if the throttle cables had jammed and we had remained immobile over the explosion!

This exercise would be repeated every quarter of an hour until dawn. The reader can see how, after a while, the novelty would wear off, and the whole thing would become a matter of boring routine.

In a later chapter the story of the Italian Lieutenant (now Admiral) de la Penne's daring and courageous attack on the harbour will be related. Suffice it at this stage to include a small extract from his account of the attack:

After 20 minutes we are off Ras-el-Tin and I hear a noise as if the torpedo (the charge which he was astride) had hit a metal cable, a noise that is repeated after a few minutes. We can see and hear people talk on the pier (breakwater). There is also a large motor boat sailing silently in front of the pier (sic) dropping bombs from time to time. The bombs prove to be rather a nuisance.

The last sentence must surely be one of the most splendid understatements of all times!

So there it was, a commendation as to our work outside the boom from one of the enemy we were there to kill or at least deter. I must not however pre-empt the account of de la Penne's attack.

Life continued in Alexandria, each day bringing grim reminders of the war. The cruiser *Phoebe* entered, having been torpedoed, but not badly. Air raids were such a nightly occurrence that it is not worth recording them except for the aftermath of one raid.

One morning I was sent in the launch to collect stores at 45 Shed. On arrival there I was met by the pleasant news that there was an unexploded bomb in the cordage store – we needed cordage as well! With the stupidity and carelessness of youth I thought it might be interesting to have a look at it. There was also a certain thrill in 'having a shufti' and besides, people were milling about apparently unconcerned.

I went in and there it was, quite a small one, probably about 250lbs., and painted red. It was right in the centre of the cordage store, and I stared at it fascinated. I had seen German bombs leave their aircraft and start their journey towards me, now I was looking at one which might have been a harmless prototype but I knew was not. The gyppo workers of course had made themselves scarce, and store handling was being done by troops. I left and hoped the defusing party would have been along before my next visit.

Instruction of the 'young gentlemen' continued apace every day. One forenoon we would be in a 15" gun turret, the next afternoon we would be having the intricacies of the Ring Main explained to us by the Warrant Electrician. The Torpedo Officer would lecture us on electric motors and then demolition. I was never quite clear as to when we were likely to have to use this latter knowledge. One of the army evacuations perhaps? I hoped I should not be near enough to the enemy again so as to put my expertise to the test. 'Last out' of Suda Bay had been enough!

Still, one of our paymaster midshipmen did get an appointment ashore and ended up in beleaguered Tobruk for a while. I thought this was going it a bit much. I had not joined the Navy to have Rommel hammering at my front door, and not in comfort either.

Nizam arrived back from Tobruk with a sizeable hole in her port bow. Apparently she had hit a wreck in the Stygian darkness of Tobruk harbour whilst doing ten knots. I reflected that it was just as well Lieutenant-Commander Clark had not done this in Suda Bay.

The whole fleet put to sea on 26 September to create a diversion for yet another Malta convoy. Poor *Valiant* was in so great a need of docking that she vibrated greatly, causing some of her rivets to be shaken out; the holes thus caused being plugged with cement! This is just an illustration of how desperately hard every ship in the Eastern Mediterranean Fleet was worked, and had the huge floating dock been put out of action there is no knowing what we would have done. Fully realising this, a large torpedo baffle was placed astern of the dock (the forward end faced the quayside) so as to forestall any torpedo bomb attacks. Rumours circulated that a large number of these aircraft had recently arrived in Libya.

A wonderful example of misplaced priorities was recorded in my journal on 29 September. A midshipman of my term serving in *Valiant*, Ronald Greenlees, was to have been sent to *Nizam* to relieve Dudley Cunliffe-Owen. This was cancelled, and the reason given? Greenlees was a powerful and valued member of the whaler's crew which *Valiant* was to enter in the fleet pulling races! The fact that *Nizam* might have left harbour or even the station before the pulling races had taken place does not seem to have entered anyone's head. Only the British at times could act like this.

On 3 October the fleet put to sea for exercises, only to learn the next day that we could not enter harbour. While we were out, the Australian cruiser *Hobart* had rammed the boom, which for a time was a danger to shipping. After another 24 hours at sea, we entered harbour to be greeted by the sight of the ammunition ship *Chinnucca*, sunk down to her funnels and masts near the breakwater. An explosion in her boiler room had caused her to sink. As she carried cordite and other explosives we all regarded her with some apprehension, hoping she would not blow up.

We were further excited by the report that there was an enemy midget submarine in the harbour. Hence, sentries with loaded rifles were stationed on the quarter-deck and on the foc'sle. De la Penne's attack was being anticipated by two months. The report was probably fostered by the sinking of *Chinnucca*, and later the harbour was declared clear. How would they know?

On 8 October, the war in Greece and Crete which we had fought and lost was once more brought home forcibly to us. At 2000 *Queen Elizabeth* entered harbour majestically, her huge bulk dwarfing all the other ships except ourselves, her sister ship. Following her was a small caique flying the Greek flag. Dignity and impudence came to mind.

My journal takes up the story: 'This caique came alongside us and we found it contained four officers and eleven men, escapees from Greece and Crete! At least eight of them were Greeks, some of whom had come from Athens. They said that a single loaf of bread cost 7/-(35p) and a pound of butter 17/6 (87p). They said the poorer people were starving due to the exorbitant food prices. Crete they said was occupied by 'a few Italians' and that there were still many men, remnants of our armies in Greece and Crete, who were hiding out in caves in the mountains, or being harboured by Greeks in Athens itself.' Poor sods I thought, all right perhaps now whilst it is hot. What price their chances in winter when they dare not leave their caves for fear of making tracks in the snow or meeting what was to come, German mountain troops searching for them?

The caique had encountered *Queen Elizabeth* outside. The latter had flashed 'Welcome' at her, and then when in harbour the caique came alongside *Valiant* mistaking us for *Queen Elizabeth*. We gave them clean clothes and baths, and they stayed on board for the night.

On 10 and 11 October we put to sea in company with the battleship *Barham*, the cruisers *Ajax* and *Hobart* (of boom fame) and destroyers. The curious thing about this sortie was that no one knew why we had put to sea.

Almost invariably, once a ship was at sea and therefore incommunicado except for WT, the ship's company was told the purpose of the mission. This was a good PR exercise, and stilled messdeck 'buzzes'. It also served to show up or commend those who had spread rumours in harbour. This time no one was told anything. Indeed at 1900 Commander Reid took the most unusual step of broadcasting to the ship's company that he had no idea why we were at sea!

We entered harbour again after 24 hours, still none the wiser.

Rumours were rife, the strongest being that enemy cruisers had been sighted off Tobruk, but no one really knew. Maybe it was as a result of an Ultra signal, which for some unexplained reason is under wraps even today.

Destroyers were still loading up for the Tobruk run and soldiers crowded the quays. This was a supreme example of the exercise of sea power in that we were able to evacuate exhausted and wounded troops, and land fresh men with their equipment, thus holding on to the 'fortress'.

Had Tobruk been say, Sidi Barrani of Kenneth Home fame ('Did I tell you Murdoch, about when I was in Sidi Barrani?' 'Yes sir, you have – many times'), there would have been no such relieving ferryboat service. A port, however blocked with wrecks, as was Tobruk, was naturally a sine qua non.

On 12 October, the fleet, except for us, put to sea. We were temporarily the flagship of the Commander-in-Chief Mediterranean, and it was with pride that we saw the plain St George's Cross of a full admiral run up to our masthead. Rear Admirals have two red balls on their St George's Cross, Vice Admirals one, and full Admirals no balls at all.

The fact that Admiral Sir Andrew Cunningham never set foot on board *Valiant* during our short time as his flagship was a pity but would doubtless have caused chaos having to accommodate all his staff. The wretched midshipmen would probably have had to trail along astern on rope's ends.

The fleet returned and just as it was entering the Great Pass, it was attacked by three German torpedo bombers. Flying in very low, they each dropped a torpedo, all of which missed their mark. Never a dull moment in Alexandria.

To emphasize this point, only one day later, a merchantman named *The Pass of Balmaha* was torpedoed off the harbour entrance at 0400. Her cargo consisted of 700 tons of petrol, together with ammunition destined for Tobruk. She never stood a chance, nor those who sailed in her. She blew up at once making a great glare on the horizon. Those who worked ships with this sort of cargo displayed the most extraordinary courage. Unarmed and sitting literally on a powder keg, they were easy prey for underwater and aerial predators. We at least were protected by double bottoms and steel armour, they had nothing. Immune as we thought we were to sudden death, we were all deeply affected by this tangible and terrible evidence of those who were in far greater danger than ourselves.

Long overdue for docking, and much slower because of the weight of barnacles on our bottom, we prepared to go into dry-dock. It is no easy task to prepare a huge battleship for docking. The laborious process of de-ammunitioning has to take place, the latter continuing for 24 hours.

Oil fuel was pumped into an oiler, but even then, so great was the load hanging on to our encrusted bottom that we did not come up to the required draught for the floating dock. Somehow it was managed and we entered the dock. Because of our draught however, the fore and after ends of the dock were still under water. No matter, the bottom of the ship and the bottom of the dock were dry. We had just made it.

Crawling under the huge belly of *Valiant* I was able to see clearly the ominous marks of the near miss caused by a German bomb which she had sustained off Crete. A foot or so nearer and I would have been looking at a gaping hole.

Rumours were rife that because of difficult repairs which had to be made to the lignum vitae propeller bush we might have to go to Durban where better facilities existed. Everyone got very excited. Durban, to sailors of that time was like Tahiti to Bligh's men – a beautiful and peaceful haven where pretty girls abounded and hospitality overflowed. I was to find this was completely true, but sadly not until three years had elapsed. The engineers repaired that bloody bush and our trip to the south never materialized.

We undocked, ammunitioned, oiled and were once again a fighting unit.

I attended the court martial of one of our seamen who had been foolish enough to desert; a heinous crime especially in wartime. Apprehended in the Jewish Club in Cairo (the Yom Kippur attack was then many years away), he was brought under armed guard back to Alexandria, found guilty and sentenced to six months' detention.

Stupid and misguided as he was, I could not help feeling sorry for him. Our Master-at-Arms, Mr Diable (well named) had told us once that when in charge of the Detention Barracks at Portsmouth he had caused iron filings to be hammered into the oakum, subsequently to be unpicked by the detainees. Charming.

On Friday 7 November, I recorded an event for which I still feel shame. 'Today,' says my journal, 'being the anniversary of the Russian Revolution, the flag of the Red Navy was flown at our masthead, probably the first time this has occurred since Russia became a Bolshevik Country.'

Having had at my prep school a number of White Russian boys including Paul and Ivan Tolstoy, I had hated Communism with a deadly hatred, and still do. Yet here we were, the Bolshevik flag fluttering aloft, its red star and hammer and sickle on a white background, a strip of green at the bottom.

'Dear old Uncle Joe' Stalin as he was misguidedly called during the war, was the biggest mass murderer in history, far outshining his enemy, but former ally, Adolf Hitler. Due entirely to Stalin and his successors we were to suffer the Cold War and treacherous defectors of the likes of Burgess and Maclean. I wanted to haul the hated flag down in spite of the fact that Russia was killing Germans. But I dared not confide that to my journal.

All this time Indian troops were being ferried to Cyprus in large numbers to reinforce the island's garrison. At the end of this task the destroyers involved entered harbour flying at their mastheads the house flags of well-known removal firms such as Pickfords and Carter Patterson. For some reason Gieves, the naval tailors was also similarly honoured. At the end of their ferry service D 14 (Captain Commanding 14th Destroyer Flotilla) signalled to his flotilla: 'As chief lorry driver I congratulate you on your last removal!'

So ended a four month period from my time spent fighting the French. A period packed with incidents of war. The next two months were to contain events of horrific proportions.

15

The Sinking of *Barham*

The sinking of two major capital ships and the elimination from active service of two others must be a case for the utmost congratulation and rejoicing in the attacking country and the deepest gloom in the country sustaining the losses.

Events which led to this terrible outcome swiftly unfolded in the latter days of 1941, both in the western and eastern Mediterranean. On Friday 14 November it was finally announced by the Admiralty that our famous aircraft carrier, Ark Royal, had been sunk, a victim of German torpedoes off Gibraltar. I say 'finally' advisedly as Ark Royal had been 'sunk' so many times by Doctor Goebbels' propaganda machine it was difficult to comprehend that this was the authentic and tragic communique. 'And where is the *Ark Royal?*', 'Lord Haw-Haw's' oft-repeated question, implying that the British were withholding information as to her loss, now had the greatest significance. We in the eastern Mediterranean, mourned her going. We were soon to have cause for mourning nearer home.

I have remarked before how lower deck 'buzzes' suddenly spring up and are often astonishingly accurate. One such originated on 17 November 1941 – *Valiant* and the whole fleet would put to sea for exercise the following day. First part correct, second part incorrect; this was to be action not 'dummy runs'.

Commander Reid broadcast that our long-expected 'push' in the Western Desert had begun. We were to 'create a diversion for enemy aircraft and to keep them guessing as to our destination'. I did not much like the thought of acting the part of the tethered goat in a tiger hunt and thought it a criminal waste of capital ships. Wisely, I did not confide these seditious thoughts to my journal, but later events were to prove me tragically correct.

The great reduction in our naval forces since 1945 is a matter of history and record. The names of ships in company with us on this sortie read like a miniature Naval Review: *Queen Elizabeth*, *Barham*, *Naiad*, *Euryalus*, *Hobart*, *Galatea*, *Neptune*, *Ajax*, *Decoy*, *Jervis*, *Napier*, *Nizam*, *Kingston*, *Kimberley*, *Kipling*, *Jackal*, *Hasty*, *Eridge*, *Avonvale* and *Kandahar*. Two battleships beside ourselves, six cruisers and twelve destroyers. A not inconsiderable goat.

A JU88 appeared as shadower. Our fighter escort had of course by then disappeared but they returned later. My journal records: '*Queen Elizabeth* tried to direct them on to the JU88 with the result that of course they missed it.' The future Fighter Direction Officer airing his criticisms!

A night at sea without further incident and then back to Alex. We wondered what effect, if any, our sorties had had on the enemy. On 23 November we had the answer. When we left harbour the first time, three large enemy convoys had been reported heading for Tripoli. As soon as our fleet was reported off Mersa Matruh, they turned tail for Italy. The tethered goat had been useful, disaster was still to come.

German tanks, retreating from Bardia, laid up in a large concentration on the Bardia-Tobruk coastal road, hoping that night would spare them. Along comes the cruiser *Neptune* and pumps 500 shells into them causing, according to my journal, 'No little damage and a great deal of confusion!' Another example, if one was needed, of the exercise of sea power aiding the military arm.

On Monday 24 November 1941, we weighed and proceeded to sea at 1630, our mission to give help to the cruisers in their interception of enemy convoys. In company were *Queen Elizabeth*, *Barham* and a destroyer screen. *Barham* would never sail into Alexandria again.

We steered 310° all night. There were the usual aircraft alarms, but no attacks. The Mediterranean fleet as usual made a majestic sight as it steamed proudly through the calm blue waters off the African coast. *Queen Elizabeth* in the van, then *Barham*, then ourselves. Had the two last positions been reversed, it is highly unlikely that this book would ever have been written.

For my part, I had become so used to being bombed, and in Syria shelled, that the deadly menace of the submarine was something I had tended to forget, or at least consign to a remote corner of my mind. It would speedily be brought to the forefront of my consciousness.

The morning of 25 November was uneventful. I had been at my action station most of the time, due to aircraft scares, much came and went, it was close to teatime. I was in the Port After High Angle Calculating Position, right down below the steel armour plating, the 6" steel hatch closed firmly above our heads. Little did we know what was approaching us underwater.

U-331 was a Type V11C boat commanded by Oberleutnant zur See Hans Dietrich Freiherr (Baron) von Tiesenhausen. She had entered the Mediterranean six weeks earlier, and was based on Salarnis, an island to the south of Greece.

At noon, U-331 was submerged off Sollum, the position in which we found ourselves four hours later. The sensitive German hydrophones picked up propeller noises coming from the north-east. Keeping his periscope barely above the surface, von Tiesenhausen saw some yellowish haze over the horizon, and soon could make out the thin shapes of masts.

Masts grew taller and as he watched, the amazed and jubilant U-boat Commander could recognise three Queen Elizabeth class battleships flanked by a screen of destroyers. He could hardly believe his luck. Hunter and quarry were, by a turn of the fleet's zigzag now on approaching courses, the weather was fine, the sun behind the hunter. What more could a submariner want?

The destroyers *Jervis* and *Griffin* led the destroyer screen, the former to starboard of the new zigzag 'leg', the latter to port. At 1615 the Asdic operator on board *Jervis* picked up an echo, range between 800 and 1100 yards. It is monotonous work listening to the 'ping' of the Asdic transmissions, but the operator concerned was not bored; he had only been on watch a quarter of an hour. He carried out the usual drill, sweeping aft to assess the width of the echo.

An echo returned from the outgoing 'ping' does not necessarily indicate the presence of a submarine. It can be bounced off a temperature layer, a shoal of fish or a whale (not in the Mediterranean!). The broad width of the echo and its loud, rather sharp sound persuaded the Asdic Officer to classify it as 'non-sub' and he told the operator to disregard it. This decision probably cost 861 men their lives. The fox was inside the henhouse.

U-331 glided between *Jervis* and *Griffin* and its commander took a quick look through the periscope. The huge bulk of *Barham* dominated the scene. The harsh command 'Los' (fire) was barked – four torpedoes left their tubes.

In the CP, the Royal Marine bandsmen who manned it had gone through the usual drills and were beginning to settle down for the watch. It was hot, no one moved unnecessarily, but watchful eyes were kept on important dials, the calculating table was silent, we awaited an aircraft attack. I sat with my back to the ship's side, headphones on. It was like many another watch. The bulkhead clock ticked, the time was 1629.

Suddenly there was a strangled yell in the headphones which connected me with Jocelyn Parker in the Director Tower: 'Start up the table, *Barham* has been torpedoed.' In the suddenness of the moment, Parker thought that it was an aerial torpedo or a bomb which had struck our sister ship, another illustration of how conditioned we were to air attack, not underwater. Had we been operating in mid-Atlantic, it would have been the reverse.

I repeated the words '*Barham* has been torpedoed' to my CP crew. They jumped to their feet, looking ashen and apprehensive. I have no doubt I looked the same. I remember to this day what I did then. I stared in fascinated horror at the bulkhead. I remember thinking quite clearly, 'My God, suppose there are several submarines around us, the next torpedoes will come through there.' It was of course quite nonsensical, had we been attacked as well, we would have known very little about it. We would either have died in the explosion or been drowned like rats in our steel-enclosed coffin deep in the bowels of the ship.

Drowning like rats was the fate of the majority of *Barham's* ship's company only yards from where we were. The whole ghastly scene was being described graphically to me by Parker from his vantage point high above *Valiant's* bridge. His strangled voice came over the headphones: 'She's keeling over. Men are jumping over the side, you can see them running up from down below. They're clambering on to the boom, some are holding on to the PV (para vane) chains, others are jumping over the bulges into the water.'

Down in the CP we could do nothing except listen to the commentary on the terrible scene being enacted so near to us. Knowing that our chances of survival were absolute zero should we also be attacked, I must admit I wished fervently that Parker and I could change places if torpedoes came, he should be all right, but for us...

I could feel the deck thrumming beneath my feet and knew that we had increased speed. A glance at the pitometer log confirmed this, we were making 23 knots, a speed we

had not attained since Matapan. There was nothing we could do for those now 'fortunate'
enough to be struggling in the sea. Capital ships do not stop to pick up survivors, that is
work for destroyers.

I write 'fortunate' in inverted commas – this is comparative. Those not fortunate enough
to be in the water were already dead or dying. More would die in a minute or so. Those
who were jumping into the sea needed to look before they leaped. Poor devils, they had a
terrible choice. Before them lay the sea, but because the great ship was now heeling over,
her bulges were exposed. A jump from the quarter-deck meant broken legs for many, and
yet if you delayed to find a better diving point you ran the risk of the inevitable explosion.

Imagine being in the sea, a broken leg or maybe both, struggling to keep afloat with oil
fuel sloshing into your lungs, choking you to death. The only fortunate factor for these
men was the temperature of the sea. Had it been the icy depths of the Atlantic, the death
toll would have been horrendous.

Parker again: 'She's at an angle of 45 degrees, more and more people are going overboard.
She's heeling right over, water is pouring down her funnel.' Then, a split-second pause and
'Oh my God, oh God, she's blown up.' As Parker stopped speaking, unable to continue as he
watched the horror unfold before his eyes, I heard the tremendous bang of the explosion as
our huge sister ship split asunder. Sea water had entered her boilers via the funnel, the rest
was inevitable.

The sinking of HMS *Barham*. (Imperial War Museum)

Parker, his voice almost inaudible, whispered, 'I shouldn't think that there are any survivors.' Fortunately he was to be proved wrong. For us in the CP those minutes which seemed to go by on the proverbial leaden feet, were moments of terrible anxiety, fear and apprehension. We could see nothing, and do nothing to help ourselves. It was Action Stations, all watertight doors were firmly shut, our armoured hatch clamped tight. My thoughts, murderous now, turned to the U-boat. I guessed she must have dived, I hoped her crew were sweating it out below as they waited for the depth charges to explode. Fear takes many forms, with me it was a not entirely irrational desire for revenge.

There was to be no revenge, but a quite extraordinary thing had happened. I did not know it at the time, but if steel had not prevented it, I could have almost touched U-331 at that moment.

Unknown to von Tiesenhausen, the three battleships had turned towards him, bringing *Valiant* practically on top of his submarine. Needing to be at periscope depth, and with the loss of trim due to the sudden discharge of four torpedoes, his boat momentarily lost buoyancy. The result was that the U-boat Commander found himself in that most horrific of situations – a forced, albeit partial surfacing right in the middle of the enemy fleet. Doubtless our great bulk in the water so close to him contributed to his being sucked towards us. Now came some frustrating moments.

Captain Morgan tried to ram U-331 as she surfaced only a cable (200 yards) away from us. But he was not commanding a destroyer, and a 30,000-ton battleship answers only slowly to her helm. Added to that, we had port wheel on to try and 'comb the tracks' of any more torpedoes which might be fired at us. Morgan realised it was hopeless and U-331 passed down our starboard side.

Now it was our turn to try and avenge *Barham*, but we might as well have used peashooters. The starboard forward (S1) pom-poms opened fire at the submarine but all to no purpose. Pom-poms are for close range anti-aircraft fire, they cannot depress low enough to hit an object on the surface at only 50 yards.

Nothing could have been more thwarting or unavailing. There we were, a huge steel fighting sea-castle, and for all the harm we could do to the Germans who had just killed so many of our shipmates we might as well have shaken our fists. I believe some did in disbelief at their impotence.

The terrible explosion which sent *Barham* so quickly to the bottom had blown whole gun turrets clean into the air. She split in half between 'X' and 'Y' turrets; the former was rocketed skywards as though it was a child's toy instead of a steel turret containing huge 15" guns weighing hundreds of tons.

Reports differ as to whether depth charges were dropped or not. My journal records that my former ship, *Nizam*, dropped two patterns, other eye-witnesses say none was dropped so as to prevent further harm to those struggling in the water. This fear is one which confronts all 'hunter-killer' commanders, and was well illustrated in Nicholas Monsarrat's *The Cruel Sea*. What do you do? Do you try to kill the dreadful submarine menace lurking beneath you which may well strike again? In so doing, you may end the lives of your

The explosion of HMS *Barnham*.

countrymen who have just escaped from one horror only to find themselves being blown up by their friends. There is no easy solution.

U-331 had escaped, but only because her Emden boat-builders had done a magnificent job. Naturally, she had 'crash-dived' after torpedoing *Barham*. Since she was bow-heavy and her propellers were still turning, she sank like a ton of stones. This had a credit and debit effect. The credit side meant that she was below the depth at which British depth charges would explode, had any been dropped. The debit side was the increasing sea-water pressure on her hull. Designed for a depth of 150 metres, she actually descended to 265 metres before the blowing of tanks stabilised her and her dive was halted. Had she gone any lower, the immense pressure of tons per square inch would have crushed her hull like an eggshell. The sea would have accomplished what depth charges did not.

Von Tiesenhausen and his crew reached their Greek base in safety. He was awarded the *Ritterkreuz* of the Iron Cross with oak leaves for his successful action.

Barham was the only British battleship to be sunk by an enemy submarine at sea during the war. *Royal Oak* was sunk in harbour whilst *Prince of Wales* was sunk by Japanese aircraft. It was a unique experience to have been so close to her at this awful end to her career; one I could have done without.

Some of our accompanying screen of destroyers were immediately ordered to pick up survivors whilst we, the two remaining battleships, left the ghastly scene as quickly as we could.

From the time of the torpedoes striking *Barham* to the time she disappeared under the waves was four and a half minutes. No one who was present at this time could believe that such a huge ship could sink in such an appallingly short time. From this it will be seen, as was indeed the case, that only those who were above the waterline at the moment of impact stood any chance at all of survival.

The survivors, which included Vice Admiral Pridham-Wippell (VA1), but not *Barham's* commanding officer, Captain Geoffrey Cooke, were now being picked up by the destroyers. Many had had their hands torn from contact with the barnacles on the battleship's side.

Pridham-Wippell was the oldest man on board, and of course the most senior. He commented: 'The behaviour of the ship's company was exemplary both while abandoning ship and in the water. There was no noise or panic and all hands took to the water in an orderly manner.'

Reports from survivors said that the sea was absolutely solid with glutinous oil. It was almost impossible to swim through it and the vomiting caused by swallowing the treacherous stuff was terrible.

Back in *Valiant*, my CP crew and myself had to endure another two hours of virtual imprisonment in our armoured steel 'cell' before most welcome release to the open air came. We had been cooped up all day down there; to say that the atmosphere was 'foetid' would be an understatement. Men sweat in heat, they sweat in fear, and we had had plenty of both. We had known the dread of there being a 'wolf-pack' of U-boats in the area, and the thought of sharing the fate of most of *Barham's* ship's company. We were not to know that V-331 was a lone wolf.

The action of the day was not at an end either, for not long after we had so hurriedly left the scene of death and destruction, four groups of aircraft were reported closing. 'That's just all we need today,' I thought, '*Barham* sunk in four minutes and now we are going to be bombed without a fighter escort.' It was not pleasant to contemplate.

Confusion reigns over these aircraft. My journal records:

I think some of these planes were our own, come to look for survivors. They dropped flares in order to aid their search, whilst the destroyers astern of us fired at them for a long time thinking the flares were looking for them!

What I had written was set down only hours after *Barham's* sinking. With hindsight, and talking to survivors in Alexandria later, I take perhaps a different view. I did not know at the time that in order to try to keep *Barham's* sinking secret, wireless silence had been ordered in the fleet. *Queen Elizabeth's* aircraft was subsequently launched early in the morning of the 26th to alert Naval HQ at Alexandria, so that arrangements for the welfare of the survivors could be made.

Painting of the view through the periscope of U-331 (bottom centre right) as the battlefleet approaches. (H.D. Freiheer von Tiesenhausen)

Some of the four groups of aircraft referred to, could hardly have been friendly, but who alerted them? Presumably it was von Tiesenhausen's initial report, but German radio only reported that a British battleship had been attacked off Sollum, and was hit by one torpedo. Secrecy was not maintained for long. We entered Alexandria at 1030 the next day and soon after that the 'buzz' got round. Hence the story that after delivering his 'Most Secret' message, the pilot from *Queen Elizabeth* took a taxi to the Cecil Hotel. There, over a drink, he discovered to his consternation that there was only one topic of conversation in the bar – the sinking of *Barham*!

I do not know who was in charge of harbour berthage that awful morning, but whoever it was ordered us to be secured, not to our normal buoy, but to B2. No prizes for correct guesses as to whose buoy this used to be. Why? Did the Harbourmaster think that the Japanese Consul could not count, or that he could not tell the difference between ourselves and *Barham*? (We were indeed sister ships but refits had left both *Queen Elizabeth* and *Valiant* looking much different to *Barham*.)

Sailors are superstitious and traditionally do not like sailing on Friday 13th. Perhaps there were many who joined their ranks when the events of the night of 19 December were unfolded.

It is now over 70 years since these events took place. Courts of Enquiry have sat, and survivors' accounts have been recorded. However, I feel that one of the most revealing, and tragic, comments was made to my brother by a senior member of the Naval Construction Service, now retired. What he had to say had been kept secret for many years.

He told my brother that after the torpedoing of *Royal Oak* in Scapa Flow in late 1939, his department was asked to look into the protection built into those battleships in active service. The department concluded that all the 'R' class battleships needed extra double bottoms fitted to render them less vulnerable to submarine attack. The same advice was given about *Barham* and *Malaya*, and it was recommended that these two ships should be so reconstructed as soon as possible. *Warspite*, *Queen Elizabeth* and *Valiant* were passed as being properly protected as a result of their recent refits.

C-in-C Med was informed of this, but his reply was that he would not release *Barham* for refit unless she was replaced by a fleet carrier. This Their Lordships could not, or would not do and so *Barham* remained on active service until she became a steel coffin for 861 officers and men. It was doubtless just as well that none of them knew of a secret report which highlighted the main reason why they died.

A second report marked 'Most Secret' and dated 28 April 1942 began:

The loss of HMS *Barham* must be primarily attributed to a failure on the part of the A/S [Anti-Submarine] screening destroyers. A quicker appreciation by either the operator or the O.O.W. [Officer of the Watch] would have shown the necessity of finding the left cut [of the A/S sweep] which would almost undoubtedly have led to the detection of the U-boat and to a counter attack in time to save the situation.

So there it was, blame was laid firmly on the shoulders of the Asdic Operator and the Officer of the Watch, which is probably right and proper. However, the author was trained as an Asdic officer, and served as such in the cruiser *Suffolk* where, incidentally, a whale did more damage to the Asdic dome than the Japanese!

As stated before, it is not easy to distinguish sometimes between the 'ping' from a temperature layer, a wreck/shoal of fish and a submarine. If you are not sure about a contact, what do you do, haul out of the line and investigate? Yes, perhaps, but then if your contact is false you have opened an arc in the A/S screen through which the real U-boat may slip. If Asdic had had IFF which radar had, how easy it would have been to identify the enemy.

Training, training and yet more training was what was needed, and what the Admiralty recommended in the signal just quoted. Against this must be set the pressure on training schools, the drafting of trained officers and ratings, and above all the provision of a real submarine on which to train. Admiral Cunningham withdrew the submarine *Otis* for just such a purpose, but how much enemy shipping might she have sunk instead of motoring up and down outside Alexandria whilst trainees 'pinged' on her?

It will assist the reader if one looks at the sketch map and drawing reproduced here by kind permission of the publishers, William Kimber, of Geoffrey Jones' book *Battleship Barham*. From both of these it will be seen how terribly lucky we were in *Valiant* not to suffer the fate of our sister ship. Any one of the three battleships could have been chosen as a target, it was simply our fortune and *Barham's* misfortune that the U-boat was in the position she was.

The morning of our return the entry in my journal reads:

Wednesday 26th November 1941. Our depleted force arrived in Alexandria harbour at 1030, The Commander broadcast that VA1 [Vice Admiral Pridham-Wippell], his Flag Lieutenant and about 450 officers and men have been rescued from Barham; a wonderful number when one thinks of the force of the explosion. Some people (sic) from one of the after HATS were picked up having been blown a long way away.

Track chart showing
how U-331 penetrated
the destroyer screen to
torpedo HMS *Barham*.

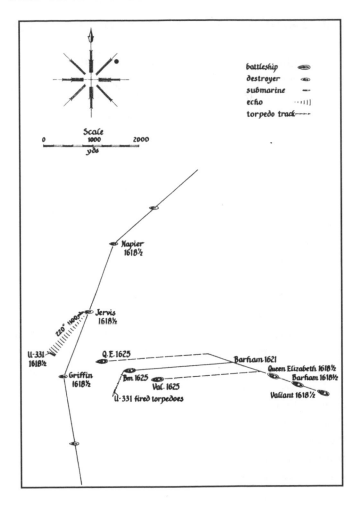

This latter piece of news was of macabre interest to me. The HATS or High Angle
Transmitting Station was, in the older *Barham*, the equivalent of *Valiant's* HACP or High
Angle Calculating Position. This was where I had been when the torpedoes struck. I mused
on the possibility of my being blown out of the bowels of *Valiant* had we been the target.

Such a number rescued is in marked contrast to the three survivors from the battle
cruiser *Hood* which blew up and sank when hit by a very accurate salvo from *Bismarck*
the previous May. The 450 rescued out of a total complement of 1310 is 34 per cent
(*Barham*). Three out of a total complement of 1500 is 0.2 per cent (*Hood*), a terrible
figure. *Barham's* survivors were luckier than they knew.

There were many survivors' stories, and nearly all of them had one common factor.
Those who have been on the brink of death, or who have been technically dead for some
seconds, speak of a long tunnel with the brightest of bright lights shining at the end.
Barham's survivors spoke of the air bubble which saved their lives. The account I have
chosen is that of my friend Peter Edwards. He had been in my term at Dartmouth and

in the same House. We were, therefore, both midshipmen of an exact age and seniority at the time.

Peter Edwards was summoned to appear before the Board of Enquiry, and what he told them, reproduced by kind permission of the Public Record Office, can be seen in Appendix Ill.

Peter Edwards later joined *Valiant*, and we all spent some time questioning him about his fight for survival. After all, it was at the back of my mind, and, I am sure, the other midshipmen, that we might be required at some time in the future to have to draw on his experiences. He had, like all survivors, lost everything that he possessed, and once again I counted myself lucky that my possessions were still intact. I thought especially of my beautiful Zeiss Delactem night binoculars which I have to this very day. It was not easy to replace clothing or anything else in those days of shortages so we helped Peter out with what we could. Poor Peter, he had been saved only to be killed later in the war.

A midshipman named McNeill, who I also met, was another whose life was in all probability saved by the air bubble. Both confirmed that they thought they were about to drown and simply had to open their mouths. To their amazement, joy and relief they sucked in air, not water, and managed to swim to the surface.

Another officer's account (he sounds like a 'schoolie', Instructor Lieutenant and was) contained the extraordinary statement that 'he went back for his *Burberry*' before abandoning ship! The search for his lifebelt appeared to have been secondary. It seemed to me like dressing for dinner in the jungle, and evidently the Burberry's waterproofing qualities were not up to keeping the Mediterranean at bay since he later discarded it in favour of his lifebelt!

Some survivors had difficulty inflating their lifebelts, and I can sympathise with them. The lifebelts with which we were issued were really somewhat primitive. I was fortunate in that I never had to put their efficiency to the test, but in survival exercises in a swimming pool I found they were hardly the lifesavers they were supposed to be. The Admiralty-issue lifebelt consisted of a small rubber 'tyre' from which hung a short length of tubing. The whole was covered with blue cloth, and tapes over one's head and behind one's back secured it to the wearer.

One was warned NOT to inflate the lifebelt before entering the water as this might burst it on impact. Imagine therefore, the wretched survivors from *Barham*, they have jumped from their sinking ship into the sea, warmish even in November, but a shock just the same. They then go down and down in the darkness with just a faint light showing above them, a long, long way off. At their last gasp, they breathe in and miraculously draw in a gulp of air. They drift to the surface, gasping once more only to find they have swallowed some thick, filthy, clinging oil fuel which is now clogging their lungs and beginning to choke them. In that situation, how on earth do you manage to put that limp tube in your oil-filled mouth and have the puff, struggling in the water, to inflate the bloody lifebelt? The answer is of course you don't, you either find a Carley raft, a piece of wreckage or drown.

In the short time available to those in *Barham*, all they could cut adrift were the said Carley floats and some picket boat seats. Ratings carried a huge knife, resembling a Stanley knife today. Officers did not, so would not be able to cut free their particular piece of wreckage. We should at least have been provided with little gas bottles which would have made our lifebelts self-inflatable like a Mae West.

When I was on leave in 1942, awaiting another sea-going appointment, I thought I might be sent to the Home Fleet. With *Barham* ' s sinking much in mind and the thought of ghastly Arctic convoys, I went to Gieves, the famous naval tailors. There I purchased a splendid kapok-filled life-saving suit and a pair of magnificent fleece-lined boots (cost – £5!). Clad in this gear, I fancied I would be reasonably snug on an open bridge in northern latitudes. The fact that I greatly resembled the Michelin man was beside the point.

This warm clothing was the best insurance I ever bought. Appointed to the 8" gun cruiser *Suffolk*, I was promptly ordered to the heat and humidity of the Indian Ocean. My Michelin suit and beautiful warm boots have never seen any more action than keeping me warm as I fetch in logs for the fire on a winter's day.

The terrible saga of *Barham* ' s sinking is best ended by the official account of the incident drafted by our Captain, Charles Morgan. Dated 26 November 1941, the day after the tragedy, it is reproduced by kind permission of the Public Record Office, Kew, in Appendix II.

Incidents of a less dramatic kind now followed, for a short time at least. One Saturday evening, John Cardew and I were told by Michael Penton, the 'snotties' nurse', that we had been invited to breakfast with the Captain the next morning. We were both delighted and a little apprehensive. In spite of the close proximity in which everyone lives in a warship, *Valiant* was big enough for me not to have seen a great deal of my Commanding Officer.

I had woken him on occasions at sea and kept out of his way at the back of the bridge, where we all noticed he had a habit of saying 'Wha' to himself. Needless to say this was copied by the more irreverent members of the Gunroom who would pace up and down, their hands behind their backs, and muttering 'Wha' at intervals.

Clad in our smartest reefer jackets and trousers we presented ourselves in the Captain's Flat at 0830 the next day and knocked on the great man's door. At his command we entered and stood respectfully on the threshold. Morgan said good morning and then suddenly uttered the question, 'Has Kent been shot yet?' We knew who he meant. Midshipman Barrie Kent (now Captain B.H. Kent, Royal Navy) was a member of the Gunroom, a survivor from the sinking of the cruiser *Southampton* on my eighteenth birthday and referred to in an earlier chapter.

We both swallowed uneasily, shifted our feet and looked pleadingly at Morgan. What could he mean? Admiral Byng was probably the last British naval officer to have been shot by his own side in the Mediterranean. Surely the efficient Barrie had not merited his demise '*pour encourager les autres*'?

Morgan laughed and explained. 'Last night,' he said, 'I had my precious sleep interrupted not once, not twice, but three times by the wretched Kent. The firing squad is being assembled now.' We listened speechless as he continued, 'My telephone has rung three times in my sleeping cabin. Each time it has been Kent telling me that I am late in relieving him on the ADP (Air Defence Position).'

Now, four-ring Captains in His Majesty's naval service do not keep watches in the ships they command. They are permanently on call at sea. In harbour they are entitled to all the rest they can get.

What had happened was that Barrie Kent had kept the Middle Watch (midnight to 0400) as Air Defence Officer on the ADP In the event of an air raid he would alert the AA gun crews and direct their fire. His watch ending, his relief had not appeared. Picking up the telephone, he asked to be connected to him. (No dialling in those days, *Valiant* had its own manual telephone exchange which a rating operated permanently.)

The cause of the incident was that Barrie Kent's relief was the Captain, Royal Marines, the equivalent in rank of a two-stripe Lieutenant Royal Navy. The telephone operator had put the hapless Kent through each time to the Captain – hence Morgan's ire!

Morgan saw the funny side of it and John Cardew and I laughed in relief as we joined him at the breakfast table. It was luxury to which we were unaccustomed. Silver coffee and tea pots, beautiful white starched table cloth, bacon and eggs in profusion, marmalade, jam, rolls or toast all served deftly by the Captain's steward.

Morgan was a charming host, and we began to feel quite at home when we were brought back to reality as he dismissed us, saying gently: 'Well, I expect you would like to get ready for Sunday Divisions.' We were ready, but we got the hint and left, thanking him profusely for what had been a delightful and diverting meal.

Senior officers must never lose sight of making such occasions possible. It means a great deal to junior officers and at the same time their seniors can assess them much better than countless occasions when on duty.

Two small entries in my journal may amuse.

Saturday 29th November 1941: At 0800 for our sins (sic) V.A.! (Admiral Commanding 1st Battle-squadron) hoisted his flag in *Valiant*. However, he has not come aboard yet and I do not think he is likely to do so for some time. He gets more money if he flies his flag than if he does not do so.

Monday 1st December 1941. There was an air raid warning at about 1745 today whilst I was ashore (in Alexandria). It was the first time that I had been on the streets here whilst a warning was on, and for an exhibition of sheer abject terror you could not beat the Egyptians when the sirens started. There were screams and yells everywhere, and people dashing for shelter. Three women came into a shop in an advanced stage of collapse. However, there was great rejoicing amongst these 'lovable people' when the 'All Clear' was sounded a quarter an hour later without any bombs having been dropped.

When my journal was later inspected by 'Nuts' Penton, our snotties' nurse, he merely put a pencilled exclamation mark in the margin beside each entry!

Another entry in my journal records that our ship's company, especially the older men, were much opposed to the conscription of women into the armed services. The BBC had given out news of this far-reaching proposal and there was much headshaking and sucking of teeth. What a change they would find on return to the UK!

The naval situation in the eastern Mediterranean in December 1941 can only be described as parlous. *Barham* was no more, and soon her two sister ships, Queen Elizabeth and ourselves, were to be attacked and put out of action for many months. Added to this, Force 'K' suffered grievous losses in the central Mediterranean. Having encountered two Italian battleships and numerous light forces off Benghazi, Force 'K' made them turn tail and flee in spite of the Italian ships being much the superior in firepower. This was the first battle of Sirte.

On 15 December the beautiful new cruiser *Galatea* was torpedoed and sunk by a submarine. This tragedy, taking place as it did within 29 miles of Alexandria breakwater, brought home to us all again how vulnerable we were to the underwater menace. She sank in two minutes. Out of a ship's company of 600, only 13 officers and 129 ratings survived.

16

The Italian Frogmen Attack

Very little has been written on the British side about the exceptionally brave and spectacularly successful attack on the battlefleet in Alexandria harbour carried out by Italian frogmen on the night of 18/19 December 1941. Perhaps this is not altogether surprising since there is an extreme paucity of any meritorious action on our part to record, whilst on the Italian side, no praise can be too high for the sheer cold courage and determination displayed by those who took part.

Put concisely, a force of six Italians immobilised for many months the two British battleships remaining in the eastern Mediterranean. They did immeasurably more with six men to alter the balance of sea power in that area than we had done at Matapan with three battleships, an aircraft carrier, numerous cruisers and destroyers. For sheer economy of effort and manpower the attack has no equal.

A film entitled *Valiant* was made of the incident and I attended its premiere along with many others of the ship's company. The leader of the Italian party, Lieutenant (later Ammiraglio di Squadra) Luigi Durand de la Penne, wrote his account of the attack and most kindly sent me a copy, but it was written in Italian and was not published in the UK.

That, so far as I am aware, is as far as accounts of this enterprise have gone. I shall now endeavour to set the record straight. My narrative of what happened is first-hand, recorded in my journal, from personal reminiscence, and from personal interviews with both Admiral de la Penne and his colleague, Commander Marceglia.

No one can say that we had not been warned. As recorded earlier, Italian frogmen had attacked the harbour of Gibraltar and so severely damaged the 8" gun cruiser *York* in Suda Bay that she had to be beached and eventually became German property.

There had then been the conference at Ras-el-Tin when the Egyptians were not allowed to know our plans for boom defence.

My journal entry of Thursday 18 December continues the story of our precautions: 'Today we were given our booms, similar to those of Queen Elizabeth. I believe this was speeded up on account of a signal to the effect that, during the prevailing calm weather and dark nights, special vigilance was to be kept for midget submarines trying to attack the fleet in harbour.'

This signal was to prove exceptionally true. The boom was laid tapering outwards from the stern and not in a straight line. This necessitated an extra good lookout when running ships' boats. Running my boat at that time was impossible as the launch had been hoisted inboard for much-needed repairs. As a result I was given my first – and only – command of a foreign vessel, an Egyptian tug! I had with me none of the sailors who normally formed my crew, only Egyptians. My journal entry says: 'None of the Egyptians spoke any English, and as my Arabic was limited, I thought that sign language would be best.

If I wanted the thing to start I had to make queer sounds and gestures supposedly indicative of a piece of decrepit machinery getting under way, which, with greater perception than I would have credited them with, they understood. We got on quite all right, and although I had anticipated having to tell the coxswain where to go, he knew.'

This latter sentence highlights the security risk which we ran permanently in Alexandria. If the Egyptian tug's coxswain, who was only one of the fellaheen, knew where *Valiant* lay, what hope had we of keeping things quiet? Feluccas plied for hire in the harbour, going from ship to ship and were frequently used by officers wishing to disembark when no ship's boat was running at the time.

The near impossibility of maintaining secrecy in Alexandria was emphasised in the C-in-C's report after the underwater attack on the harbour. Egypt is not the Orkneys and Alexandria is not Scapa Flow where the sheep would be the only likely breaches of security.

Alexandria harbour is unlikely ever to see again such intense activity as there was on the night of 18/19 December 1941. Chronologically, what took place was this: At 2030 on 18 December, the *Sciré*, an Italian submarine, surfaced off Alexandria harbour. On board, beside her crew, she carried six men, three officers and three ratings who were about to embark on a very hazardous mission indeed. Their equipment consisted of three 'chariots' which were virtually explosive charges capable of being propelled electrically, were submersible, and each of which carried two men sitting astride rather like a pilot and observer in an open aeroplane cockpit.

The commander of this expedition was Lieutenant (later Admiral) Luigi Durand de la Penne. Accompanying him was Petty Officer Bianchi. The next 'chariot' was commanded by Captain Martellota, and the third by Lieutenant (later Commander) Antonio Marceglia. They also carried a rating behind them.

The signal made by C-in-C Med referring to extra harbour security, had correctly anticipated the frogmen's mission: 'In view of the activity of the Italian fleet at sea covering important convoys, it is reasonable to anticipate that endeavour will be made to immobilize the fleet at Alexandria.' As they would say in Australia, "Too right, mate.' C-in-C Med went on to say: 'Steps to increase vigilance have been taken by ordering out the greatest number of patrol craft, 51b. charges were dropped at irregular intervals at the El Khot anchorage and outside the boom, defences were inspected and lookouts increased.' Irregular intervals' is rubbish. (As one of those who actually dropped the charges, we shoved them over the side at regular intervals I fear!)

The Italians' 'chariots' were placed in the water by the submarine's crew, and the small but extremely deadly fleet started its journey towards the African coast. De la Penne found that water was being let in to his submersible suit. It is possible that this may, in a strange way, have saved both his life and mine for the reason that he grew colder and colder during the operation. This resulted in his not being able to place his lethal charge in the position where it could well have blown *Valiant* in half, and us with it.

The sea was calm, it was a dark, clear, still night after recent storms. De la Penne decided that the journey to Alexandria harbour would be made on the surface without breathing gear so as to conserve air. His chariot was slower than the other two, and so Martellotta and Marceglia had constantly to adjust their speeds to that of the slowest 'ship of the convoy'.

After about an hour he could see cliffs and the royal palace. Two hours later they were off Ras-el-Tin (Naval HQ Alexandria). Having checked their position and the current, they calmly opened their food tubes and had 'breakfast'! They were not to eat again for a long time.

We must now turn to the vital question of what was happening to the Boom Gate at the harbour entrance. It was here that the monumental cock-up occurred, for had this not been operating like a zoo turnstile on a Bank Holiday, the attack would in all likelihood have failed.

The Boom Gate was opened no less than three times that fateful night, and was open for a total of no less than six hours ten minutes for traffic to pass in and out. I have used the phrase 'the fox was in the henhouse' in the account of the sinking of *Barham*. The amount of time the boom was open on 18/19 December 1941 amounted to giving de la Penne and his crews a master key to the harbour entrance, a gift of which they took full advantage.

C-in-C Med's report after the attack stated that in his opinion, the Boom was open for an unnecessarily long period, and that in future was only to be opened at night in cases of emergency. For stable doors read Boom Gates.

Between 2017 and 2031 the Boom Gate was opened to allow the tug *Roysterer* (sic) to pass out to bring in the *Flamingo*, which, escorted by the *Farndale* and the *Falk*, was returning damaged from Tobruk. All right, so she was damaged, but she had made the passage from Tobruk safely, so a few extra hours at sea would not have come amiss. The escorting ships passed in at 2122 followed at 2356 by *Flamingo* in tow and the gate was closed at 2359.

The Boom Gate was reopened at 0040. This was to facilitate the entry of the 7th Cruiser Squadron and the 4th Destroyer Flotilla. It was closed at 0150. It was opened yet again at 0242 for the 14th Destroyer Flotilla to enter and closed at 03 15.

Agreed, there were enemy submarines about that night – we know of one already. The destroyer *Jervis* attacked one in position 297° Ras-el-Tin 37 miles at 2245. Another contact was attacked by the *Kingston Cyanite* in position 284° Ras-el-Tin 23 miles.

But this submarine activity was an ever-present danger, and one we had to contend with all the time. These ships' ETAs (estimated times of arrival) should have been revised to first light – a far different story might then have been told.

Which master key did the Italians use in order to gain entry to the harbour? De la Penne must have thanked his lucky stars that he was being offered such a fantastic chance. He did not hesitate. He ordered his tiny 'fleet' to submerge so that only the 'driver' had his head above water without breathing gear. The after man was quite invisible just below the surface and breathing in oxygen. This variable trim was a great technical feat for such a small craft.

De la Penne approached the breakwater. The time was 2300. He had, although he was not then aware of it, chosen the midnight performance. He was by this time so close that he could see and hear men talking on the breakwater, and could see 'a large motorboat sailing silently in front of the breakwater dropping bombs from time to time. These bombs prove to be rather a nuisance.' A marvellous example of understatement.

So here it was that de la Penne and I nearly came face to face for the first time. 'The large motorboat' to which he refers was in fact *Queen Elizabeth's* 1st picket boat doing exactly what I had done only the night before and on many nights previously. *Queen Elizabeth* and *Valiant* shared this duty on alternate nights. There was no need for me to 'drop bombs' the next night.

De la Penne then noted: 'Lights delineating the sailable courses have come on outside the port.' Marvellous, it was as if the Harbour-master had been a Quisling, and done everything in his power to act as a guide to the enemy attacking force. (In fact, a rumour went round the fleet after the attack. It was to the effect that a signal had been received at Ras-el-Tin: 'No more charges to be dropped at harbour entrance after midnight.' No one knew where it had come from.)

De la Penne realised at once that the lights had come on only for one purpose a ship or ships was about to enter or leave harbour. He decided to take this wonderful opportunity now blazing before his eyes. He would ride in under cover of the entering vessels!

He took a quick look round. No sign of Martellotta or Marceglia, but dark shapes were approaching rapidly which he correctly identified as cruisers. He positioned himself so that he was only inches away from the bow of the leading cruiser. Her bow wave threw him under, but he regained control of his craft and returned to the surface.

He entered the harbour under cover of the second cruiser, but then the wash from the third cruiser threw him into the full light of the harbour beacon. He managed, he says, to pass by her stern without anyone spotting him.

Courage, bravery and initiative had brought their reward. He was inside and undetected. So, he supposed and hoped were his companions. Little did the 7th Cruiser Squadron realise what a signal service they had performed for the Royal Italian Navy. In spite of dire warnings, how easy it had been made for de la Penne. We were to pay a very heavy price indeed for the crass decision to open the Boom Gate during the hours of darkness.

By this time, de la Penne was having further trouble with his submersible suit. Because it continued to let in water, he began to feel very cold. For once, luck was deserting him and favouring those of us who were unconsciously awaiting his intentions.

He now relates that, 'In the area where I must operate there is a lot of light because a ship is loading.' It was unusual, since Alexandria and particularly the harbour, observed a strict blackout. Once again, de la Penne was in luck. The lights guided him, but he was undetected. It was then that he saw a dark shadow. It was *Valiant*. He had found his target.

De la Penne then found himself up against 'an obstruction' 50 metres from us. He said it was of an unknown type. It was composed of a steel cable connecting spheres; obviously our anti-torpedo boom. Only placed in position the day before, no one had anticipated that it would be of use so early. De la Penne tried to lift the cable but it was too heavy, so instead of going under it he decided to go round it. The reader must remember that these two men, de la Penne and Bianchi, were not just frogmen swimming freely. They had their big 'chariot' to manoeuvre, and this, in the cold dark waters of Alexandria harbour, was to prove no easy task. De la Penne's hands were now almost numb with cold and his whole physical condition was worsening.

He decided to go over the net on the surface, but then the 'chariot' became entangled with the net, causing a lot of noise. In this position he was like the proverbial fly caught in the spider's web. Had the armed sentry which we had in the bows seen or heard him then, it is likely de la Penne would have received a burst of submachine-gun fire. Nothing happened, luck was still with him and he heaved a sigh of relief.

He finally disentangled himself and the 'chariot' and now there was nothing between him and ourselves. He was 'about 30 metres from the ship'. The time was 0200.

Where was I whilst all this enemy activity was going on, whilst de la Penne was making preparations to blow me and hundreds of others to kingdom come? I was fast asleep, blissfully unconscious of what was going on, one of about a dozen midshipmen who had their camp beds on the deck of the Admiral's Flat. Whilst we slept, a pump hummed in a nearby compartment. That pump was to contribute greatly to our nearly premature departure from this earthly existence.

What follows now is a saga of de la Penne's iron determination to succeed in his mission. He was to need all the courage and willpower upon which he could call during the course of the next 40 minutes.

When only seven metres from *Valiant*, de le Penne submerged and slowly motored towards us. He hit the hull. Would no one hear? No one did. The reason why he hit the ship's side was that his hands were so stiff with cold that he could not manipulate the engine controls in order to stop.

He had turned into a sort of deadly dodgem car driver, and had hit the side of his target. Now at last luck deserted de la Penne, and nearly aborted his attack. His 'chariot' moved away from our side and fell to the harbour bottom, a depth of seventeen metres. In its fall, the 'chariot' sent up clouds of mud. De la Penne thought he would never find it.

Now, he had to re-surface in order to check his position. This was not easy because of his faulty diving suit. The latter, having let in so much water, was pulling him down a great deal, and made any movement extremely clumsy. To add to his troubles, de la Penne had to inflate his oxygen bag to give him the necessary impetus to reach the surface. Once there, he knew that the oxygen leaving his mask would be bound to make undue noise and this worried him.

He knew that we had an armed sentry on patrol, but when he surfaced, there was no sign of him. The reason for his re-surfacing was to find the optimum position in which to place the charge.

Whilst most of *Valiant's* ship's company slept, de la Penne dived again and tried to start the chariot's engine, but this refused to turn. What was he to do? Being within an ace of the successful completion of his mission, he felt angry and frustrated at this reversal in his fortunes. Here he was, with the huge explosive charge near his target, but probably not near enough to cause serious damage, if any at all. He had been highly trained for this, travelled hundreds of miles, entered the harbour in a brilliantly successful fashion, and now he was facing failure through two technical faults, his suit and the engine.

Lesser men might have given up, set the charges and tried to make for safety. Not de la Penne, he was made of very stern stuff indeed, and what Harold Macmillan, in another context called 'little local difficulties', were not going to deter him. He looked for Bianchi in order to ask him to check the propeller. It was only then that he realised Bianchi was no longer in the 'rear cockpit'. De la Penne assumed that Bianchi had fainted and floated to the surface.

This presented yet another problem for the troubled de la Penne. Stray frogmen's bodies floating in Alexandria harbour were not likely to be an everyday occurrence, and the discovery of Bianchi would undoubtedly disturb a hornets' nest. Up again to the surface therefore, and a quick look round for signs of Bianchi. What de la Penne would have given for the use of a periscope!

On the surface, de la Penne found himself only four metres away from our bows. He at once came within the strong beam of the projector light operated by our sentry. De la Penne thought that he was done for, but the light passed him by and he heaved a sigh of relief. The light had had one bonus for him however, if it could be called that. It had illuminated the water and revealed no sign of Bianchi.

De la Penne never lost sight of the supreme object of his mission – to destroy or immobilize the British battlefleet. Everything must be sacrificed toward that end, and whilst he was naturally concerned at Bianchi's disappearance, he could not afford to waste any more time. If Bianchi was discovered, he was discovered, and that was that – meanwhile he had work to do.

Everything was still quiet, and so like a huge sea lion de la Penne submerged yet again in search of his 'chariot'. Finding it, he discovered the cause of its immobility. A metal cable had become entangled with the propeller. It was impossible to disentangle the cable, but fortunately the latter was slack, leaving de la Penne with only one course open to him. He must try to drag this huge object along the harbour bottom and position it under *Valiant*. There was now no question of adhering to the original plan of securing the explosive charge to our hull. He must hope that the explosion, when it came, would do sufficient damage to justify his mission.

The task facing de la Penne was Herculean. Six hours had elapsed since he and his companions had left the submarine. Those hours had been packed full of tension caused by the risk of discovery. At times submerged, at times only with his head above the surface so that he swallowed sea water with every ripple, he had naturally become exhausted. His submersible suit was faulty and acting like a lead weight; the tension and everything else had tired him almost to breaking point. He had tried not to think that he was astride a high explosive charge weighing 500lb. which might go off prematurely. He had lost his companion and was alone on the bottom of an enemy harbour with the prospect of midshipmen like myself dropping charges on him at intervals. (He did not know that we only performed this duty at the Boom Gate – for all he knew, we might be throwing over a charge any minute.)

He began to haul, push and shove at the 'chariot'. It was immensely heavy work and he could only move it a few inches at a time. To add to his troubles, his exertions raised clouds of mud all around him and his eye pieces began to mist up. He was beginning to become disorientated. How could he be sure he was moving this huge object towards *Valiant*? Perhaps he was actually moving it away.

It was then that he heard the beat of a pump, that bloody pump to which I referred earlier – de la Penne now had the perfect direction sign. It was as though he had heard a reciprocal foghorn, a noise which was not to warn him to keep away, but which beckoned him like the Lorelei's song. The cardiac thump of this machine which he knew could only emanate from *Valiant*, was to aid him immeasurably in the success of his mission.

It is not meant as any denigration of de la Penne to say that the noise of the pump gave him the vitally needed shot of adrenalin which contributed to his final motivation. His courage and determination were such that he would probably have been successful anyway, but he admits that, 'The nearness of my target gave me strength.'

Every now and then he had to rest from his almost superhuman exertions. Not only was he extremely exhausted, but his submersible suit was giving trouble once more. This time it was the folds of it which were cutting into him. Did he need any more adversity?

Nearer and nearer he got, inch by inch he moved the 'chariot' towards the noise of the pump. The noise grew stronger. He knew he must be underneath some vital part of the ship. De la Penne was working like an automaton, not knowing what he was doing, understanding nothing except the beat of the pump calling him on.

The weight of his waterlogged suit, the weight of the 'chariot', the total numbness of his fingers, all added to the immense amount of will-power which he required to carry on. He became light-headed, and like someone who has taken a drug overdose, he needed to be slapped in the face and exhorted in stentorian tones to 'Get on with it – don't falter now'.

It took de la Penne 40 minutes to move the 'chariot' to a satisfactory position. The noise was much louder now – suddenly the face slap was almost administered. He bumped his head against a very solid object. It was our hull!

The shallowness of Alexandria harbour was another bonus for de la Penne. His 'chariot' was now lying only five feet below us. Any lower and its effectiveness would naturally have been greatly reduced. There was no time to lose, and having reached his goal, he made final preparations to blow us up.

He returned to the 'chariot', eager to complete his task before any minor depth charges descended on him. He was, in his own words 'totally exhausted' but his brain had to function, and to motivate his fingers, otherwise all would have been for nothing.

What was there left to be done? Why, the fuses had to be set of course, without those vital instruments, there could be no explosion. So he set these, and then fearful that the illuminated instrument panel of the 'chariot' could be seen from above, he covered it in mud.

He had with him some incendiary bombs, but decided that their use could easily give away his presence. (In point of fact Martellotta used them – see later.)

De la Penne could do no more. He had positioned his 'chariot' with its 500lb. explosive charge where it would undoubtedly do a great deal of damage, if it did not succeed in sending *Valiant* and everyone in her sky-high. Crammed full of explosives and ammunition as we were, this was by no means impossible. He had set the fuses. If an explosion did not occur it would not be his fault.

He swam to the surface. Once there he took off his respirator and threw it away. He had surfaced on a level with my old friend 'B' turret. He gasped, gulping in great draughts of fresh air. He longed to have something to which he could hold on thus conserving his strength.

De la Penne, who by now could only make feeble strokes in the water, swam a little further. Then, he says: 'After about ten metres someone on board calls me.' What could he do, he had hardly the strength to swim, let alone shout. So reasoning correctly that if he did not swim he would not be able to answer, he continued to swim away from the ship.

Our sentry in *Valiant's* bows, was not asleep nor stupid. He shone the projector light full on de la Penne, and then the latter heard the sound of a machine gun and bullets splattered the water close by. He had been well and truly discovered. Events moved very quickly from then on.

De la Penne swam underwater for as long as he could, making towards our stern. With no respirator and in a state of almost total collapse, this was no easy matter. At our stern he found Bianchi who told him that he had fainted and found himself on the surface. He had been of little use to de le Penne. The latter told Bianchi that the charge was in place and fuses set. Meanwhile de la Penne, who was not at all without command of some English, could hear what was being said on our quarter-deck, and was able to understand most of it.

Someone was saying: 'Ities in the water – how typical, they can't get anything right. We've discovered them before they've had a chance to do anything.' Laughter and agreement.

De la Penne smiled to himself and said to Bianchi, 'In a couple of hours they will have more respect for the Italian nation.'

At this time I was still soundly asleep, my camp bed in the Admiral's Flat being literally only feet from where the two Italians were when swimming round our stern. Did someone say anything about 'ignorance being bliss'?

De la Penne and Bianchi now swam up our starboard side and found themselves at our bow buoy to which we were secured. Somehow they managed to climb on to it (these buoys are huge anyway) and then sat there in a state of near collapse.

De la Penne now misunderstood what was being said to him and it nearly cost him his life. Thinking he was being ordered to board us by the anchor chain he endeavoured to climb up it only to receive a burst of machine-gun fire for his pains. Wisely he rejoined Bianchi on the buoy. The time, according to de la Penne, was 0330.

Shortly after they had been fired upon, one of our picket boats approached the buoy. 'It carried,' he said, 'two men (actually Royal Marines), armed with submachine guns.' They ordered the Italians to put up their hands. De la Penne refused, and the Royal Marines did not insist. The Italians were searched for arms, none were found, their watches were taken away and the prisoners were conveyed to the after gangway.

The C-in-C's report now comes in: 'At 0325, *Valiant* signalled that two foreigners had been found on her bow buoy. The C-in-C at 0332 made a general signal that the presence of human torpedoes was suspected in the harbour. Patrol vessels were ordered to drop explosive charges, harbour defences were brought to the first degree of readiness, and steam raised in tugs. All ships were ordered to pass bottom lines (a sort of keel-hauling without a victim) and send boats to drop explosive charges. The Boom Gate opened at 0352, it was closed by 0432 after the *Hotspur* and *Hasty* had passed out. It was opened once more from 05 10 to 0544 to allow the *Griffin* to pass out.'

So here we have the zoo turnstile once more turning merrily whilst no one, least of all Midshipman Holloway, knew what on earth was going on.

De la Penne and Bianchi were now climbing the quarter-deck ladder, again only feet away from my recumbent form. They were taken to the Ward Room where they were put in the charge of a party of armed ratings. De la Penne said, 'They made menacing gestures towards us.' So they might well have done, they were probably extremely frightened since they did not know what was going to happen.

De la Penne requested assistance in taking off his submersible suit. He says: 'I was rather sharply helped.' Just then one of our officers came in and asked the two Italians who they were and where they came from. He told de la Penne, 'You have had no luck.'

With hindsight this was a very stupid statement, but it must be remembered that those who took part at that moment were apprehensive and quite untrained in Intelligence work. No HM ship carried any officer so trained. If prisoners were taken (which was very seldom) they were landed and then interrogated. The job was best left to experts and de la Penne just ignored it.

De la Penne handed over identity papers and refused to answer further questions as he was quite entitled to do. Captain Morgan then joined in and asked him, 'Where did you put the charge?' This was a change of tack to the previous question and showed that we were now admitting that the Italians might have succeeded.

The prisoners were then taken under heavy escort to the picket boat and transferred to Ras-el-Tin.

It was during this trip across the harbour that de la Penne did a most kindly thing. Many years later, in a letter to me he asked if I could remember the name of the midshipman who was in charge of the picket boat that fateful morning. I told him that unfortunately I did not know and it was very difficult to find out now after so many years had elapsed. The reason he wanted to know was that he managed to whisper to the midshipman that if he could find some excuse not to return to *Valiant* then he should do so. This really was a very kind thing to do. There was de la Penne, a very exhausted prisoner of war, with many perils still ahead of him, and yet he was trying to save the life of at least one member of our ship's company.

Of course, the unknown midshipman could not take advantage of the warning de la Penne had so kindly given him. He could hardly have had a sudden attack of appendicitis or discovered that he had urgent business on the Coal Wharf or Quarantine Breakwater. As we shall see in a moment, de la Penne was soon to be his passenger again, but for a short while that midshipman was in receipt of more enemy intelligence than anyone else in Alexandria, meagre though it was. De la Penne had proved himself to be not only a very brave man indeed but had by this warning proved himself to be of a very kind and caring nature as well.

The reader may snort and say, 'What utter cant.' This man had just planted a device which could well send over 1000 men to their deaths. True, but this was war, and to quote Admiral of the Fleet Lord Fisher in 1913, 'The essence of war is violence and moderation in war is imbecility.' In the violence of war de la Penne had shown as much gentleness as he could in the circumstances.

On arrival at Ras-el-Tin, the two Italians were taken ashore. Bianchi was questioned inside a hut. On emerging he managed to gesture to de la Penne that he had not said anything.

It was now de la Penne's turn. In de la Penne's own words: 'I meet an officer armed with a gun. He asks me in Italian, where I have put the torpedo, and advises me to answer him because he is very nervous since I have woken him up at such an unearthly hour of the night.' De la Penne refused to answer, whereupon the officer said that he might as well speak since Bianchi had told him everything.

I have earlier mentioned 'expert interrogators'. So far, the questioning at Ras-el-Tin would have disgraced an American B-movie and only lacked the time-honoured phrase, 'We have ways of making you talk.'

Believe it or not, this was the statement uttered next by the officer at Ras-el-Tin. Whether he is now a high-ranking officer in MI5 or MI6, history does not relate. De la Penne still did not answer and was marched out of the room.

Into the picket boat again, and racing across the harbour back to *Valiant*. The midshipman could not avail himself of his warning. Midshipman Holloway was still asleep.

It is four o'clock in the morning. The Italian prisoners are met on our quarterdeck by Captain Morgan who asks de la Penne once more for the position of the torpedo. He receives no answer.

Action is prompt. De la Penne and Bianchi are marched forward under the same heavy escort. De la Penne said they were taken 'through corridors where people are still asleep'. He does not mention me! They stopped in front of a steel door with a ladder leading down. He noticed 'lots of heavy iron [sic] chains and other instruments hanging from the deckhead'. The description sounds like the reception room of the Spanish Inquisition, but where they had been taken was actually our cable locker.

De la Penne asked where they were and was told 'between the two turrets'. He guessed that only feet separated him from the 500lb charge, its fuses activated, and ticking away. So this was it. He and Bianchi had been put down in the most dangerous part of the ship. A good guess had been made – they were literally only feet from the charge. This was calculated to concentrate their minds.

Now, the wets and the liberals, the purists and the jurists, what have they to say to this? By the Geneva Convention of which Great Britain was a signatory, no prisoner of war should be incarcerated in any place where he is in further danger. Hence, for instance, no POW camp must be sited near a military installation which could itself become a target. Do we see Mr Ludovic Kennedy foaming at the mouth and demanding that the British guilty men be brought to account for this alleged breach of the Convention? Well nobody has complained yet, least of all de la Penne.

As for myself, much as I admire de la Penne's courage, I would heartily support any move which would have assisted us in preventing the torpedo from exploding. *Valiant* and everyone in her was in great jeopardy. There should be no pussyfooting about as to how the information concerning the whereabouts of the torpedo was to be obtained. De la Penne found out something himself though. He says that the ribbons on the sailors' caps bore the ship's name *Valiant*.

Their Lordships had decreed during the war that ships' names should disappear from cap ribbons and be replaced by HMS. This was good security but it did not appear to have filtered through to our ratings by December 1941.

When de la Penne calculated that there were only ten minutes to go before the explosion, he asked to speak to the Captain. Accordingly he was brought before Charles Morgan. De la Penne told him that there were only a few minutes left before the charge would blow up. Morgan was told that there was nothing he could do to prevent it and the Italian suggested that *Valiant's* ship's company should be taken to a place of safety.

Morgan was not having any of that. The idea of abandoning his ship on the advice of a junior foreign officer was not one that he would have entertained for one second, well meant though de la Penne's suggestion was. What would the Commander-in-Chief have said if he had seen scores of boats surrounding *Valiant*, jam-packed with sailors abandoning their ship? It was unheard of and in any case there was very little time left.

Events again unfolded swiftly. Morgan demanded that de la Penne reveal the whereabouts of the torpedo. De la Penne refused. He was at once taken back to the cable locker and the door slammed shut. It is only now that I in common with 98 per cent of *Valiant's* ship's company, come into the picture.

Morgan had quite rightly decided that on the discovery of our Italian frogmen, there would be little to be gained and much to be lost by alerting everyone on board. Hence my assertions, oft repeated, of my total ignorance that I might be about to meet my Maker, propelled there by Italian explosive. There was really nothing that anyone could have done at that stage, except to pass the bottom line which had revealed nothing. Had we known that the explosive rested on the sea bed and was not attached to us, we might, conceivably have been towed to another berth. However, this would not have been an easy operation or a quick one and it might have ended in our being nearer other ships when or if, we were blown to smithereens. The only thing that had not been done was now about to be carried out – the closing of all water-tight doors.

One was so used to constant noise in a warship in wartime that everyone had slept soundly. I was suddenly shaken awake by John Cardew who said urgently: 'Come on, get up, hurry up and go on deck. The Italian underwater cyclists have arrived.' This was the somewhat theatrical term which we used for enemy frogmen, and because he had used it I did not at first believe him. I did however, believe the loudspeakers which were relaying the order: 'Close all 'X' and 'Y' doors,' followed by the most unusual order in any ship: 'All hands on deck.' That means what it says, you leave whatever you are doing wherever you are and you beat it hell for leather to the upper deck. Things must be serious. The time was 0555.

The Commander's voice then came over the loudspeakers. In a calm tone he told us that there were two Italian prisoners on board who had been seen in the water by the bow sentries. They had told us that, 'Something would go off at 0600.'

I was sleeping in my pyjamas. The niceties of dressing gowns were not for us. The ladder leading to the quarter-deck was only in the next flat (compartment). It was a beautiful wide ladder with wooden steps and polished oak handrails rather like the ones which can be seen preserved in HMS *Victory* to this day.

I did not know where my lifebelt was. I had never thought I would need it in harbour. I grabbed my reefer jacket, slipped my feet into Egyptian sandals and obeyed the order.

I had only just placed a foot on the ladder when there was a violent explosion from somewhere up forward. I was nearly thrown off the ladder. De la Penne had succeeded in his mission, but we were still alive.

17

The Battlefleet Disabled

I arrived on the quarter-deck shaken, bewildered, but strangely not frightened. I had certainly and without equivocation been frightened many times. On being bombed, on leaving Suda Bay, with the German Army so close, on being shelled, and when *Barham* was torpedoed, yes, I was certainly frightened. But not at this moment. It was something new being blown up and I suppose the implications had not really sunk in.

My journal entry even at that time, has a certain ironic ring to it:

Friday 19th December 1941. I arrived on the Q.D. [quarter-deck] to find the ship had a 5° list to port. This was contrary to Daily Orders which said that the ship would be listed to starboard for scraping the side.

The quarter-deck was full of officers, all in varying stages of undress. Most were dressed like me in pyjamas under reefer jacket. The most extraordinary sight was presented by the Dental Officer. He was dressed in pyjamas, uniform cap, and lifebelt. Added to the fact that he sported a huge black piratical beard, and one will see that he looked somewhat out of place. 'Toothy' was the only officer wearing a lifebelt and I remember thinking he was 'windy' at the time. Looking back after 70 years, he was perhaps more sensible than one thought then, but we all took the view, 'Well, we have never worn lifebelts in harbour, why start now?' Another officer wore a reefer jacket, pyjama bottoms and a pilot's helmet. Whether he thought that would help him if blown into the water I know not. Alexandria was not all that cold even in late December so he could not have wanted to keep his ears warm.

My Divisional Officer, Lieutenant-Commander Fairbairn (the Torpedo Officer), decided on a gallant but foolish course of action. He jumped overboard and swam round the ship trying to find what he assumed would be a second explosive charge. He did not know that there was no second charge and had no hope whatsoever of finding out without diving equipment. I remember looking at him and thinking he was brave but misguided.

A note of the purest comedy was introduced at this time by the inimitable Henry Barnes. Clad in British Warm, white scarf and uniform trousers, he had eschewed the rig of lesser mortals like ourselves whose pyjama bottoms were much in evidence. The order to clear Lower Deck had not deterred him from dressing like an officer and a gentleman. He was thus better arrayed for the possibility of meeting his Maker.

It was not his attire however which caused us to laugh behind our hands, but what he was doing. Henry B. had sent for the drummer, Royal Marines, a pimply and somewhat bolshie youth whose duty it was to sound bugle calls. Accustomed as he was to sounding Reveille and the Last Post, Action Stations and Repel Aircraft, the drummer had obviously been at a loss when it came to sounding off 'Clear Lower Deck'. He was not alone in this; it happened so seldom that most of us were ignorant of its cadences.

The drummer now stood stiffly to attention in front of Henry B. Henry berated him in parade ground terms: 'How dare you make such an appalling mess of sounding off Clear Lower Deck!' And then came the gem of it all: 'Don't you know there are foreign officers on board?'

It was delicious and only Henry B. could have said it. Visions of a ceremonial visit in peacetime to an Italian port were conjured up. The failure of the drummer to have sounded the proper bugle notes would then have been a heinous crime. H.M. Bateman would have delighted in describing the scene as 'the drummer who sounded the wrong bugle call when the Italian Admiral stepped on board'. Now here we had Lieutenant de la Penne Royal Italian Navy, soaking wet and our prisoner, together with Petty Officer Bianchi paraded before us, but Henry B. was determined to show that even in moments of crisis and adversity the Royal Navy does not forget its ceremonial. Long live the Empire, and Henry B. for First Sea Lord. There was no panic, but on the other hand no one seemed to know what they ought to be doing. If attacked by aircraft or surface ship, we went to our action stations and worked whatever gun or instrument we had been taught to operate. But an 'underwater cyclist' attack in harbour left us completely unprepared. After all, what was there to do, except what we had done, get up on deck having closed the watertight doors? We felt, and were, completely impotent and were horribly conscious of the fact.

Those who had been on deck earlier told me that at 0558 there was an explosion under the stern of the Norwegian oiler *Sagona*. This damaged the bows of the destroyer *Jervis* which was alongside her at the time.

A little while later, a number of incendiary bombs came to the surface and exploded. They did no harm, only causing some consternation in an already rather taut situation. The Italian plan had been for No. 1. (Martellotta) to attack an aircraft carrier, failing which his target was to be an oil tanker. The object of the exercise was to blow open the tanker and spill her oil into the harbour. This would then be set alight by the incendiary bombs. Charming, I thought, just another little '*divertissement*' to add to the night's activities.

A note of comedy had crept into Martellotta's actions. The official report says that he 'identified the Vichy French battleship Lorraine with his torch'. Unofficially it was said that he surfaced alongside her, and asked the sentry: '*Valiant?*' The sentry gladly pointed us out and with his thanks Martellotta dived! What is not in dispute is that whilst under the oiler's stern Martellotta was hit on the head by a felucca oar! It must have been the only pro-Allied action ever undertaken (albeit unwittingly) by an Egyptian during the entire war.

The Dentist fiddled with his lifebelt, alternately inflating and deflating it. He seemed to be having trouble with the red lamp attached. Since it was by then broad daylight I wondered what his purpose was. Perhaps he felt like peering into someone's mouth with it.

The officer with the pilot's helmet pulled at his ear-flaps uneasily. He seemed to be having difficulty hearing anything said to him and was oblivious of the somewhat obvious cause.

Our snotties' nurse, Michael Penton, strolled around sucking at his dead pipe. I mused on the fact that the only navigating he would be doing in the next few months would be to bring us into the floating dock. Why do navigators puff at pipes? I think his must have been part of his uniform.

Sidney B. Taylor, our Schoolmaster Commander, wandered about looking cantankerous as usual. Perhaps he was speculating on the possibility of more visits to the Union Club (barred to Lieutenants and below) now that we were so crippled. Midshipmen talked in excited groups. We all waited.

We left de la Penne hearing the steel door of the cable locker clanging shut behind him for the second time. As he was being taken below again he muttered to Bianchi: 'It is all over for us but we can congratulate ourselves because we have succeeded in our mission.' Bianchi did not answer for the very good reason that he was not there. Whilst marching the pair forward, someone had detached Bianchi from his commanding officer. The thinking behind this was that a lonely de la Penne might be more inclined to talk than if he was imprisoned above the charge with a companion.

Whoever separated the two Italians had reckoned without de la Penne's great courage and iron will. He says: 'This time I was alone with half a ton of explosive under me and only a few centimetres (a little more than that – Author) of sheet iron (sic) between myself and the charge. I must find strength, not talking had been hard, I did not want to die, I was young. I did not want to give in for many reasons; our dead, Italy, the wish to show the English sailors how an Italian sailor behaved. I waited and I prayed.'

De la Penne continued: 'After a few minutes an explosion occurred. The ship was violently shaken. All the lights went out and the compartment was filled with smoke.'

Incredibly, he was unhurt except for a badly bruised knee where the force of the explosion had slapped one of the anchor chains against it. If anyone had stared death in the face, behaved with exemplary courage throughout and emerged virtually unscathed, it was de la Penne. He was now far better off than before the explosion but his position was still a precarious one. He was the only man on board *Valiant* who knew that there would be no more explosions. His charge had detonated, there were no more attached to the ship, and so from that point of view he was able to breathe more freely. However, breathing was the operative word. He very soon realised that he might soon cease to exercise this essential bodily function.

The explosion had obviously blown a great hole in *Valiant*. This was evident from the 5° list to port. At the moment this was not being increased, but for how long?

De la Penne looked apprehensively at a porthole some feet above him. He managed to open it and found that he could practically touch the sea. The ship's list had so heeled *Valiant* that he believed he was in grave danger of drowning. He said: 'I could feel the ship was reaching the bottom.'

Having survived the explosion, he realised he was now in imminent peril of its aftermath. His account of that moment is a wonderful understatement: 'I decided that it is not a good idea to remain any longer in this compartment.'

His only thought now was to prevent himself from a slow death by drowning in the steel compartment which could well be his coffin if he did not act. What could he do? He looked longingly at the porthole. Light was streaming through it. He entertained thoughts of escape to safety and freedom and then realised it was hopeless. Naval portholes are made to let in air and light. They are not escape hatches and the one in the cable locker was no exception. He could not possibly crawl through it.

He looked up at the huge anchor chains which hung down from the deckhead. Could he climb up these and then gain the comparative safety of the foc'sle? He was reminded somehow of a cathedral as he gazed up at these pendant arteries of possible escape soaring upwards.

A climb skywards was not to be for him. He was desperately tired, exhausted by his efforts on the harbour bed, the swimming and the general tension of the operation. Moreover it was again the horror of Alice in Wonderland. He was still too big to crawl to freedom through the hawse pipe.

He turned his attention to the steel door. He mounted the steps to it, gave it a tentative push, and found it opened to his touch. There was no one there, and breathing a sigh of relief he walked out of his prison and near-death cell.

Now this was surely disgraceful, but perhaps capable of explanation in the dire circumstances prevailing at the time. Where was Master-at-Arms Diable and the other guards who had been detailed to watch over the prisoner? Had they been guilty of gross dereliction of duty, or had they been obeying orders when 'All hands on deck' was piped? This is probably something we shall never know. The stark fact remains that a very important prisoner of war, one who might have given valuable information, had been left completely unguarded, an event which might well have resulted in his escape.

One thing however was in de la Penne's favour, and perhaps also in favour of his absent guards. They had not left him locked in, doomed to drown like a rat in a storm sewer. He found his way to the foc'sle, where some members of the ship's company were sitting on the deck. They stood up as he went by, seeing for the first time the man who had crippled their ship and who had nearly ended their mortal existences. To them de la Penne looked harmless enough, but what else had he up his sleeve? Why, they must have wondered, had he been allowed on deck? Had he told someone of another explosion to come?

My account of what happened next is at variance with that of de la Penne. My account was written in my journal on the afternoon of the explosion, de la Penne's was not recounted until much later. His account is perhaps at variance with mine more because of omission than anything else. At the risk of seeming immodest, I am therefore going to say that my account complements that of de la Penne! I can certainly vouch for its veracity.

De la Penne, having arrived on the foc'sle, found there Commander Reid who, he says 'was giving orders for the safety of the ship'. Of course the question uppermost in everyone's mind at that time was the one I have just posed – was there another explosion to come and if so, where? It was to this ghastly problem that Reid was addressing himself.

The appearance of de la Penne alone and unguarded, must have shaken Reid to no uncertain degree. The architect of the disaster now stood before him. De la Penne had the temerity to ask Reid, 'Where is my assistant (Bianchi)?' Reid did not answer him and he was roughly told to keep quiet by another officer.

We now come to the diverging account. My journal says:

> As I was standing on the quarter-deck, a Marine brought one of the Italians aft. The Captain (Morgan) was standing there. The Marine told the Captain that the Italian had been very unwilling to come aft, and that he was making signs indicative of there being something under our stern.

I looked with fascinated interest at the enemy standing only feet away from me. He had discarded his submersible suit and was clad, like our own submariners in dark blue naval uniform and roll-neck pullover. He seemed to be very wet.

A good-looking man I thought – now here before me, a prisoner, stands the man who has tried to kill me and everyone else on board *Valiant*. I did not feel though, any animosity towards him, just curiosity and a hope that he had nothing else up his sleeve. Oh no, I thought, not that! We had survived the explosion under our bows. What would an explosion under our stern do to us – split us in half like *Neptune* off Tripoli?

Morgan did not take long to act, and fortunately for those of us milling about on the quarter-deck, he decided that discretion was the better part of valour. If he could not save his ship he might be able to save his officers' lives. The order came: 'Everybody to the ship's waist.' The non-naval reader will doubtless understand that this is the middle of the ship. The motley collection of officers, including the bearded and lifebelted dentist, stumbled forward. We tried to look as though we were not hurrying. ('Who me, Sir, frightened Sir, certainly not Sir.') But shall we say we did not exactly tarry.

We arrived on 'X' gun-deck and waited. De la Penne and Morgan, still on the quarter-deck, appeared to be in conversation. De la Penne had been misunderstood. There was no other explosive charge, at least not attached to *Valiant*. We were not long left in doubt as to the location of the third.

We had been on 'X' gun-deck for about five minutes when there was a tremendous explosion astern of us, but not fortunately under our stern. A huge column of black smoke erupted from the single funnel of our sister ship and flagship *Queen Elizabeth* and she began to settle in the water. Antonio Marceglia had been as expert as his commanding officer. More so in fact, for not only did he attach the charge to his target but he made good his escape, even if only temporarily.

Eruption was the right word to use. De la Penne says:

> I see from one of the officers' watches that it is 0615. I look at the ship *Queen Elizabeth*, her crew are gathered in the stern. She is about 500 metres from us. After a few seconds she explodes and is lifted out of the water. Pieces of steel, other objects and soot are ejected from her funnel, making everyone on *Valiant's* upper deck very dirty.

The force of the explosion capable of doing this to a 30,000-ton battleship ' was now plain for all to see.

One of our officers then again approached de la Penne, and asked him to say on his word of honour, if there were other charges underneath *Valiant*. De la Penne refused to disclose anything.

As we all watched, bemused and mesmerized by the attack, some more explosions occurred in the harbour, though these were on a smaller scale. The explosions were in fact the ignition of small fire bombs which came to the surface near the oiler *Sagona*. This was the work of Martellotta, referred to earlier. Following on his refusal to supply the information we required, de la Penne was taken below once more. This of course was a futile exercise since he knew full well that apart from drowning in the cable locker, he was safe – from his side at any rate!

A quarter of an hour elapsed, and those in authority began to think the worst was over. After all, what further targets could there have been? The two battleships would not put to sea for many months. Most of the rest of the fleet had been out that night anyway and were unlikely to have been the object of attack. De la Penne was therefore released and taken to the Ward Room. There he found Bianchi, but they were not allowed to speak to each other.

Down the ladder again, and the two Italians were once more taken to Ras-el-Tin. As they rounded the ship, de la Penne noted that *Valiant's* bow anchor was submerged. His porthole had not been far from it. De la Penne was questioned on the journey as to his mode of entry into the harbour, but as before he remained silent.

Arrived at Ras-el-Tin the frogmen were locked in separate cells. No attempt was made to question them, but soon de la Penne began to feel very cold and shivery, a result of his long exposure to the harbour elements. He asked to be taken out into the sun in order to get warmer. He was given a very perfunctory examination and told brusquely that there was nothing wrong with him. After what he and his compatriots had done to the fleet, . there was not at that time a great deal of compassionate or caring feeling on our side.

That evening de la Penne and Bianchi were taken to a POW camp near Alexandria. It is interesting here to add that although I had now spent over a year based at Alexandria I had no idea there was a POW camp near the city. One learnt of Germans living near Belsen and other horror camps who have said repeatedly that they never knew of their existence. Perhaps they had a point.

No food was given to the Italians and they were forced to lie on the floor. No facilities were given to de la Penne to dry himself and he spent the night sopping wet, trying to get some sleep. It is a wonder he did not contract pneumonia or hypothermia. The next morning his knee injury was attended to and some Italian orderlies gave him a tasty plate of pasta. Had they not done this de la Penne might have starved until he and Bianchi were taken to Cairo for questioning 24 hours later. Perhaps that was the idea, soften him up for the interrogation to come?

It is now time to follow the movements of Commander Antonio Marceglia. It will be remembered that it was he who so successfully immobilised Queen Elizabeth and who very nearly escaped capture.

I have had, since 1975, a sporadic correspondence with Luigi de la Penne. To him I owe a great debt as he has always been most willing to provide as much detail as he could of the attack.

When I told him in 1986 that my wife and I were proposing to spend a week in Venice, Admiral de la Penne suggested that we visit the Maritime Museum. 'You will see one of our 'chariots' there,' he said, 'and you should ask Admiral Gottardi, the Curator, to put you in touch with my old friend Marceglia, who lives in Venice.'

On a beautiful autumn morning, my wife and I took a vaporetto from our hotel to the Naval Museum. We were taken to Admiral Gottardi's office, he was kindness itself. Fortunately for us, Admiral Enzo Consolo was there to act as translator. Gottardi spoke no English and my Italian was limited to, 'I wish to get off at the next stop.' I did not feel that would be adequate in making my investigations.

We descended the stairs, and there in the centre of a huge room was a replica of the engine of destruction which had caused so much damage that fateful night in December 1941. I looked at it fascinated. The 'chariot' was large and solidly built. Painted dark green, it stood menacingly facing us. There were two spaces for its 'riders' to sit astride, whilst the forward space had a rudimentary dashboard with small splash screen. Levers at the side controlled the electric motor and the operating depth. The explosive charge, like any torpedo, was in the nose.

At that moment, a figure appeared clad in blue trousers and cardigan. He introduced himself rather shyly as Antonio Marceglia. I thought he looked like a senior clone of Gregory Peck. Marceglia fortunately spoke good English and told us his story.

His target was the battleship *Queen Elizabeth*, and he had little trouble identifying her. He and his crewmate successfully attached the charge to the great ship's bottom in what must have been a text-book operation. Not for him any trouble with his submersible suit, or the

The 'Chariot' at the Naval Museum, Venice. (Museo Storico Navale, Venezia

Antonio Marceglia, the author, his wife and Admiral Gottardi at the Naval Museum, Venice. (Author's collection)

lack of a crewmate to assist him. How de la Penne must have wished he could have had Marceglia's good fortune.

Having fixed the charge, Marceglia set the fuses to a time delay of three hours. He and his companion then made for a small beach in the harbour near the abattoir. The ingeniously constructed 'chariot' was still capable of transporting its riders although it was now of course without its deadly nose cone.

Once at the beach, the two frogmen stripped off their underwater gear and donned overalls. Marceglia said these had badges of rank on them, doubtless to give them POW status. However, this would surely have made them more easily identifiable. Perhaps his English misled me.

They then set destruction charges on their 'chariot' and headed into the city. They made their way to the railway station with the idea of catching a train to Rosetta in the Nile Delta. It was part of the attack plan that an Italian submarine would surface for three hours there on Christmas Eve and Boxing Day. Why Christmas Day was missed out is an unanswered question!

When I asked Marceglia what means they had of getting in touch with the submarine, he replied, 'Only our voices!' They had no signalling equipment whatsoever. It does seem odd that such an apparently well-planned and undoubtedly successful operation such as this should have relied on a completely primitive method of rescue.

At the station, their hitherto unbroken run of efficiency and good fortune received a setback which later proved fatal to their freedom. The cause was not attributable to them, but to Italian intelligence. The latter had provided them with English pound notes for use in their escape. Italian intelligence had most certainly not done its homework. The currency in use in Egypt at that time was Egyptian pounds, not the pound sterling. (100 piastres equalled £1E.) Hence the already quoted plaintive cry: 'All right Captain, you have my sister, only 20 acker [piastres].' Moreover, the use of the Egyptian pound note was being insisted upon more and more by the British at that time. The reason was that Hitler was flooding Britain with counterfeit pound sterling notes in an effort to unbalance the economy. The British had no wish to see this duplicated in Egypt.

Proffering their English pound notes at the ticket office the two Italians were told sharply that they must buy their tickets in Egyptian currency. Disconcerted, they were about to return to the waiting-room when a note of pure English comedy was heard. A British Major, hearing of their plight, took pity on them. 'That's all right old boy,' he said, 'you just stay in the station buffet while I change your money for you.'

Basil Radford and Naunton Wayne could not have done it better. The Italians thanked the Major politely, whilst the latter went merrily off to assist the two men who had just put paid to his chances of receiving bombardment support when he returned to the Western Desert!

The transaction took some time however, and by the time it was completed, and the Major had returned in triumph with the Egyptian pounds, the train to Rosetta had left. Marceglia and his crewmate decided that perhaps trains were not for them and set out for Rosetta on foot.

En route to Rosetta, they were picked up by a party of Egyptian police. This party later released them. However, a little later on they were picked up by another Egyptian police patrol, arrested and eventually made prisoners of war.

I told Marceglia how unlucky he had been as the Egyptian police had not been renowned for their efficiency, or indeed, for their liking for the British. Perhaps there was some reward for handing over the enemy.

I also told Marceglia that I had been one of the midshipmen who were dropping charges at the entrance to the harbour to prevent his entry. He replied that he had heard them but in the end, as they followed our destroyers in, the charges presented no great problem. My broken sleep and time spent patrolling up and down outside the boom had gone for nothing!

Marceglia then asked me one question. 'Were any men killed on board Queen Elizabeth?' He seemed surprised, not to say put out, when I told him nine men had died as a result of his action.

Of the six Italian frogmen who entered Alexandria harbour that night, none escaped. All were sent to POW camps in India and remained there until Italy surrendered.

That, however, was not to be the extinguishing of the light which surrounded de la Penne. He was to have a quite unique reunion with someone he had met briefly before.

In the Naval Museum in Venice, there hangs a large white board on which a short narrative is written in black. It hangs in what, for want of a better word, I will call the 'chariot room'. The wording is in English and at the foot is a signature which I know well – it appeared once a month in my journal when it was inspected by the Captain. The signature was C.E. Morgan. It says:

Decoration of Lieutenant de la Penne with the Italian Gold Medal for Valour.

On the 19th December 1941 the British Fleet in Alexandria Harbour was attacked by three Italian 2-men torpedoes. The Senior Officer of the Flotilla, Lieutenant de la Penne, Royal Italian Navy, together with his Artificer Diver, attacked HMS *Valiant* of which I was their Commanding Officer. They were captured swimming in the water alongside the ship at 3 a.m. and for the next three hours Lieut. de la Penne was my prisoner on board the ship. As he refused to say whether he had attached anything to the ship I placed him down below close to that part of the ship's side where I thought the explosive charge might have been fixed.

At about 5.45 a.m. I was told that Lieut. de la Penne wished to speak to me and I had him brought up to the Wardroom.

All he would say was that very soon there would be some explosions, but he still refused to say whether or not any charge had been attached to the ship.

I therefore had him taken down below again, closed all watertight doors, cleared the lower deck, and ordered all officers and men on to the upper deck.

At four minutes past six an explosion occurred under the ship which blew a very large hole in the hull abreast 'B' turret, 21 feet below the waterline. There were no casualties, but as a result of the damage, the ship was out of action for over five months. Neither Lieut. de la Penne nor his assistant were injured by the explosion as they were in a compartment well for'd of the damage. [Not entirely accurate – see de la Penne's account of his knee injury.]

Later on I learned from de la Penne that the charge was not slung under the ship as he had intended, but owing to a mishap had to be placed on the bottom of the harbour below the ship, and he was uncertain what effect the explosion would have on the ship with the bomb in this position.

Lieut. de la Penne was taken ashore about 6.30 a.m. and I did not meet him again until he was repatriated from India in 1944 when I was Admiral Commanding Taranto and the Adriatic. After this he came to see me quite frequently, and not only gave me his version of the attack on HMS *Valiant* but explained many other matters of which I had been in doubt. He was also most helpful in keeping me supplied with valuable information on the attitude and reactions of Italian naval officers, especially the younger ones, to certain events which were taking place in Italy at that time.

He subsequently played a most gallant part in the attack on La Spezia, and I did my utmost to obtain a British decoration for him. However, as we were officially still at war with the Italian nation, no awards were being granted to Italian naval officers.

In March 1945, the Crown Prince of Italy came down to Taranto to inspect the Italian ships and establishments. I lunched with him on the second day and accompanied him during his inspections which included a visit to St. Vito Barracks where a presentation of medals was to take place. The first officer to be decorated with the Italian Gold Medal for Valour (equivalent to our Victoria Cross) was Lieutenant de la Penne, for his attack on HMS *Valiant* on December 19th 1941.

After the citation had been read out to the parade, Lieutenant de la Penne came forward on to the platform.

As he did so, the Crown Prince turned round and said: 'Come on Morgan, this is your show!'

I stepped forward, took the medal from the Crown Prince's hand and pinned it on Lieutenant de la Penne's breast.

I thus had the pleasure and honour of decorating Lieutenant de la Penne with the highest award granted by the Italian Navy for the very courageous and gallant attack he made on my ship three years and three months before!

C.E. Morgan
18th October 1946

It is nice to think that the age of chivalry had not entirely vanished at that time. It is also interesting to speculate if, had a similar situation had arisen in the Pacific, whether a Japanese would have been decorated by Mountbatten. I doubt it very much and would have hoped fervently that it would not have happened.

The so-called chivalry of the Japanese has long ago been exposed for the cruel sham that it was by Lord Russell of Liverpool in his book *The Knights of Bushido*. In it he said:

'To describe the Japanese treatment of their prisoners as bestial is an insult to the animal kingdom.' How right he was.

When a successful frogman attack had been made by British forces on Japanese-occupied Singapore, the enemy issued a statement. This threatened that if such an attack took place again and the attackers were captured, they would be castrated. Charming people. Perhaps we should have sent a party of Wrens to attack Singapore!

Steps were taken at once, both to repair the two battleships and to endeavour to keep as secret as possible the extent of the damage which had been caused to them. This latter, in an Egyptian harbour, was an almost impossible task.

Valiant was immediately prepared for entry into the floating dock and although the engineer officers concerned had doubts about our being able to have sufficient buoyancy for such an operation, we were marginally ensconced in the dock on Sunday 21 December. Talking to one of the dock officials, I was told by him that he was really very worried that we, and the dock, might sink on to the harbour mud and stay there. Not a cheerful thought!

A ship in dock is a ship in dock and there is little or no way of concealing that from reconnaissance planes. However, it was decided to do the best that could be done in the circumstances.

My journal entry of 22 December says:

An Army camouflage expert came aboard during the morning and ordered brown painting to be carried out round 'Y' Turret and on top of all the 15" guns. The idea is to create the effect of making us look like a 6" gun cruiser.

I could not help thinking that Lord Haw-Haw might soon be demanding, 'And where is the *Valiant?*' He might well ask.

As for *Queen Elizabeth*, what happened to her would not have disgraced a 'Carry On' film. The day after the attack, a civilian concert party organised by the indefatigable Gabriella Barker, was due to come on board to entertain the ship's company. My friend Joan Tubbs was one of the junior but most glamorous members of the party. The Captain of *Queen Elizabeth* rang up Gabriella Barker. He spoke in what he hoped was a calm tone, and most apologetically said he would have to forego the pleasure of having the concert party on board that night. 'We may,' he said, 'be involved in some night exercises.'

'Night exercises?' replied Gabriella tartly. 'What rubbish, your ship is sitting on the bottom of the harbour!' So much for Alexandria security. The Japanese Consul would, by that date, have been removed from Alexandria since we were at war with his country. However no doubt the Spanish Consul would have been active. In fact, it was Marceglia's intention to seek protection from the Spanish Consul if his rendezvous with the submarine should fail.

A further feature of the 'Carry On' film syndrome was demonstrated every morning after the attack. Gabriella was right, and *Queen Elizabeth* was sitting firmly on the bottom of the harbour. The shallowness of the harbour however, was a great boon, for her upper deck was well above water – so were many of her scuttles or portholes.

A Gilbertian pantomime was therefore enacted daily at 0800. A Royal Marine Guard and Band would parade on the quarter-deck whilst the ceremony of hoisting the White Ensign was carried out with all due solemnity!

How much this fooled the enemy or for how long was of course not known at the time. I am afraid I was entirely cynical. Aerial photographs would have revealed, and indeed did so, the presence of a submarine alongside the flagship. What, the enemy would ask, would a submarine be doing alongside? Queen Elizabeth was not a depot ship. The only explanation must be the correct one, namely that the submarine was supplying electrical power to a stricken ship. Moreover, as I saw when I took my Seamanship examination in *Queen Elizabeth*, many of the scuttles had huge trunking coming out of them. The pumps were working night and day.

The harbour after the attack was a hive of activity. The acid comment in My journal reads: 'A new policy was introduced – that of closing the stable door after the horse had bolted.' Perhaps not an apt simile. Three stallions had entered the stalls and caused havoc to two very valuable mares perhaps? No matter, grievous damage had been done, and now everyone was scurrying around trying to prevent a recurrence.

Patrol boats were everywhere dropping charges, myself in the launch doing my part. The launch was slow, and I saw to it that the charges were thrown well clear as we chugged around! The official Report takes up the story:

> Commenting on this attack, which resulted in crippling the only two battleships in the Mediterranean, the C-in-C remarks that as the possibility of attack was expected, the defences were on the alert, but that protection must not rely on the comparatively out-of-date methods of lookouts, boats and nets.
>
> Warning of approach by modern scientific methods is essential. Some method of neutralizing a charge once it has been placed is important; in this instance there was three hours' warning.
>
> He considered that the boom was open for an unnecessarily long period, and that a patrol boat should have fired more charges while the destroyers were entering.
>
> Although after the event, we knew more and were in a better position to deal with such attacks, the C-in-C in writing in February 1942 stated his reluctance to guarantee certain prevention of another such attack. He also referred to the question of security at Alexandria which could not be considered entirely satisfactory whilst Egyptian civil and military authorities were allowed to participate in the defence of the harbour.

Of course, Cunningham had a couple of points here when he touches on security, one I have mentioned previously, and one incapable of solution. Although in some respects the British were an occupying force in Egypt, some semblance of having control over their own affairs had to be left to the Egyptians, otherwise we might have had a 1916 Irish situation on our hands. That was the last thing we wanted when we were fighting a war for our very existence.

The result was that, hopelessly inefficient as they were, and pro-Axis when it came to security, we had to work with the gyppos rather than keep them away from the harbour, as we would have liked to have done. A protectorate has its limitations.

Why on earth were there no hydrophones at the harbour mouth? Why were divers not sent down to inspect the hulls of ourselves and *Queen Elizabeth*? They would probably not have found our charge buried as it was in the mud, but they could have cut the umbilical cord of *Queen Elizabeth's* charge and perhaps rendered it safe. The work of bomb disposal experts was no less hazardous and often very effective.

The Italian attack had been brilliantly successful, an enterprise carried out with good planning and great courage. That it carried with it some good luck (the boom opening) does not make for any derogation. Good commanders have throughout history had some luck on their side. This has not detracted from their fame.

It is appropriate here to illustrate what might have taken place had de la Penne's charge been fixed to our hull and *Queen Elizabeth's* nearer her magazine.

Both battleships might well have blown up with the force with which the ill-fated *Hood* exploded when hit by a salvo from *Bismarck*. Virtually no one would have survived; 3000 officers and men including myself would have perished instantly. Furthermore, the oiler *Sagona* would have been blown open, her oil spread over the harbour. The oil would then have been ignited by the incendiary bombs, and the whole area would have been ablaze. A more Dantesque picture it would be hard to imagine.

Nevertheless, even if the above did not happen, I have described the operation as being brilliantly successful, and so it was. Two 15" gun battleships were immobilized for six months at least.

At the cost of six men taken prisoner the Italians had dealt a devastating blow to British sea power in the Mediterranean. Taranto and Matapan had been avenged.

Epilogue

My service in the Eastern Mediterranean Fleet was drawing to its close. Unless I and my contemporaries were appointed to other ships, we certainly had no prospect of further sea time. Quite frankly, we were not displeased at the thought. We had really been through and seen a very great deal of action since our arrival in Alexandria in October 1940. We felt, and with some justification, that we were entitled to some rest.

Another factor was the imminence of the dreaded Seamanship exam. Before every midshipman could be promoted to Sub-Lieutenant, he had to pass a very searching viva voce examination in seamanship. He also had to pass two navigation examinations.

Our examinations were due to take place in mid-January, less than a month away. If we passed, we had to get safely home to the UK and would be promoted Sub-Lieutenants on 1 May 1942. With the coveted gold stripe on our sleeves we would then undergo 'Subs' Courses' in signals, gunnery, torpedoes and navigation. It therefore made sense for us to remain in our crippled ships and work for our exams. At least, I thought, we will not be watch on, watch off every four hours as at sea. How we would have worked for our exams in that situation I did not know. I sent up a silent prayer to whatever patron saint was in loco parentis for Italian frogmen.

I went to look at the damage done to us by de la Penne as soon as the ship was lifted clear of the water. *Valiant* was damaged along 80 feet including her keel. Great jagged pieces of metal hung down. 'A' magazine was very near. For a while I replaced my prayer to the patron saint with a curse. We had been very, very lucky. Did I say I thought we were going to get some rest? Stupid and naive I must have been. Although not keeping the tiring watches which we kept at sea, I was still very busy running the launch.

On 23 December I recorded that I had to do a liberty trip at 0100. At 0300 my crew and I relieved the 2nd picket boat on Boom Patrol. At 0615 we returned to the ship and at 0700 we began a ferry service for liberty-men. Sleep? You must be joking!

Christmas Day 1941 came and with it Hong Kong fell to the cruel Japanese. Whilst many in *Valiant* were the worse for wear, I could not help thinking of our countrymen, 9000 miles from home passing into the custody of a barbarous enemy. I was, in 1945, to be a member of the task force which took Hong Kong's surrender.

My journal entry said: 'Christmas Day was duly celebrated on board, and at the end of the day there were more than a few recumbent bodies lying around.'

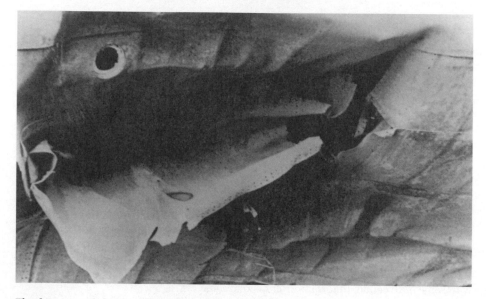

The damage to *Valiant's* hull. (Imperial War Museum)

On Boxing Day 1941, a signal was received – 'Operation Alert'. This was the executive signal for ships to have patrols around them all night. Why on earth had this not been done before?

The 2nd picket boat was immediately armed to the gunwales with depth charges and scurried round the floating dock like a wet hen dropping them at ten minute intervals. After half an hour the whole exercise was cancelled. Rumour had it that 'something' had been caught in the 'Loop'. The latter was an electrical circuit at the harbour mouth designed to detect people like de la Penne. If they entered its warning area, huge galvanometer needles would quiver and alarm bells would ring.

Avoidance measures? Enter as de la Penne had, concealing yourself with the enemy's cruisers!

It was fortunate no Italian frogmen thought fit to attack us the next day. The 2nd picket boat ran on to the slipway at 201 Group, damaging screw and shaft, and bending one rudder at right angles. Result? Hoisted inboard and out of action for a week. My journal omitted to detail what happened to the wretched midshipman in charge. He was probably considered fit to share de la Penne's POW cell.

New Year's Eve 1941 arrived, and my journal entry recorded somewhat laconically: 'The New Year was seen in with great enthusiasm (sic) by a large crowd of officers on the quarter-deck including Rear-Admiral Rawlings (*Valiant's* previous Captain) and Mr Hartin the *Daily Mail* correspondent.'

Considering that this gathering of New Year's Eve revellers was celebrating on the quarter-deck of a badly damaged battleship which was only just being kept afloat by continual pumping, there would seem to have been an air of somewhat misplaced jollity.

New Year's Day 1942 was marred by a somewhat disgraceful incident involving my former appointment, the Australian destroyer *Nizam*. Let my journal record what happened:

> *Nizam* came alongside the starboard side of the floating dock at 0900. There was a strong wind blowing and as Lieutenant Commander Clark is not particularly brilliant at ship-handling at the best of times, she took a long time to arrive, making several attempts. Finally she dropped an anchor underfoot, found she had let out too much cable, and heaved in only to find that she had fouled one of the dock moorings round the anchor flukes!
>
> *Nizam* had come to mend her A.S.V. [Anti-Surface Vessel] radar which had been damaged by an over-enthusiastic Oerlikon gunner.

What happened next reflected no credit on *Nizam*, her officers, or the Royal Australian Navy. When the hands were piped to 'All Watches' at 1315 My journal says: 'With typical Australian bloody-mindedness the ship's company refused to turn to and remained on their messdecks.' Their reason (it could not be an excuse) for disobeying orders was that they considered they should have a make-and-mend (half-holiday) due to the amount of time they had spent at sea.

The action of *Nizam*'s lower deck was of course nothing short of mutiny. Mutiny in peacetime is bad enough as with the Royal Navy at Invergordon in 1931. Mutiny in wartime could carry with it the death penalty. It is doubtful if any of the Australians aboard *Nizam* had read British naval history. Had they done so, they might have recalled Lord St Vincent's famous utterance at the Mutiny of the Nore in 1792. Taking one final look at the figures of the mutineers swinging from the yard-arm, he turned on his heel to go below, remarking to his Flag Captain as he did so: 'Discipline is preserved, Sir!'

It was not Invergordon however. No sailors' soviets were formed, the Red Flag was not hoisted at *Nizam*'s yard-arm. The Captain and the First Lieutenant walked round the messdecks, and after this my journal records: 'They condescended to return to work.'

That day I took a party of sailors from *Nizam* to the shore. They were destined to return to Australia. Whether or not these were the ringleaders of the mutiny I never discovered. I reflected later however, when news of the brutal treatment of their prisoners by the Japanese began to leak out, how these mutineers would have fared had they become Jap prisoners. A stint of holding a heavy rock above their heads, and beaten severely if they faltered, might have well been their mildest fate.

On 7 January five midshipmen joined us, all survivors from the sinking of *Barham* the previous November. We helped them out with kit as much as we could and listened horrified as they told their stories of survival. Pleased as we were to see them, it made conditions in the Gunroom very crowded. It was fortunate that it was winter so that the overcrowding was not as oppressive as it might have been.

My journal entry of 9 January 1942 reads as follows:

This morning's papers [i.e. the Egyptian English language press] gave prominence to an Italian naval communique which stated that 'assault units of the Italian Navy penetrated the defences of Alexandria harbour on the night of December 18th and caused considerable damage to a battleship of the *Valiant* class. This damage forced her to remove into drydock where she now remains.

It was nice to know that *Valiant* had given her name to the class instead of *Queen Elizabeth*.

A German reconnaissance plane had flown over Alexandria four days previously. Although subjected to an intense anti-aircraft barrage, and chased by fighters, it made good its escape. Doubtless the photographs it took resulted in the communique we were now reading. My journal entry comments acidly: 'And so our camouflage has fooled no one.'

Perhaps, but there was no mention of two battleships having been damaged, so perhaps the charade enacted on *Queen Elizabeth's* quarter-deck every morning was fooling someone? Not Gabriella Barker anyway! 'London declined to comment.'

Saturday 10 January 1942 was my nineteenth birthday. I wrote that 'I was thankful that it was in no way like my last!' Celebrations were not to be, and I kept the Middle Watch (midnight to 0400) as Officer of the Watch on the brow. This was not a particularly exacting task and consisted of standing at the gangway which connected us to the side of the floating dock, and making desultory conversation with the quartermaster and his side party. Technically I was temporarily in sole charge of a 30,000-ton battleship and Walter Mitty thoughts raced through my brain. When I came down to earth however, I was not doing much more than shouting '*Imshi*' at any itinerant gyppo who might try to gain unauthorised entry to our damaged home.

The next day saw *Valiant* bristling with top brass. We were honoured by no less than the Commander-in-Chief, Sir Andrew Cunningham, the Vice Admiral commanding the First Battle-squadron, and the Rear-Admiral commanding Alexandria. My thoughts wandered in an acid manner concerning the latter, for here was the man responsible for the breach in the harbour defences. He was now boarding one of the battleships damaged as a result of his negligence. I grew excited, was there to be a Royal Marine firing squad formed up on our quarterdeck? Had the top brass come to witness the execution of another Byng, so fittingly had the venue been chosen? The answer was no, they had not. What they had come to see was two films, one Italian and one British.

The Italian film produced as propaganda was captured at Asmara in East Africa. How it got there I do not know since we effectively sealed off the eastern Mediterranean when Italy declared war against us in 1940. However, no matter, it purported to show the Battle of Calabria which was fought in July.

The British had three capital ships to the Italian two, but the latter were greatly superior in cruisers and destroyers. After the battleship *Cesare* had been hit the Italians turned away and retired under cover of a smoke-screen. In the final phase, there was heavy but ineffective bombing by Italian shore-based aircraft, most of which was aimed at their own ships!

This was not shown in the film which I saw myself later that day. My journal comment was: 'In parts it was greatly exaggerated in favour of the Italian fleet, which was certainly churning along at great speed whenever it appeared on the screen!' It was not clear however, as to which was their chosen heading. Roskill commented: 'Though the failure to bring the enemy to battle was disappointing, the brief encounter was of interest because it indicated the unwillingness of the Italians to stand and fight.' Except for de la Penne and his men, this was all too true.

The second film to be shown to the senior officers, and later ourselves, was the sinking of *Barham*. It did not make pretty viewing. I reflected ruefully that our usefulness as a contribution to the war effort had now been reduced to being little more than a semi-secure Gaumont cinema for senior officers. How are the mighty...

My fellow senior midshipmen and I were now preparing hard for our exams and this occupied much of our time. We sat our navigation exam; whoever set it must have had a sick sense of humour or was devoid of imagination. Three hours were devoted to questions on the set chart. The latter was of Hong Kong harbour; our beautiful former naval base had been in the hands of the Japanese for the past three weeks.

The date set for the dreaded Seamanship exam was announced and duly arrived. We had questioned each other endlessly. How was a kedge anchor laid out? What was the use of a Senhouse slip? How do you tow forward or aft? How do you rig an awning? How do you come to a buoy?

All these and many others had preoccupied our thinking. At last our knowledge was to be tested. With my inferiority complex concerning this, to me, boring subject, I was more apprehensive than most.

Our viva voce was to be conducted in the flagship *Queen Elizabeth*. Her midshipmen in turn came to us. The picket boat drew alongside Queen Elizabeth's gangway and we trooped on board, dressed in our No. Is of blue doeskin and shining shoes.

Taken below, the next few hours were very reminiscent of our Dartmouth interview except for two things. Firstly, we were spared writing that ghastly 'SA', which the reader will remember almost strangled at birth my desire to follow in Nelson's footsteps. Secondly, the noise; *Queen Elizabeth* was resting on the bottom of Alexandria harbour but she was fighting a constant battle against water entering her through the huge hole blown in her bottom by Antonio Marceglia. Pumps heaved and thumped and through many scuttles, including those in the cabin where our exam was held, great pipes snaked, convoluting like huge hydrostatic colons. This did not make for concentration. I strained forward towards my examiners, pretending as far as I dared that the pumping was putting me off, which it was. I did not quite dare to cup a hand to my ear and pretend I could not hear the questions, which unfortunately I could.

The Captain of *Queen Elizabeth*, his Commander and First Lieutenant faced me for what seemed like hours. Surprisingly, utterly surprisingly, I found myself giving what appeared to be the correct answers to the questions, anyway, no one said, 'Nonsense boy', or 'Rubbish', and I began gradually to gain confidence, even so much as to entertain thoughts of passing.

At last the ordeal came to an end and we raced over the harbour, back to the floating dock. Excited chatter broke out over lunch – like all examinees we exchanged questions and answers, compared notes. I then thought well, maybe I had passed but I hoped against hope that I had done better than that. The reason was that no *Valiant* midshipman had ever achieved less than a Second class pass in Seamanship and certainly no one had ever failed. I waited in trepidation.

The next day the results arrived by *Queen Elizabeth's* picket boat. The snotties' nurse, Michael Penton, came into the Gunroom with a piece of paper in his hand. He rarely smiled, but now a slow, almost delighted smile creased his face. 'Well done all of you,' he said. 'You've all been awarded Second class passes.' A cheer went up and I almost fainted in disbelief. Me – with a second in seamanship? There must be something wrong, but no, it was true, and I was glad I had not let Michael Penton down. After lunch I asked him for permission to go ashore. 'Of course, old Holloway,' he said, again with a trace of a grin. He had never addressed me with such warmth before. I felt ten feet tall.

As used to be said in Latin, 'That having been done', we could all relax and now only awaited passage home. We were madly excited as we had not spoken to any of our loved ones in the UK for sixteen months. No prisoner incarcerated at Her Majesty's pleasure has to wait that long for a visit. We were given permission to cease writing up our journals. My last entry is therefore dated Tuesday 20 January 1942. Beneath it is a flowing signature, the same writing that stares at visitors to the Naval Museum in Venice – C.E. Morgan, Captain.

I was really sorry. I had come to regard my journal as a friendly chore, but now I no longer had to write it up I felt somehow bereft. I had written it up every day since October 1940. I had written it up immediately after being bombed or shelled, after the torpedo passed under *Nizam*, during and after the ghastliness of Crete, and after de la Penne had nearly blown us to Kingdom come. I had never lost it, it had never been damaged. It even had some drawings in it as demanded, the best I could do with no draughtsman's ability.

It had not been a female teenager's 'Dear Diary' confessional. Occasionally I had made some acid comments but I had always been mindful of senior officers perusing it. I was also mindful of the note printed on its first page: 'This journal is to be produced at the examination in Seamanship for the rank of Lieutenant, when marks to a maximum of 50 will be awarded for it.'

Now my journal had to be given in and I would not see it again until the war's end. It was treated as a confidential book, for that is indeed what it was, containing as it did complete records of the movements of many of HM ships. Back it would go to England, there to be stored away in some safe place. Its journey home must have been without incident and its wartime eyrie a safe one, as it was indeed returned to me in 1946 encased in a plastic cover. I have it before me as I write. The ink and drawings are as legible as they were 70 years ago. I can only hope that its contents have been of some small interest to readers.

News came of how we were to return home. Some of us would be flown across Africa to Lagos, there to proceed by sea to the UK. John Cardew and I together with 20 others would take passage in the 6" gun cruiser *Ajax* of River Plate fame. Our return journey would be through the Suez Canal and then back round the Cape of Good Hope, a re-run of our 12,000-mile journey in 1940 in the *Dominion Monarch*. I was glad it was not then.

Even our return journey was not to be without incident. Stopping at Durban, and then Simonstown, we had just left the latter when we had orders to search for a German armed merchant cruiser to the south of us.

Down into the awe-inspiring Roaring Forties we went, right down to 44°S. It may have been summer in the Southern Hemisphere but it was highly unpleasant whilst it lasted. The winds did roar, right up from the Antarctic and the piercing chill factor went to the marrow of our bones. I was so cold on watch that a kindly petty officer gave me some of his rum 'tot' to keep me warm. The waves tossed our 6000 tons of steel about like a cork. I was seasick too, and we never saw that bloody German ship.

Blue seas again as we turned north, we sunbathed and almost forgot the war. Then, instead of blue skies, blue uniforms and the grey skies of the Bay of Biscay. Much vigilance, this was submarine country and we were a prime target. All was well and on 2 April 1942 we dropped anchor off Greenock. We were home at last.

A very different country greeted us. We had left when shortages were almost unknown. Now everything was rationed, the people looked haggard, women were in uniform, and there was talk of 'being browned off', an astonishing expression which was quite new to us. From occasional lapses into Walter Mitty, I had now become Rip van Winkle. I did not care for it. A long and exhausting journey in a dirty, crowded and blacked out train brought us to Cheltenham the next morning. My parents and the Cardew's were there – it was a wonderful reunion. Only those who have undergone such an enforced separation can realise what it meant to us to be back again in loved and familiar surroundings.

What can one say, as one reflects on all this from a viewpoint 70 years on? We had left England when the enemy was literally about to descend upon our island and to deprive us of the liberty we all held so dear. What would have happened had he done so? Our parents would have been enslaved, with German soldiers perhaps billeted at Winacres. Starvation and subjugation would soon have been their lot. As for us, where would we have ended up? Canada or the States perhaps, to begin a life of exile in a strange land. None of that happened but it could so easily have done.

We had left England as raw schoolboys of seventeen. We had returned, and this is no boast, as battle-hardened veterans of nineteen. We had seen enough action to last many a man a lifetime, certainly far, far more than many of the senior officers in the Navy today. All of us were destined to see three more years of war and action before it was finally ended. There were some who never returned to their homes and loved ones. They lie now in steel-hulled coffins off the coasts of Greece and Crete, Libya and Cyrenanica, in the depths of the eastern Mediterranean.

This book is dedicated to their memory.

Afterword

Fast forward to the Royal Naval Dockyard at Plymouth, 4 June 2004. A beautiful, sleek destroyer lies moored alongside, the ensign of the Italian Navy fluttering at her stern. The ship is named *Luigi de la Penne*, a familiar name.

Three of us, survivors of the Italian frogmen's attack on our ship *Valiant* in Alexandria harbour 63 years previously, had been invited on board the destroyer named after her attacker. There were present on the British side Captain Barrie Kent, RN (who had been a midshipman with me) and Lieutenant-Commander Tom Hunt (who had been our observer), together with the latter's daughter, myself and my wife. On the Italian side there was Professor Francesco Berlingieri and Signora Berlingieri. The Professor had trained as a frogman but had not taken part in the attack at Alexandria. He was a respected maritime lawyer with a practice in Genoa.

Then came what Harold Macmillan would have called 'a little local difficulty'. Some time previously I had had an operation on my knee; it was stiff and I had to use a stick. Due to the high tide the gangway was at a 45-degree angle. I looked up and saw that not only would I have to climb up it but there was a 'side party' on the quarterdeck composed of the Officer of the Watch, a petty officer and three ratings. The Captain stood facing the gangway. What is more, the shrill wail of the bosun's pope trilled in our ears ... we were to be piped on board! Never had I thought that I would be accorded such an honour, an honour reserved for commanding officers of ships, admirals and foreign naval officers ... it suddenly dawned on me that that was of course what we were.

'There is nothing that the Navy cannot do' was a mnemonic written up at Dartmouth. A pompous saying, but very well I thought, I would have to live up to it. Tightening my grip on my stick (the thought of falling overboard made me shudder), I braced my shoulders and commenced the climb up the gangway. There were wooden rungs on it which did not help.

Then another thought came to me. An officer salutes the quarterdeck and the reception I was to receive certainly demanded an acknowledgement of some kind. I was not of course in uniform. In those cases, if officers are in civilian clothes, they should doff their hat and stand for a moment stiffly to attention at the top of the gangway.

I had no hat but having reached the top I stood as smartly as I could while the pipes wailed and all the Italians saluted. I tried to conceal my stick behind me. Then of course there was the 45-degree descent to the quarterdeck which I managed without too much difficulty.

My hand was shaken by the commanding officer, Captain Ricca, a tall, charming man who I feel sure would draw gasps of admiration from the fairer sex. Other officers from the ship introduced themselves and we were taken on a tour of the upper deck and its armament. I would have liked to have seen the bridge and the operations room but that was evidently not on the agenda.

Drinks were served in the Ward Room anteroom and we then sat down to a delicious lunch. At the end of the meal Captain Ricca made a charming speech in very good English. I replied and was sorry I could not do so in Italian. My knowledge of the language was limited to '*é pericoloso sporgesi*', a phrase that used to be shown on every window in continental trains and is translated as 'it is dangerous to lean out of the window.' Since modern warships have no scuttles in case of atomic attack, the advice seemed superfluous.

A photographer from *Navy News* took a great many photographs. The one reproduced here shows me doing my best to hide my stick behind me. I did not wish to appear too geriatric.

And so ended an unforgettable day. I have little doubt that the late Admiral Marchese Luigi Durand de la Penne would have been delighted that the *rapprochement* had taken place. He was a distinguished aristocrat, an officer and gentleman, who undertook a most hazardous operation with brilliant success. After his death I used to receive Christmas cards from his wife.

In a world which is still torn apart by revolutions, terrorists and wars, it is at least comforting that chivalry and forgiveness are not forgotten.

Appendix I

Summary Of V/S Signals During the Night Of 18/19 December 1941

0106

– Explosion *Neptune*.

– Explosion *Aurora*.

– Explosion close to port side of *Penelope*.

– From *Neptune* by W/T: 'Turn together to 180°.' (This was assumed to be in error for 'Turn 180° to starboard together.')

– From *Aurora*: 'My course and speed – 030° 10 knots.'

– Two more explosions alongside *Neptune*. – From *Aurora* to destroyer: 'Send a destroyer alongside *Neptune*.'

– From *Aurora* to *Penelope*: 'Form astern.'

– From *Aurora*: '*Neptune* has been badly damaged. Have detailed one destroyer to go alongside.'

– From *Neptune*: 'Lost all power and unable to steam.'

– From *Aurora* to *Penelope*: '*Neptune* seriously damaged. Am detaching one destroyer to go alongside her. Stand by her. Am damaged myself. Am taking three destroyers and steaming for Malta.'

– From *Penelope* to *Aurora*: 'My six-inch control out of action due to explosion, otherwise all right. Can I help *Neptune*?'

– From *Aurora*: 'Do what you can for *Neptune*. Keep clear of minefield. Give me two destroyers.'

0153

– From *Penelope* to *Lance*: 'Pass me. I am going back to *Neptune*.'

– From *Penelope* to *Lively*: 'Follow me.'

– From *Penelope* to *Lively*: 'I must keep clear of minefield. Close *Neptune* and let me know what I can do. Go on. Good luck.'

– From *Neptune* to *Aurora* (Made to *Penelope*): 'Have told *Kandahar* to lay off till I have drifted clear of the minefield. Am preparing to be taken in tow then.'

– From *Penelope* to *Lively*: 'I will circle round here. I will come in if there is any chance of towing *Neptune*.'

– From *Penelope* to *Kandahar*: 'Have told *Lively* to close *Neptune*. I will close and take *Neptune* in tow when signalled.'

– From *Lively* to *Penelope*: '*Neptune* mined, cannot steam. Ordered to tow. Am going back to her now.' – Exchanged identities with *Neptune*.

– From *Penelope* to *Neptune*: 'Am ready to tow you. Shall I come now.' – From *Neptune* to *Penelope*: 'Close on my port side.'

– Explosion in *Kandahar* about two miles away.

– From *Neptune* to *Penelope*: 'Keep away.'

– From *Penelope* to *Lively*: 'Ferry survivors to me if necessary.'

– *Penelope* calling *Aurora*. – From *Lively* to *Penelope*: '*Kandahar* mined.'

– From *Penelope* to *Neptune*: '*Aurora* not in company, has gone to Malta damaged.'

– From *Kandahar* to *Penelope*: 'After Engine Room bulkhead is holding and ship can be towed. But realise this is impossible.'

– From *Penelope* to *Kandahar*: 'Regret I must keep clear.'

– From *Lively* to *Penelope*: '*Kandahar* mined. She has ordered me out of field.'

– From *Kandahar* to *Penelope*: '*Neptune* has touched off another mine.' (Reply: 'I clearly cannot help. God be with you.')

– From *Kandahar* to *Penelope*: 'Suggest you should go. Consider sending submarine to pick up survivors.'

– From *Penelope* to *Lively*: 'Course 010° Speed 15.'

– From *Lively* to *Penelope*: 'Suggest I go for *Neptune's* survivors.'

– From *Penelope* to *Lively*: 'Regret not approved.'

– G.20.

– From *Lively* to *Penelope*: 'Suggest a submarine could be asked for.' (Reply: 'I am going to do that. I hate to leave them, but am afraid we must.')

Appendix II

Letter from CO HMS *Valiant* to C–in–C Med

From – THE COMMANDING OFFICER, HMS *VALIANT*.
Date – 26th November, 1941. No. – 5106/196
To – THE COMMANDER-IN-CHIEF, MEDITERRANEAN STATION.

The following report on the sinking of H.M.S. *Barham* in latitude 32° 29' North Longitude 26° 27' East at 1630 on the 25th November, 1941, is forwarded for information.

2. The Battle Fleet was formed in single line ahead in the order Queen Elizabeth, *Barham* and *Valiant*. Course 290°, speed 17 knots, and carrying out zig-zag, number 10. In accordance with the instructions for this zig-zag, course was altered together 22° to port to 268° at 1621. *Valiant* was steady on the new course by 1623, and at this time was on the correct bearing from *Barham*, the distance being just three cables.

3. At 1625 the Officer of the Watch, Sub Lieutenant D.F. Trench, Royal Navy, was taking the distance of *Barham* with the Stewart's Distance Meter, when he observed a large explosion on the port side of *Barham* abreast the mainmast. He realised immediately that *Barham* had been struck by a torpedo fired from somewhere on the port side and quite correctly ordered 'Hard-a-port.'

4. I was not on the compass platform at the moment of the explosion, but on reaching the front of it ten seconds later, I observed a very large column of water and smoke alongside *Barham*, only the after end of the quarter deck being then visible.

5. I immediately ordered 'Full speed ahead together'; at the same time the Officer of the Watch informed me that the wheel was hard-a-port, and I observed that the ship was just beginning to swing to port under the influence of full port rudder.

6. About fifteen seconds later a submarine broke surface between 5° and 10° on the port bow at a distance of approximately 150 yards and moving from left to right. By then *Valiant* had swung about 8° to port, and was therefore heading approximately 260°. The submarine was steering between 050° and 060°, and her speed appeared to be about 4 knots.

7. Immediately on sighting the submarine I ordered 'Amid-ships', and then 'Hard-a-starboard' in an endeavour to ram her, but before the rudder was hard over it was obvious that it would not be possible to check the swing to port before she was across the bow. Actually the swing was just about checked when the submarine passed down the starboard side, and she submerged again when abreast *Valiant's* bridge at a distance of about 50 yards.

As she appeared on the starboard side S.1 pom-pom fired 19 rounds at her with the maximum depression, but all rounds appeared to pass over her. The wheel was then again reversed so as to keep clear of *Barham*.

8. The only portion of the submarine which appeared above water was the periscope and about 2 to 3 feet of the conning tower, which was flat topped. A certain amount of disturbed water before and abaft the conning tower indicated the fore and after ends of the hull, and enabled an accurate estimate of her course to be made.

9. As soon as the smoke and spray had cleared away and *Barham* became visible again, it was seen that she had developed a very heavy list to port, probably about 20° to 30°, as it was observed that the water was level with the after screen door into the lobby at the fore end of the quarter deck. She appeared to hang in this position for about a minute, when she began to roll over on approximately an even keel.

10. She continued to roll over and sink deeper in the water until the water was seen to be entering the funnel. A moment or two after this there was a loud explosion amidships, and a very large column of black and brown smoke with flame from the explosion in the middle of it shot into the air. This explosion occurred at 1630, or 5 minutes approximately after the torpedoes hit, when *Barham* was just abaft the beam from *Valiant's* bridge.

11. All observers are agreed that, as the torpedoes hit, there were three explosions, a first one, followed about one or two seconds later by two in quick succession, and that the explosions all occurred amidships between the funnel and the mainmast. It is not certain what caused the final explosion, but the general opinion was that it was the 6" magazine. It did not appear large enough nor loud enough for a 15" magazine, and it was certainly not 'A' nor 'B' magazines, as the centre of the explosion was abaft the bridge, and I am of the opinion that it was not as far aft as 'X' magazine.

12. A rough sketch showing the approximate tracks of *Valiant*, *Barham* and the enemy submarine is attached.

Appendix III

Midshipman P.B. Edwards' Account of the Loss of HMS *Barham*

At 1626 I was sitting reading in an armchair at the far side of the Gunroom. There were three or possibly four explosions, all within a few seconds of each other and the ship lurched over to port taking a list of 110°. All the lights went out, cordite fumes and water came in from somewhere. There were about twelve altogether in the mess, all of whom rushed out onto the halfdeck. I was I think the last through the door. I did not stop to pick up my life belt. The halfdeck was flooded and it is possible that the first few out of the Gunroom door may have been swept for'ard by the initial gush of water. It was about a foot deep when I waded through it and I went up the ladder past the Gunroom heads and so on to the boatdeck. I climbed up to the starboard side where I waited for about 20 or 30 seconds. I found Midshipmen JENNINGS, R.N.R., JOCELYN, R.N. and CLASTE, R.N., and a large number of ratings there. At this time several men were freeing P.B. seats so they would float off and I saw Lieutenant Commander COBHAM walking for'ard along the boatdeck. The ship now started to roll over to port again instead of righting herself as I expected. A lot of men were now going over the side and several attempted to jump from the boatdeck itself and landed on the bulge breaking various limbs and thus standing little chance of surviving. Midshipman JOCELYN did this and hit the lower bulge with both his legs. Others including myself ran and slipped down to the lower bulge and then jumped from there. By the time I had got there the ship was nearly on its beam. I kicked off my shoes and jumped with about a 50ft drop. I was sucked down and seemed to stay under her for a considerable period, during which time I had a breath of air from what was probably an air bubble as it was still pitch black ... When I came to the surface smoke was hanging low over the surface and it was impossible to see her. The Flag Lieutenant was the only person anywhere near me and we clung to part of a writing desk, changed to a P.B. seat, followed by a broken Carley float and were eventually picked up by HMS *Hotspur's* whaler. The surface was covered with oil fuel and wreckage.

I have no recollection of the magazines or any boilers blowing up.